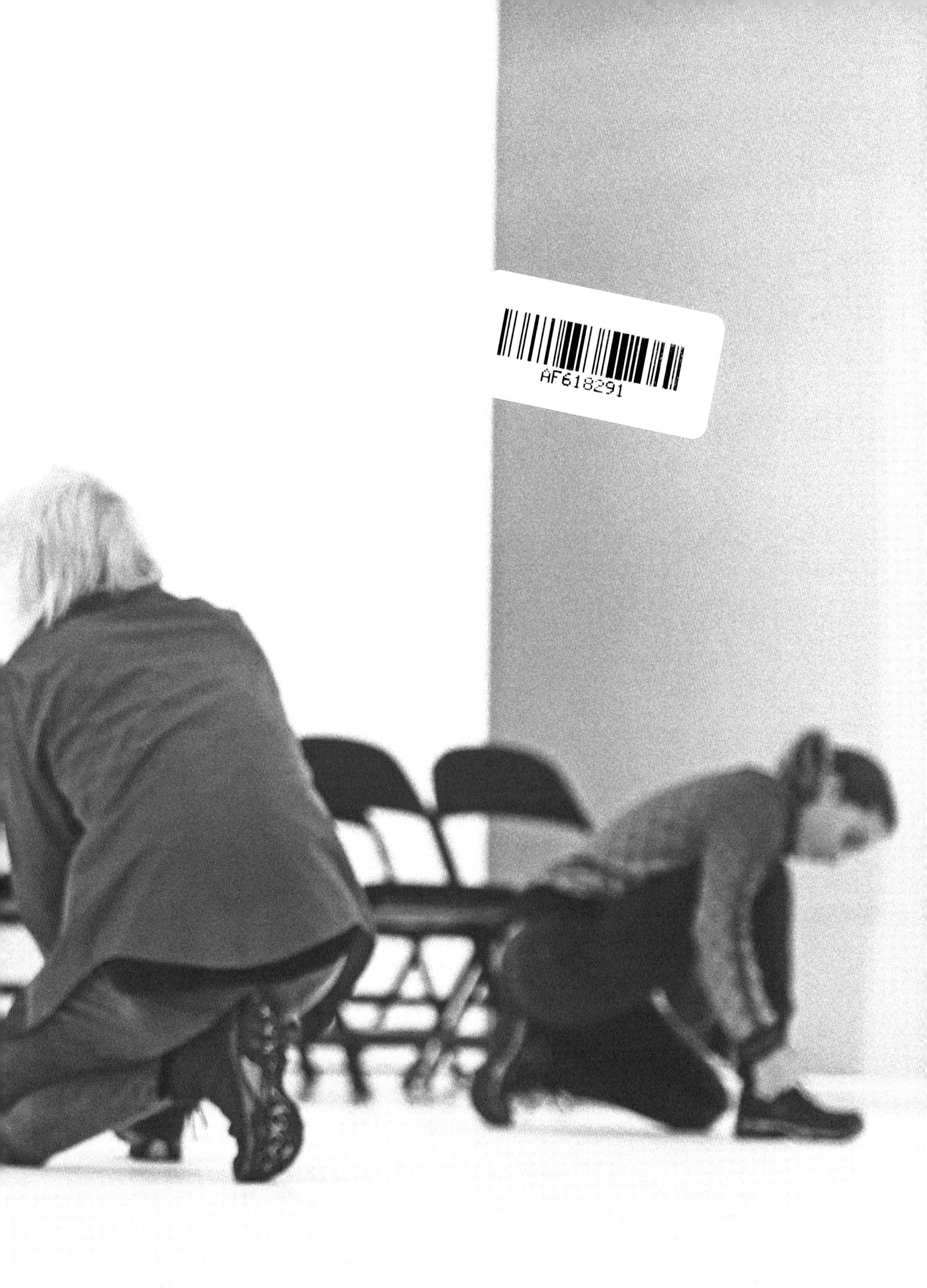

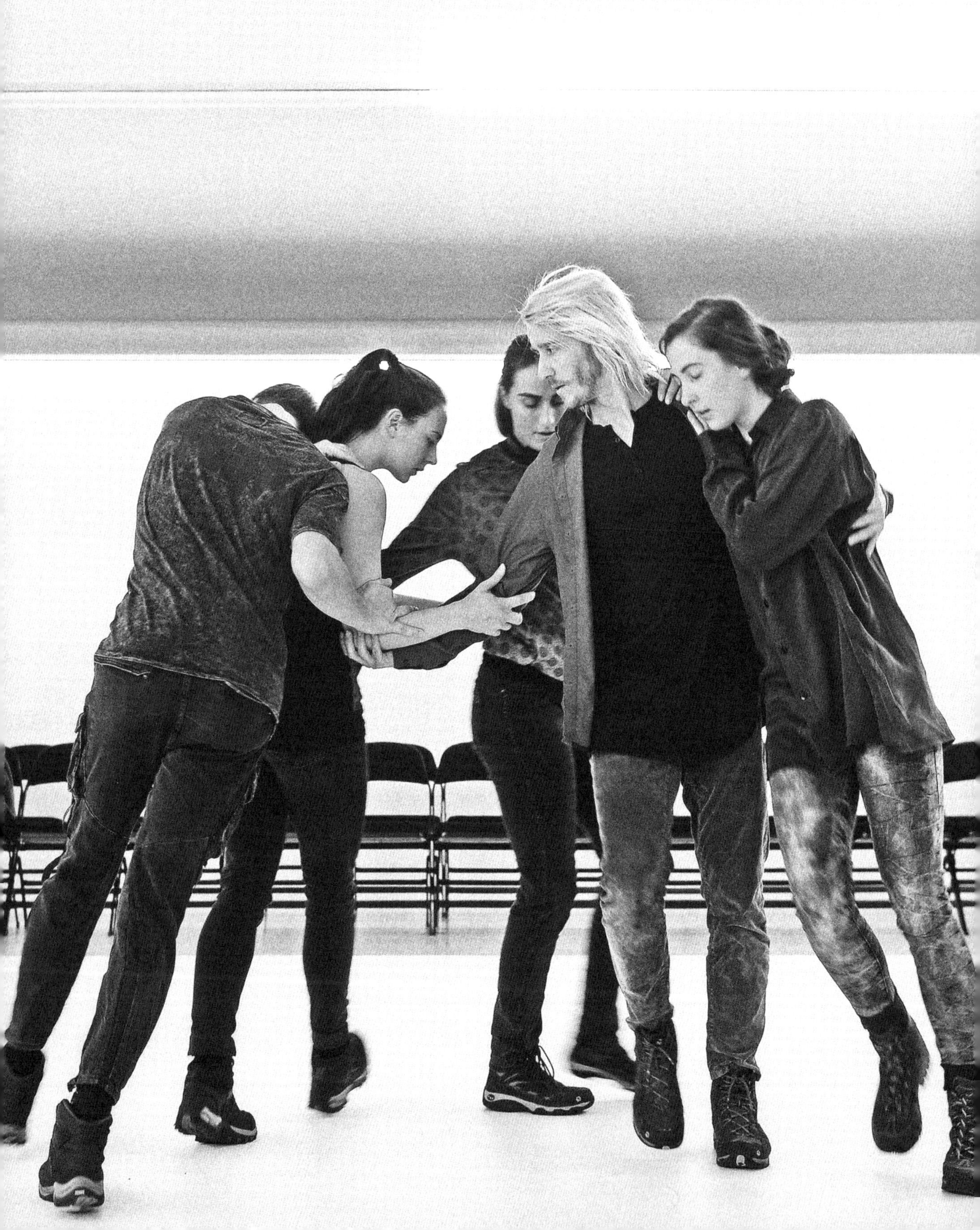

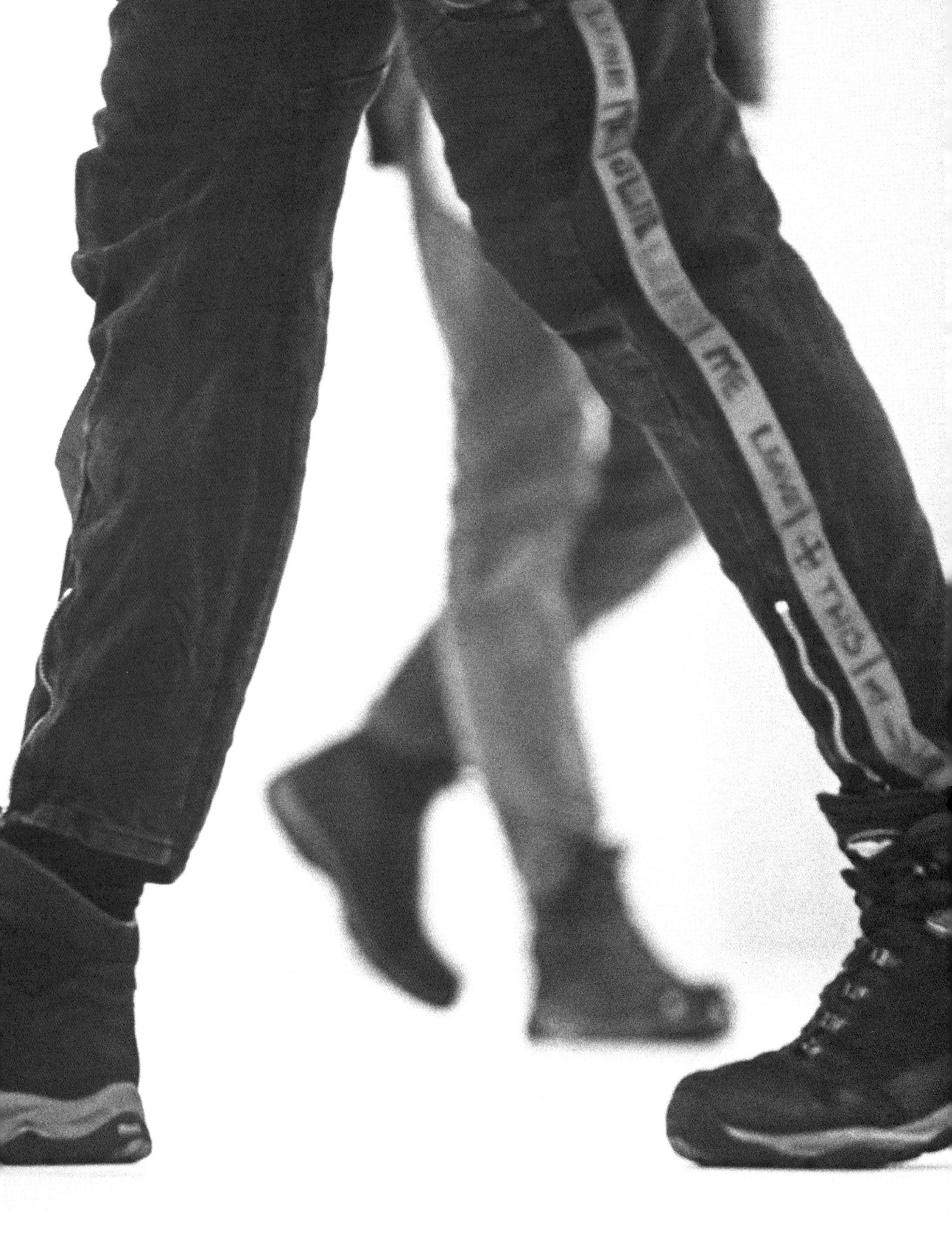

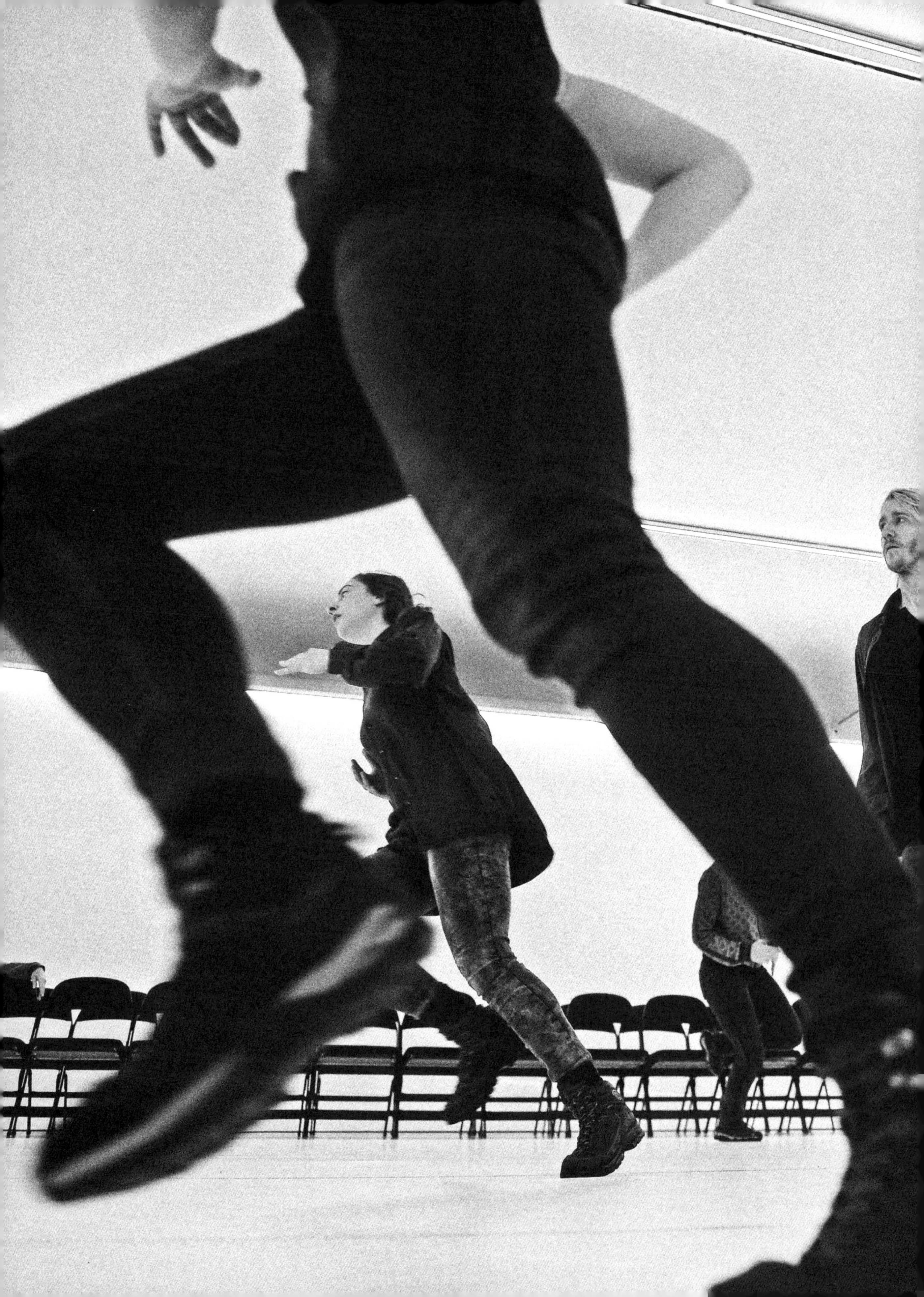

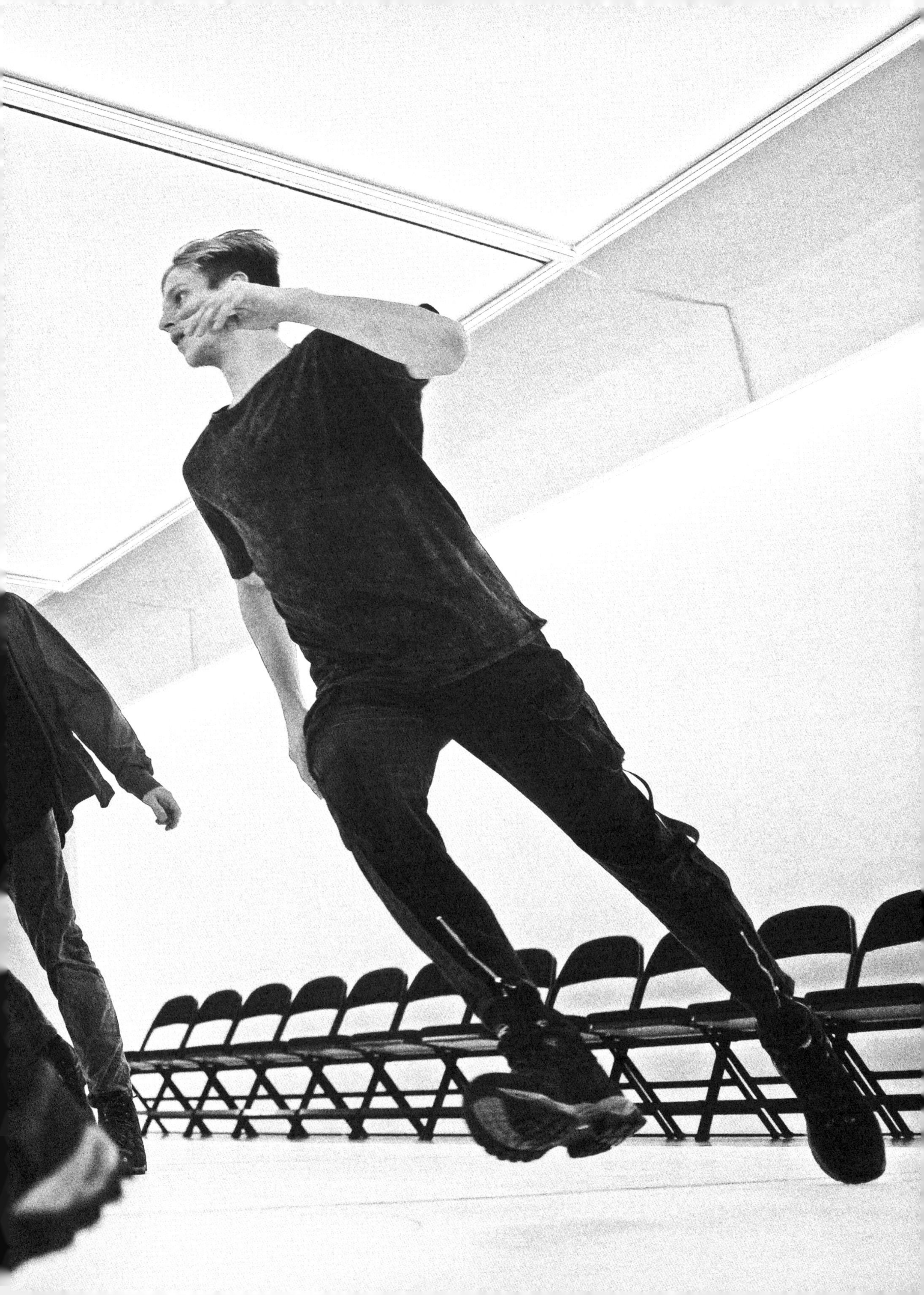

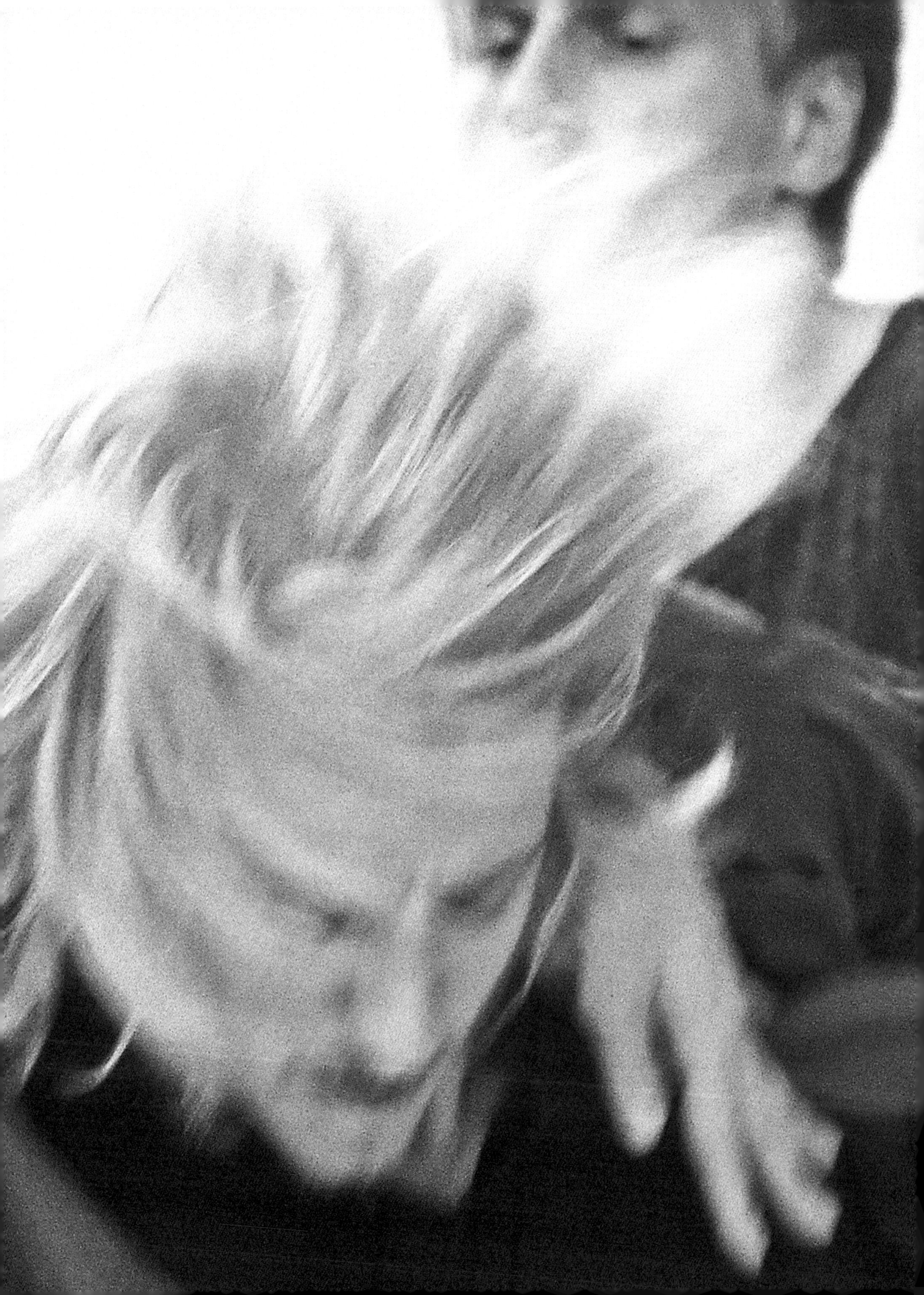

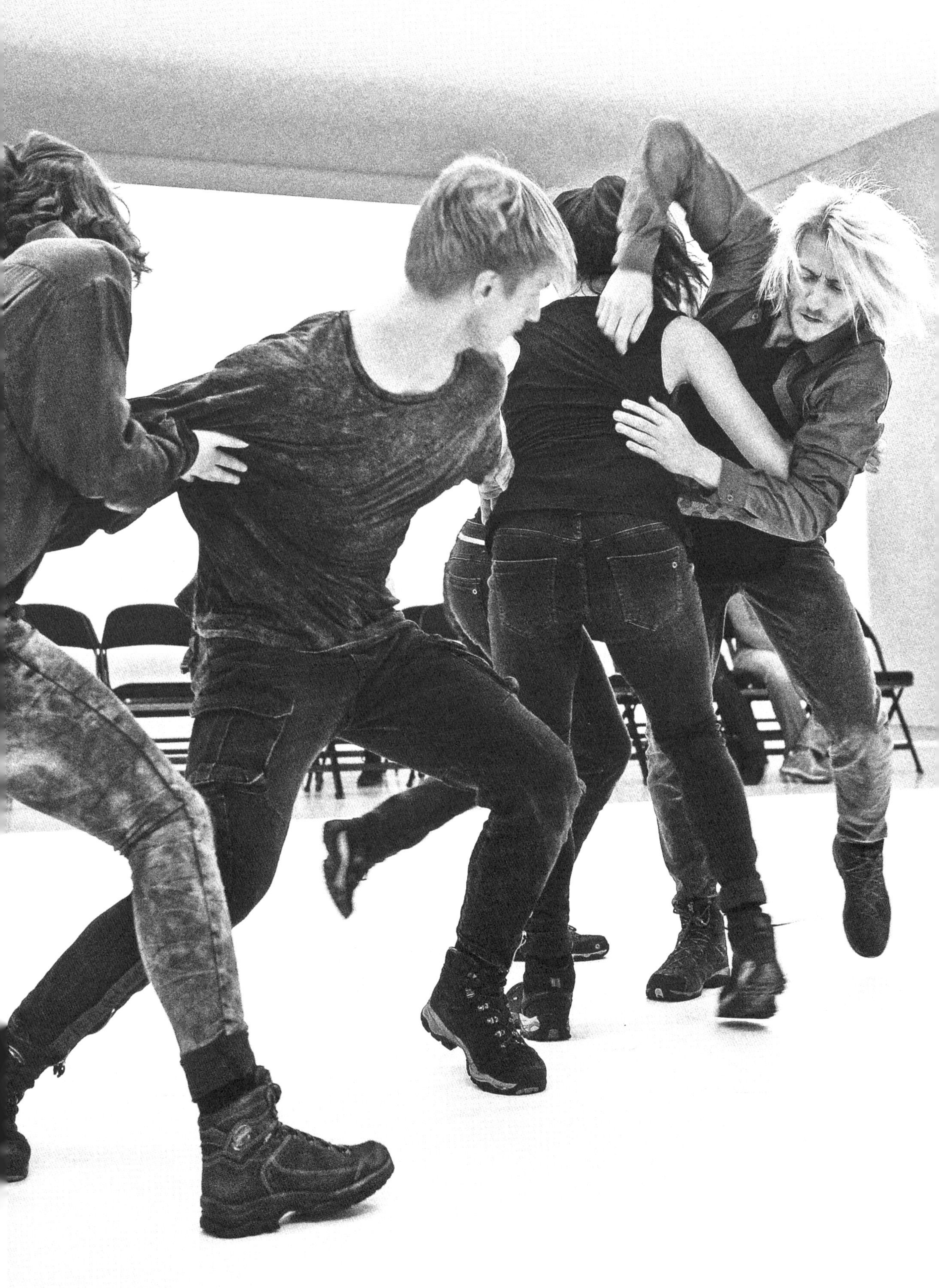

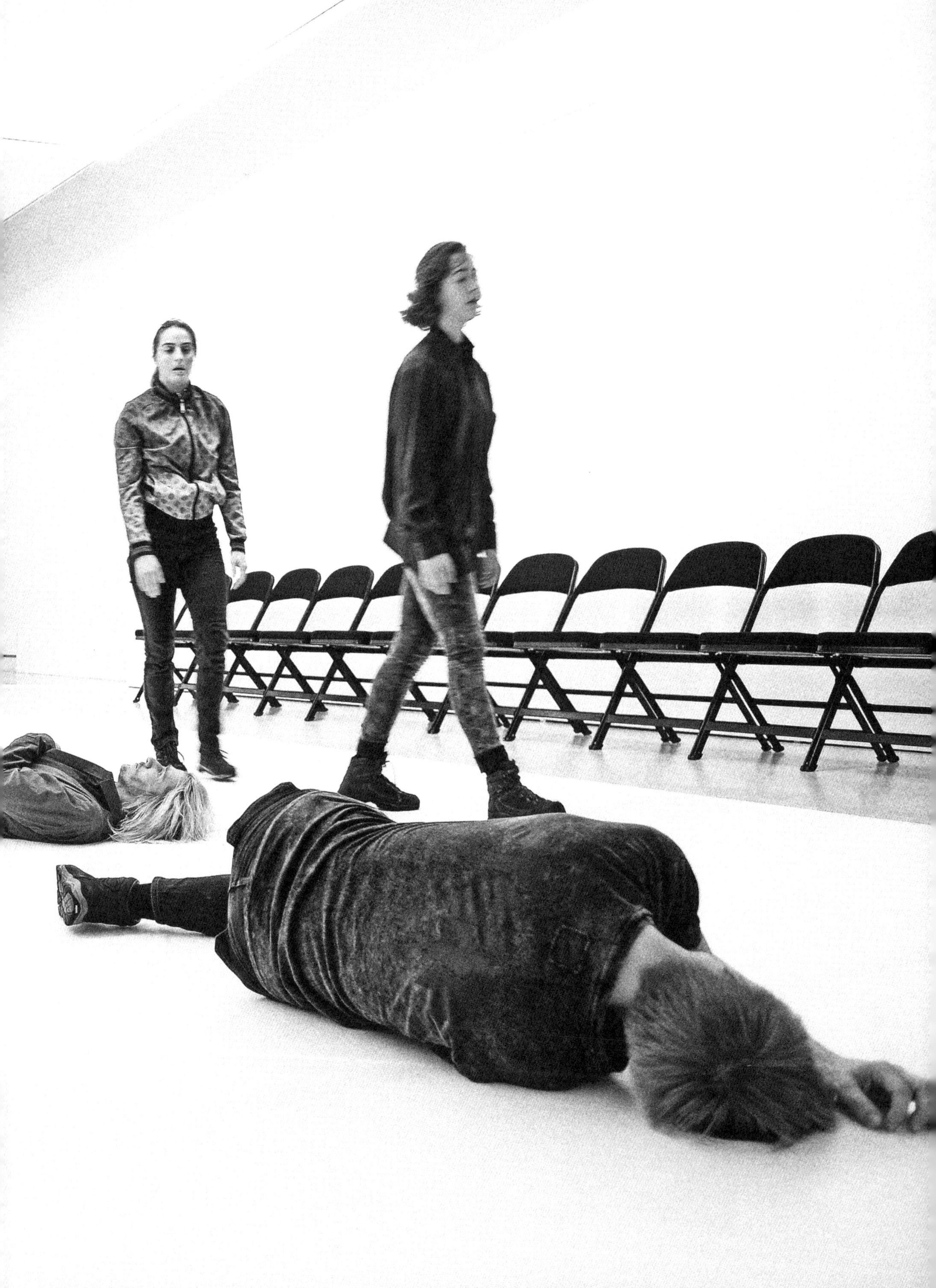

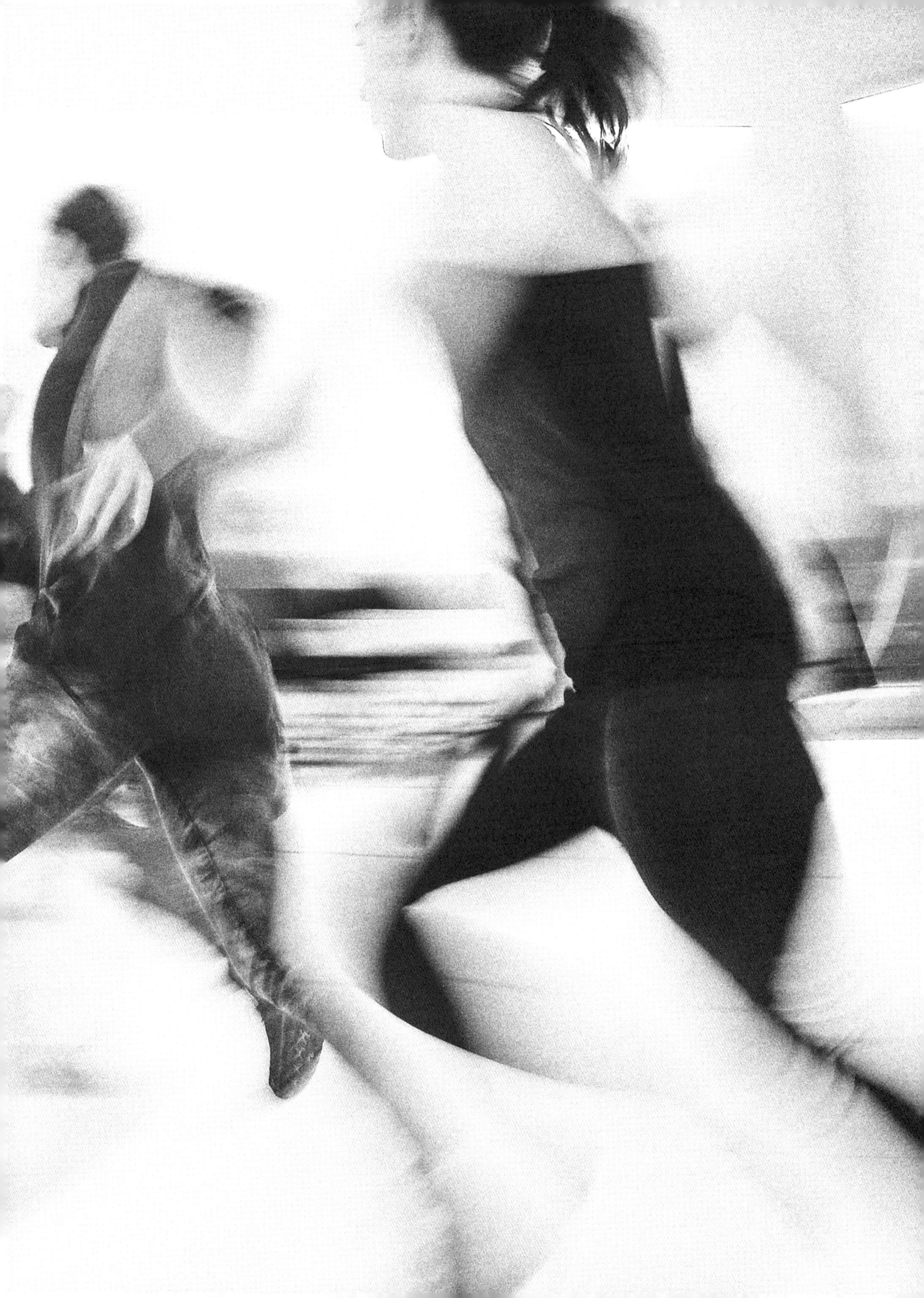

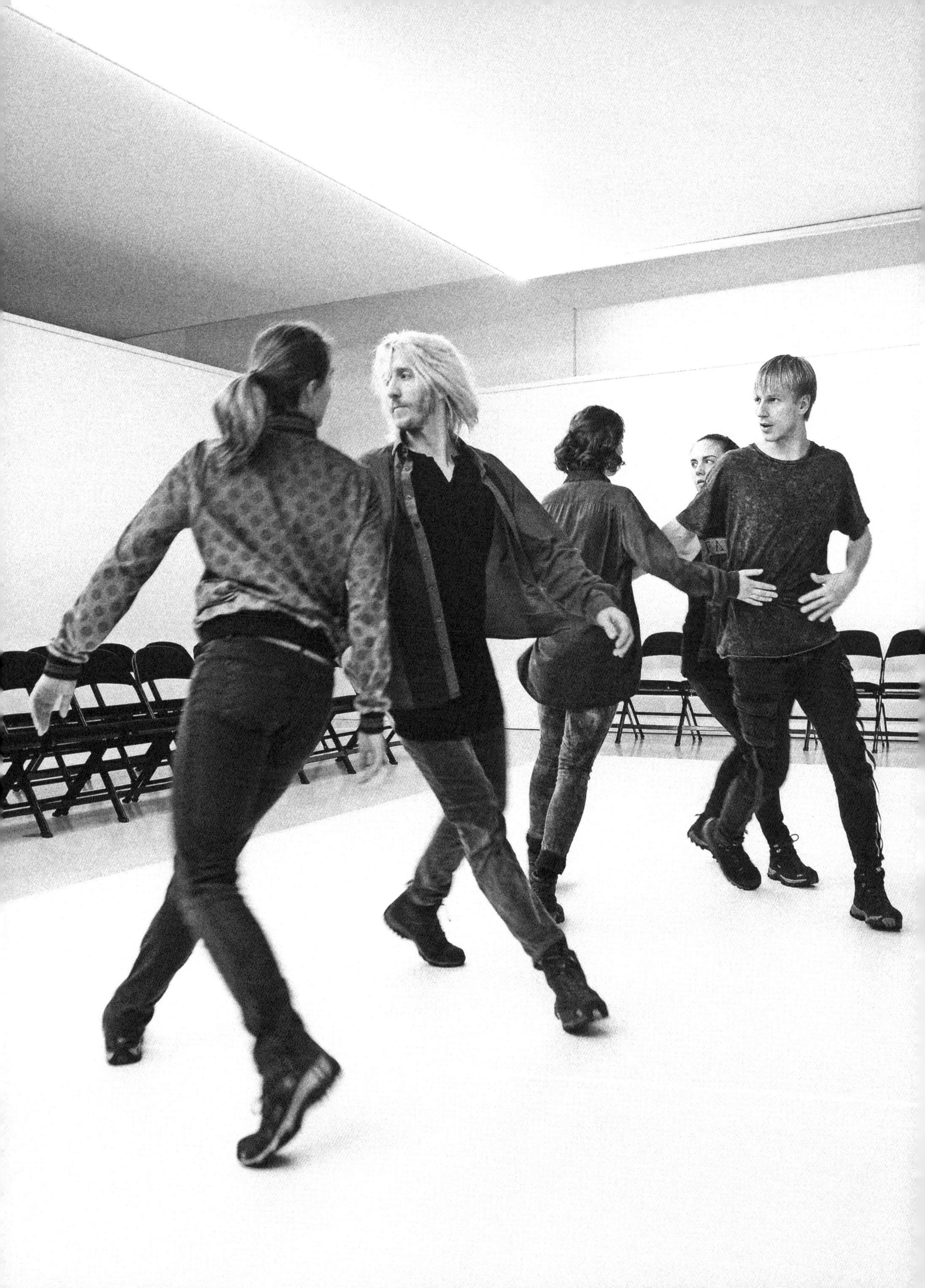

0:00	**Putting On Shoes**
3:12	**Circles**
12:34	**Small Circle**
14:04	**Running**
16:00	**Mirror**
18:11	**Alessandra Solo**
18:39	**Hugs**
19:45	**Looks**
21:10	**Blackholes**
24:31	**Carousel**
26:25	**Falling**
27:06	**Finn Solo**
29:39	**Amber Solo**
29:45	**Magnet**
30:37	**Superman**
32:19	**Figure 8**
34:06	**Buckle-Up**
34:21	**Six Steps**
35:51	**Spider Web**
36:51	**Tail**
37:12	**Lift**
37:19	**Backwards**
40:25	**Falling Backwards**
41:01	**Taking Off Shoes**
41:27	**Raindance/Techno**
42:44	**Ritual Dance**
44:51	**i-A**
48:06	**Game**
52:19	**Leaving One by One**

Inhalt
Content

Vorwort Welche Konzepte lassen sich von einer Disziplin in die andere übertragen, und was reflektiert von dort zurück? Welchen Einfluss können choreografische Strukturen und deren Digitalisierung auf die bildende Kunst haben? Welcher Mittel, welcher Sprache bedarf es, um diese Übertragung zu ermöglichen? Was passiert mit einer Information, wenn sie verschiedene Ohren, Münder, Köpfe, Körper oder Disziplinen durchläuft? Was bleibt übrig – was kommt hinzu? Das sind nur einige der Fragen, die sich uns im Rahmen von *Between Us* stellten. In diesem Buch werden der Umgang mit ihnen, Art und Inhalt unserer Zusammenarbeit nachvollziehbar. Was sich lange Zeit als abstrakt und hochkomplex darstellte, gewinnt durch Bilder visuell Gestalt sowie durch Interviews zwischen sämtlichen Beteiligten inhaltlich Kontur. So bringt dieses Buch nicht nur die Vielschichtigkeit von *Between Us* zum Ausdruck, sondern bildet den nächsten Schritt dieses facettenreichen Projekts, erweitert es durch Beiträge des Choreografen, der Tänzer*innen und Künstler*innen. Sie alle geben Einblick in Entstehung und Wachstum einer einzigartigen Kooperation, die keine bloßen Antworten generiert, sondern mit jeder Wendung auch zukünftig neue Zugänge, Blickwinkel, Interpretationen und Bilder kreiert.

Between Us ist ein interdisziplinäres Projekt, das drei Institutionen – Staatstheater Mainz, Kunsthalle Mainz, Hochschule Mainz – und damit die Disziplinen Tanz, bildende Kunst, digitale Tanzforschung und -vermittlung über Fragestellungen des Austauschs von Informationen und Wissen zusammenbringt. In drei Disziplinen, drei Ansätzen, drei ästhetischen Formaten spürt *Between Us* der Übertragung und der Umwandlung von Informationen nach – auf struktureller wie inhaltlicher Ebene. Die Basis dieser Kooperation bildet die Choreografie *Effect* des finnischen Choreografen Taneli Törmä, die er mit fünf Ensemblemitgliedern von tanzmainz für *Between Us* entwickelte. *Effect* nimmt das Motiv des Kreises auf. Während 55 Minuten umzirkeln die Tänzer*innen ein unsichtbares Zentrum, generieren Kreise, variieren, vervielfältigen oder dekonstruieren sie. Sie untersuchen körperlich, wie sich Bewegungsimpulse weitertragen, sich gegenseitig und verschiedene Individuen beeinflussen. In einem zweiten Schritt wurde die Choreografie der Tänzer*innen mittels Motion-Capture-Verfahren vom Forschungsprojekt Motion Bank der Hochschule Mainz aufgezeichnet und in Datenströme umgewandelt. Gemeinsam mit der vollständigen Dokumentation der sechswöchigen Entwicklungsphase des Stücks, zusätzlich erfassten Hintergrundinformationen sowie der Aufzeichnung mehrerer Durchläufe ist der Entstehungsprozess von *Effect* vermutlich der am besten dokumentierte weltweit. Die durch Motion Bank gewonnenen Daten und die Choreografie selbst bildeten wiederum die Arbeitsgrundlage für sechs internationale Gegenwartskünstler*innen. Tim Etchells, Tamara Grcic, Žilvinas Kempinas, Søren Lyngsø Knudsen, Isabel Lewis und Sissel Tolaas schufen, von dem Quellmaterial inspiriert, neue Werke. Damit wurde ein bis dato einzigartiger Rezeptionsprozess angestoßen, der ein Tanzstück weder dokumentiert noch übersetzt oder interpretiert. Vielmehr senden die künstlerischen Beiträge neue Impulse aus, öffnen eine Choreografie in ganz unterschiedliche Richtungen und erweitern dadurch ihre Bedeutung.

Anhand der Verzahnung von Kunst, Forschung und Tanz wird deutlich, wie komplex Informationen und deren Übermittlungsverfahren sind. In dem Moment, in dem eine Idee oder Botschaft ihren Absender verlässt, gerät sie in einen Kreislauf der permanenten Neuformulierung. So spielen auch in *Between Us,* wie in allen Austauschprozessen, die individuelle Wahl und die Gewichtung eine entscheidende Rolle. Rhythmus, Tempo, Distanz, Bewegungsart oder -sequenz sind nur einige Elemente der Choreografie, die von Motion Bank analysiert und von den bildenden Künstler*innen in ihren Werken aufgegriffen und transformiert wurden.

In der Kunsthalle Mainz öffnet sich das Projekt *Between Us* schließlich nach außen. Dort verbinden sich Produktion und Ausstellung, Prozess und Aufführung, Erfassung und Vermittlung. Zwölf Aufführungen von *Effect* begleiten die Beiträge von Motion Bank und den bildenden Künstler*innen in den Räumen. Auf diese Weise formiert sich ein Parcours, der die Besucher*innen in Analysen und Visualisierungen, in Installationen, Soundarbeiten und partizipatorische, multisensorische Settings hineinführt. Die Kunsthalle Mainz zeigt und öffnet einerseits den Prozess und die Ergebnisse dieser einzigartigen Zusammenarbeit, bildet andererseits einen lebendigen Ort des Erfahrens und Erforschens. *Between Us* erweist sich so in seiner Präsentation als genauso herausfordernd, experimentell, bereichernd und lebendig, wie es der gesamte Entstehungsprozess war.

Stefanie Böttcher,
Honne Dohrmann,
Florian Jenett

Preface What concepts can be transferred from one discipline into another, and what is reflected back into the original discipline after such a shift? What influence can choreographic structures and their digitization have on visual art? What media and what language is required in order to make such a transposition possible? What happens to information when it traverses different ears, mouths, heads, bodies or disciplines? What remains—and what is added?

These are just some of the questions we asked ourselves in the context of *Between Us*. This volume traces the way we approached them, as well as the nature and content of our collaborative work. What has for a long time presented itself as an abstract and highly complex undertaking has now taken shape in images, gaining contours in terms of content through interviews conducted between all those involved. This book thus not only expresses the multi-layered nature of *Between Us*, but also forms the next step to this many-sided project, extending it through contributions by the choreographer, dancers and artists. They all provide an insight into the development and emergence of a unique cooperation that has not simply generated answers, but with each loop performed also created new access paths, perspectives, interpretations and images.

Between Us is an interdisciplinary project that brings together three institutions—Staatstheater Mainz, Kunsthalle Mainz, University of Applied Sciences Mainz—and through these three, the disciplines of dance, the visual arts, and digital dance research and communication, in a conversation on issues concerning the exchange of information and knowledge. *Between Us* pursues the transfer and transformation of information—both at the structural and content-related levels—in three disciplines, three approaches and three aesthetic formats.

The choreography *Effect* by Finnish choreographer Taneli Törmä, which the latter devised with five members of the ensemble of tanzmainz for *Between Us*, forms the basis of the cooperation. *Effect* revolves around the theme of the circle. In the piece, the dancers circle around an invisible center for 55 minutes, they generate ring-shapes, vary, multiply or deconstruct these. With their bodies they investigate how movement impulses are spread, what influence they have on other such impulses and on different individuals.

In a second step, the dancers' choreography was recorded using motion capture methods by the Motion Bank research project at the Mainz

University of Applied Sciences and then translated into data streams. In addition, exhaustive documentation of the six-week-long development phase of the piece was carried out, and additional background information, as well as numerous run-throughs were recorded: all of this probably makes the process of the formation of *Effect* the best-documented of any such piece world-wide. The data captured by Motion Bank and the choreography itself in turn provided the basis for works created by six international contemporary artists. Tim Etchells, Tamara Grcic, Žilvinas Kempinas, Søren Lyngsø Knudsen, Isabel Lewis and Sissel Tolaas created new works inspired by the source material. A hitherto unique process of reception was thus launched that neither documents, nor translates or interprets a dance piece. Instead, the artistic contributions provide new stimuli and open up the choreography in entirely new directions, thereby expanding its meaning.

The interweaving of art, research and dance makes it clear just how complex are information and the processes used to communicate it. In the moment in which an idea or message leaves its sender it enters into a circle of permanent reformulation. Individual choice or emphasis thus play a crucial role in *Between Us*, just as they do in all processes of exchange. Rhythm, tempo, distance, type or sequence of movement are just some elements of the choreography analyzed by Motion Bank and addressed and transformed by the visual artists in their works. At Kunsthalle Mainz the project *Between Us* then opens outwards. Here, production and exhibition, process and performance, capture and communication are tied together. Twelve performances of *Effect* are carried out alongside the contributions by Motion Bank and the visual artists in the rooms. A course is formed in this way that leads viewers through analyses and visualizations, installations and sound pieces and participatory, multi-sensory settings. Kunsthalle Mainz on the one hand shows and opens up the process and the results of this singular collaboration, while on the other providing a vivid space of experience and exploration. The presentation of *Between Us* magnificently reflects the challenging, experimental, enriching and lively process of its formation.

Stefanie Böttcher,
Honne Dohrmann,
Florian Jenett

TANZ
DANCE

Choreografie
Taneli Törmä

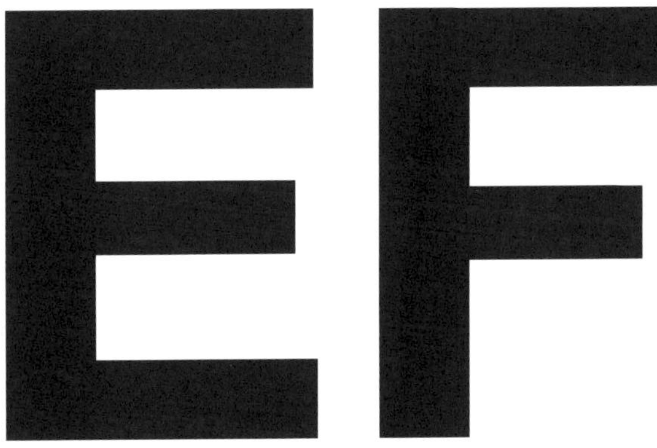

FE

Kostüme
Ute Noack

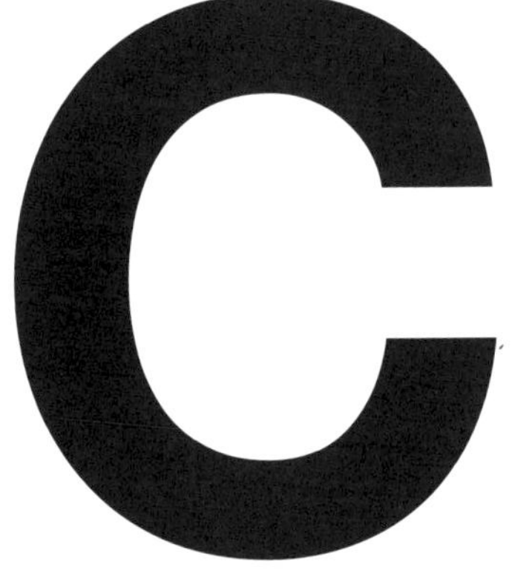

Sounddesign
Søren Lyngsø Knudsen

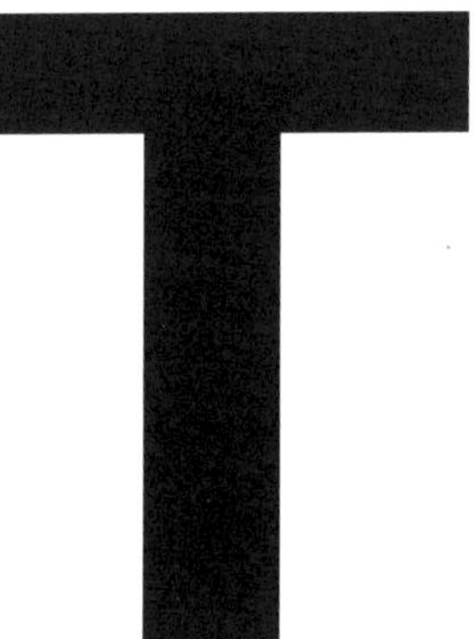

Lichtdesign
Petri Tuhkanen

E

Choreography
Taneli Törmä

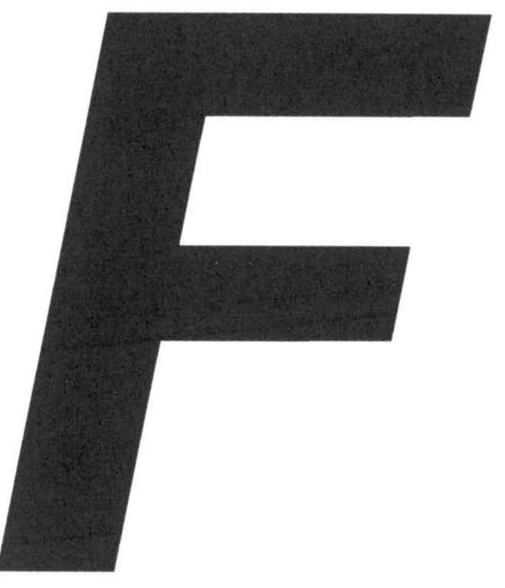

Costumes
Ute Noack

Sound Design
Søren Lyngsø Knudsen

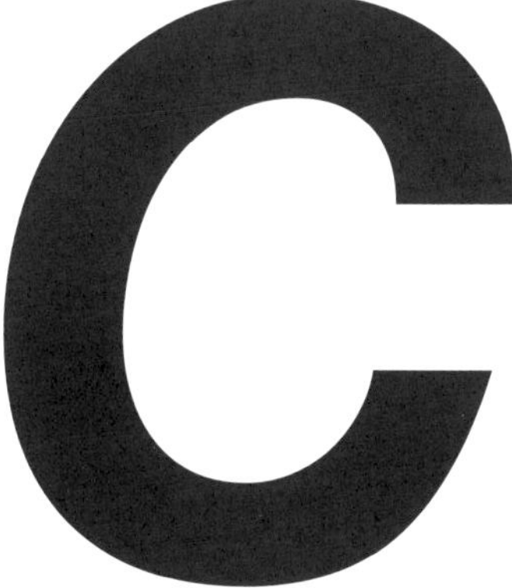

T

Light Design
Petri Tuhkanen

Stefanie Böttcher
Zachary Chant
Honne Dohrmann
Lina Louisa Krämer
Finn Lakeberg
Bojana Mitrović
Amber Pansters
David Rittershaus
Taneli Törmä
Milena Wiese

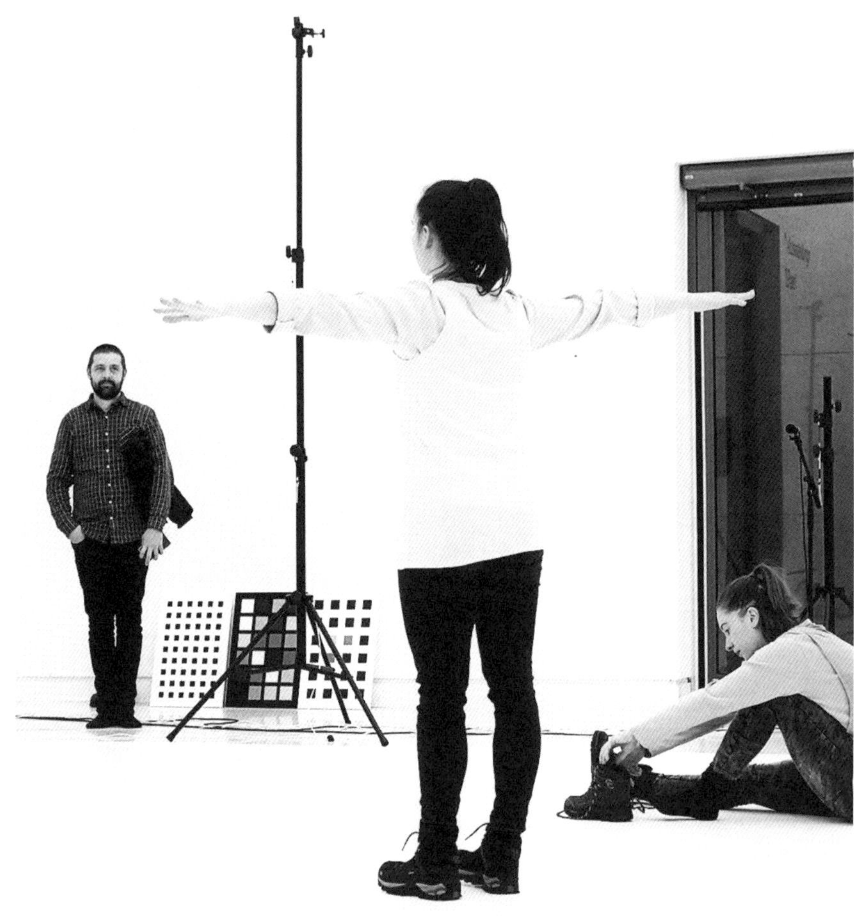

„Es geht nicht um Wiederholung, vielmehr erschaffen wir das Stück bei jeder Aufführung neu."

Amber Pansters

David Rittershaus: **Als wir das erste Mal über die Idee für *Between Us* sprachen, sagte Honne Dohrmann augenblicklich: „Ich kenne den perfekten Choreografen für dieses Projekt." Warum hast du sofort an Taneli Törmä gedacht?**

Honne Dohrmann: Aus unterschiedlichen Gründen. Zunächst einmal kennen wir uns schon längere Zeit, und ich habe auch schon einige von Tanelis Arbeiten sowohl als Choreograf als auch als Tänzer gesehen. Seine ausgesprochen formalisierten Tanzstücke, die ungeheuer menschlich und berührend sind, haben mich sehr beeindruckt. Zu jener Zeit wusste ich noch nicht, wie *Between Us* genau aussehen würde, aber es war klar, dass eine große Flexibilität und Offenheit gegenüber dem gesamten Projekt vonnöten sein würde.

Stefanie Böttcher: ***Between Us* ist ein gemeinsames Projekt, das sich mit Beziehungen und Einflüssen auseinandersetzt. Taneli, welche Aspekte des Projekts waren neu für dich? Und welche hast du als Inspiration empfunden?**

Taneli Törmä: Ich fand die Frage interessant, wie ich den Kern einer Bewegung darstellen könnte. Daher wollte ich die Performance auch

„Ich fand die Frage interessant, wie ich den Kern einer Bewegung darstellen könnte. Daher wollte ich die Performance auch so minimalistisch anlegen.“

Taneli Törmä

so minimalistisch anlegen. Was würden Motion Bank und die bildenden Künstler*innen mit einer solch reduzierten Information anfangen können? Ich fand es spannend, auf welche Teile der Choreografie sie sich dann konzentrierten und was das Stück ihnen persönlich vermittelt hatte. Außerdem inspirierte mich die Vorstellung einer Tanzaufführung in einer musealen Umgebung und wie das die Wahrnehmung des Publikums beeinflusst. Und nicht zuletzt wollte ich sehen, wie sich das Stück selbst durch diesen Prozess verändern würde: Konzeption des Stücks im Tanzstudio, seine Aufführung in einer Kunstinstitution mit einer begleitenden Ausstellung und später dann mögliche weitere Entwicklungen, sobald die Performancedaten als Open-Source-Material zur Verfügung stehen. Und, ganz abgesehen davon, auch die Frage: Was kann ich als Choreograf noch steuern, wenn ein Tanzstück so viele Impulse von außen erhält?

David: **Ein Großteil des Stücks wurde von alltäglichen Bewegungen abgeleitet. Mich würde interessieren, wie es für euch als Tänzer*innen war, mit dieser Art von Bewegungsmaterial zu arbeiten, das ja zunächst einmal nicht so „tänzerisch“ ist wie bei anderen Stücken?**

Zachary Chant: Auf den ersten Blick mag es etwas nüchtern und einfach aussehen, aber es war ausgesprochen diffizil, Tanelis Vorstellungen hier umzusetzen bzw. durchzuhalten: die Vermeidung jeglicher Theatralität oder Absichten, so als würde etwas völlig überraschend aus dem Nichts auftauchen. Das Stück ist ganz anders und hat seine eigene und besondere Sprache.

Bojana Mitrović: Gewöhnlich proben wir ja etwas, das immer gleich bleibt. Ein bestimmter Moment in der Musik geht immer mit einer bestimmten Position im Raum einher, hier ist das allerdings ganz anders. Wir müssen trotzdem einen gewissen Ablauf beibehalten. Er findet jedoch immer wieder an verschiedenen Orten und mit anderen Personen statt. Es ist wie eine Art Multitasking auf einem anderen Niveau und hat wenig damit zu tun, was wir sonst machen. Insofern ist es eine Herausforderung und sehr inspirierend.

Amber Pansters: Es geht nicht um Wiederholung, vielmehr erschaffen wir das Stück bei jeder Aufführung neu. Das ist sehr erfüllend, erfordert aber eine hohe Konzentration, Hingabe und Aufmerksamkeit. Vordergründig wirkt die Arbeit einfach, sie ist jedoch sehr speziell und eröffnet ständig neue Optionen. Es ist, als müsse man im Sekundentakt Entscheidungen treffen. Man spürt dadurch ein gewisses Verantwortungsgefühl für die Gruppe und für die einzelnen Beteiligten. Wir machen das zusammen und stellen gemeinsam sicher, dass es funktioniert. Das gefällt mir sehr gut an diesem Stück.

Finn Lakeberg: Ich schätze besonders das Gefühl des hundertprozentigen Eingebundenseins, sowohl während der Entwicklung des Stücks als auch während der Aufführung. Das Engagement des Einzelnen und miteinander in der Gruppe und die anhaltende Aufmerksamkeit, die für das Gelingen des Stücks notwendig ist, sodass wir wissen, wo wir uns räumlich und zeitlich gesehen befinden, und uns nicht auf die Füße treten. Diese Reise, die wir als Gruppe während der Vorbereitung und jeder Aufführung durchlaufen haben, ist etwas sehr Besonderes.

Honne: Ich würde an dieser Stelle noch gerne hinzufügen, dass es diese Art von eher konzeptueller Arbeit ist, die für die Entwicklung von tanzmainz so wichtig ist. Schließlich möchten wir ja unser Repertoire durch neue Tanzformen erweitern.

David: **Taneli, du hast gesagt, das Stück sei geometrisch angelegt. Dieser Aspekt wurde besonders klar, als Motion Bank die aufgezeichneten Bewegungsdaten visualisierte. Welche Rolle spielte die Idee im Entwicklungsprozess, dass der Körper im Raum eine Zeichnung auf der Oberfläche des Bodens hinterlässt?**

Taneli: Diese Idee habe ich schon in vielen Choreografien genutzt. Ich glaube, viele Choreograf*innen zeichnen in gewisser Weise im Raum. Aber wenn ich es jetzt bedenke, dann hatte mein Wissen, dass die Künstler*innen die Daten nutzen würden und sie Teil des Projekts sind, vielleicht Einfluss auf die Konzeption. Ich habe auch an Dinge gedacht, die man später mit den Daten zeichnen kann.

Amber: Im Entstehungsprozess ist die Visualisierung von Wegen sehr hilfreich. Aber später weiß der Körper, wohin er sich bewegen und welcher Person er folgen muss.

Lina Louisa Krämer: **Taneli, du hast zuvor schon mit Søren Lyngsø Knudsen gearbeitet, der einer der Künstler und auch der Komponist**

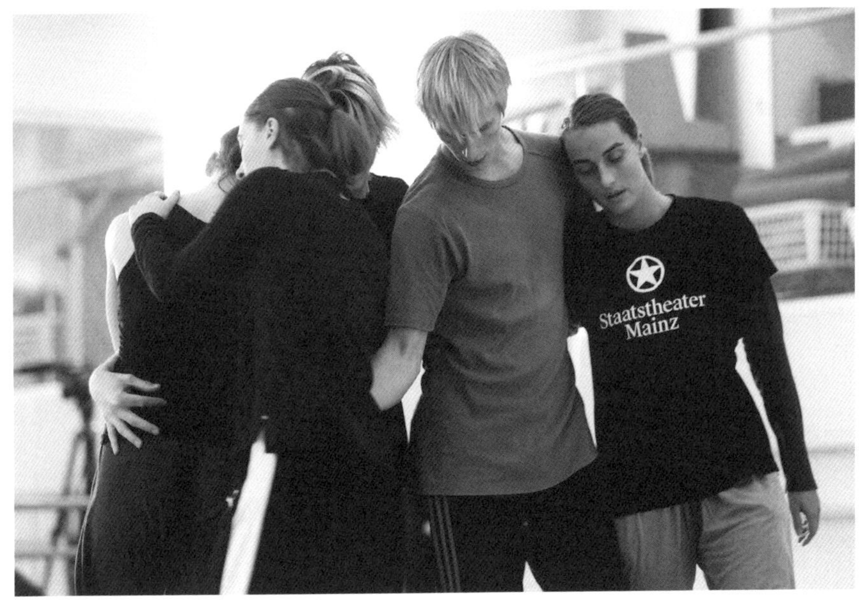

des Sounds für *Effect* ist. Soweit ich mich erinnere, habt ihr zeitgleich an der Komposition und der Choreografie gearbeitet. Wie sah diese Zusammenarbeit aus?

Taneli: Søren hat den Sound für *Effect* während der ersten Probenmonate entwickelt, danach habe ich meistens alleine mit den Tänzer*innen gearbeitet. Als das Stück zur Aufführung fertig war, begann er auf der Basis der von Motion Bank aufgezeichneten Daten, seine eigene Klanginstallation für die Ausstellung zu entwickeln. Ich finde es sehr interessant, beide Arbeiten im Rahmen des Projekts *Between Us* zu präsentieren.

Stefanie: **Siehst du einen Zusammenhang zwischen den künstlerischen Arbeiten und *Effect*?**

Taneli: Nehmen wir die Arbeiten von Tim Etchells als Beispiel. Wenn ich seine Sätze lese, assoziiere ich sie sofort mit meiner Choreografie, aber ich habe das Gefühl, sie nicht ausgesprochen zu haben. Das finde ich ausgesprochen interessant. So ist das zwischen uns: Vielleicht habe ich diesen einen Satz gesagt, aber für mich bedeutete er etwas anderes. Und eine weitere Person versteht ihn vielleicht wiederum anders. Was bedeutet es wirklich, wenn es diese Form von Übertragung gibt? Auf diese Weise wirkt sich der Prozess auf die Regie, die Choreografie und darauf aus, wie diese Art von Stück mit fünf internationalen Tänzer*innen entsteht.

David: **Während der Proben wurdest du permanent für die Dokumentation des Entwicklungsprozesses von einer Kamera gefilmt. Hat dies bei der Konzeption des Stücks etwas verändert?**

Taneli: Ich hatte etwas Sorge, ob sich dies auf die Konzeption des Stücks auswirken würde. Die Kamera war jedoch vom ersten Moment da, und ich war überrascht, wie schnell sie in Vergessenheit geriet. Wäre sie nur einmal die Woche eingeschaltet gewesen, hätte sich dies wie ein besonderes Ereignis angefühlt. Aber da sie immer da war, wurde das schnell normal.

David: **Im Allgemeinen wird Wissen im Tanz von Körper zu Körper übertragen. Das heißt, der Arbeitsmodus besteht darin, zur selben Zeit im selben Raum zu sein. Wie wirkt sich der Prozess der Digitalisierung auf die Tanzkonzeption aus?**

Bojana: Heutzutage machen sich vermutlich die meisten Choreograf*innen die Kamera zunutze. Zuvor musste man sich immer alles merken, aber jetzt ist das einfach: Wir machen eine Aufzeichnung und schauen uns dann das Video an. Das ist hilfreich. Manchmal ist es aber auch schwierig, weil man sich auf etwas verlässt, was zu weit von deinem Körper, deinem Verstand und deinem Gefühl entfernt ist.

Milena Wiese: Ich glaube, man kann das Körpergedächtnis nicht ersetzen, und das ist es, was man letztlich braucht. Du hast diese Beziehung mit der anderen Person und mit dem Raum und fühlst körperlich, was du tust. Ich glaube, es ist gut, sie als Werkzeug zu benutzen, aber wenn du tanzt, musst du mit allen deinen Sinnen anwesend sein, um ständig Entscheidungen treffen zu können.

Honne: Auf meine Arbeit hat die Digitalisierung natürlich einen Einfluss, da ich so viel zu sehen bekomme. Man kann ja jede Aufführung als Aufzeichnung anschauen. Man kann jedes Stück googeln und zumindest Teile davon sehen. Das ist mitunter sehr aufschlussreich, da man mitbekommt, welche Entwicklungen es gibt, und man bekommt neue Ideen. Allerdings muss man sich angesichts dieser Fülle auch klarmachen, dass die Qualität darin besteht, dass wir in der Realität und mit realen Menschen tanzen. Und dass jede Aufführung einzigartig ist und diese Nähe zum*r Zuschauer*in haben muss, um auf die persönliche und körperliche Wahrnehmung wirken zu können.

Effect

Stefanie Böttcher
Zachary Chant
Honne Dohrmann
Lina Louisa Krämer
Finn Lakeberg
Bojana Mitrović
Amber Pansters
David Rittershaus
Taneli Törmä
Milena Wiese

'It's not about reproducing, it's about recreating it every single time when we perform the piece.'

Amber Pansters

David Rittershaus: **When we first discussed the ideas for *Between Us* Honne said almost immediately: 'I think I know a choreographer who would be perfect for this project.' Why did you immediately think of Taneli?**

Honne Dohrmann: For different reasons. First of all we know each other for quite a while and as a dancer and as a choreographer, I've seen several works of Taneli and was really amazed how he was developing and creating very formalized dance pieces that are very humane and touching. At that time I couldn't really see what *Between Us* will look like, but it was clear that there's a demand for flexibility and openness towards the whole project.

Stefanie Böttcher: ***Between Us* is a collaboration that deals with relations and influences. Taneli, which aspects of the project were new for you? Which ones inspired you?**

Taneli Törmä: I was interested to see how I could present the core of a movement. That's why I wanted to make the performance so minimalist. What could Motion Bank and the visual artists do with such reduced information? It was exciting for me to see on which parts of the choreography they then focused and what the piece conveyed to them personally. I was also inspired to make a performance in a museum environment, and interested in how that would change the audience's experience. How the piece would modify through the process was also interesting for me, creating it in a dance studio, presenting it in an art institution together with an exhibition, and later on to see what else might develop when the performance data is provided as open source material. And aside from all this: when a dance piece gets so many impulses from the outside, what can I, as the choreographer control?

David: **A lot of the piece was derived from everyday movement. I'm interested in how it was for you as dancers to work with this kind of movement material that is at the first moment not as 'dancy' as in other pieces?**

Zachary Chant: Firstly it looks very pedestrian, it looks very simple but it's actually incredibly complex as well to maintain or to achieve what Taneli is after: removing extra theatricality or intentions, if something can appear, almost from nowhere and become almost surprising. It is so different, it has its own special language.

Bojana Mitrović: Usually we are trained to rehearse something that is always the same. You are always at this or that point in space, at that moment in the music, but this time it's never the same. Still, we have some structure that we have to maintain, but it always happens in different places, with different people.

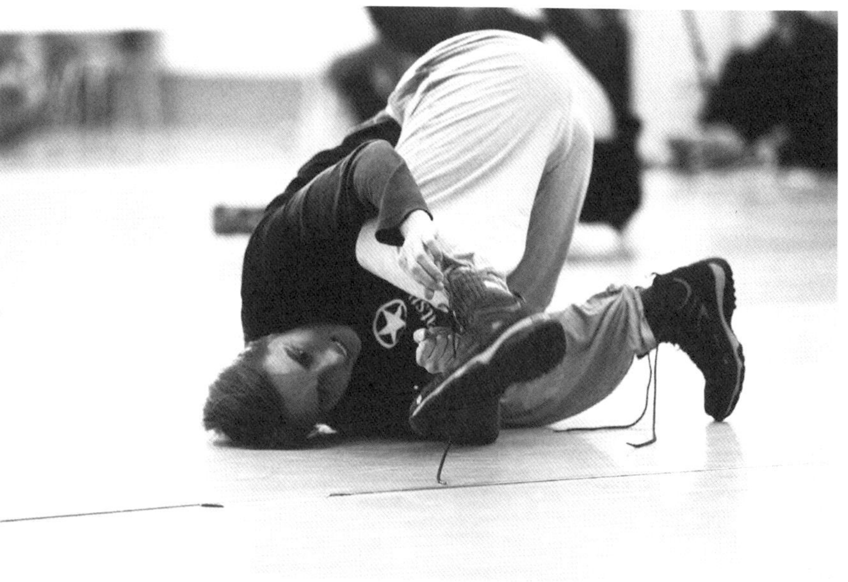

It's multitasking on another level, not what we usually do. Challenging in that sense and very refreshing.

Amber Pansters: It's not about reproducing, it's about recreating it every single time when we perform the piece. That's very fulfilling in a way with a really high concentration, and engagement and being there, awareness. The work seems very simple, but I think it's highly specific and because it's so specific there's a lot of options, it feels like you have to make a decision every second of the piece. That gives you the feeling of having responsibility for the group and for the individuals in the group. We do it together, make sure it works together, and that's why I like this piece very much.

Finn Lakeberg: Especially this feeling of being involved 100% during the creation and also during the performance is, for me, the most valuable thing. And it is the involvement as individuals and with each other as a group, this awareness that you have to have throughout the piece to make it work and to not run into each other and to know where we are in time and space. This journey, which we as a group also went through during the process and during every performance, is something very special.

'I was interested to see how I could present the core of a movement. That's why I wanted to make the performance so minimalistic.'

Taneli Törmä

Honne: I would like to add that this kind of work, which is more conceptual, is totally important for the development of tanzmainz. Because our aim is to extend the languages of dance in our repertoire.

David: **You said the piece is geometrical and this aspect becomes very clear when you visualize the recorded motion capture data. This idea of the body drawing in space on the surface of the floor: what role did it play in the creation process?**

Taneli: I have used it in many choreographies and think many choreographers are somehow drawing in space. But now when we speak about it I think that it was affecting the process that I knew the artists will use the data and it's part of the project. I was also thinking of things that you can later draw with the data.

Amber: In the creation process it really helps to have this visualization of pathways. But now the body knows where to go and which person to follow.

Lina Louisa Krämer: **Taneli, you worked with Søren Lyngsø Knudsen before, who is one of the visual artists and also the composer of the sound for *Effect*. As far as I remember you partly worked on the composition and the choreography simultaneously. What was the collaboration like?**

Taneli: Søren created the sound design for *Effect* during the first months of the rehearsals and after that I mainly worked alone with the dancers. When the performance was ready he started to create his own sound installation for the exhibition based on the data Motion Bank was recording. I think it is super interesting to present both works in the project *Between Us*.

Stefanie: **Do you see any connection between the artworks and *Effect*?**

Taneli: Let's take, for example, Tim Etchells's pieces. When I read the sentences I immediately associate them with my choreography, but I feel like I have not said them. That is interesting for me. It's how things are between us: maybe I said the

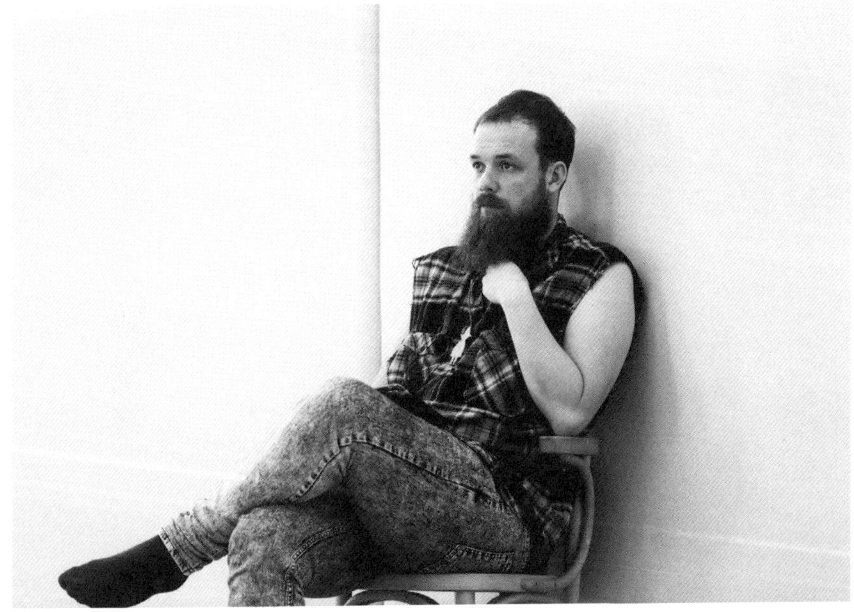

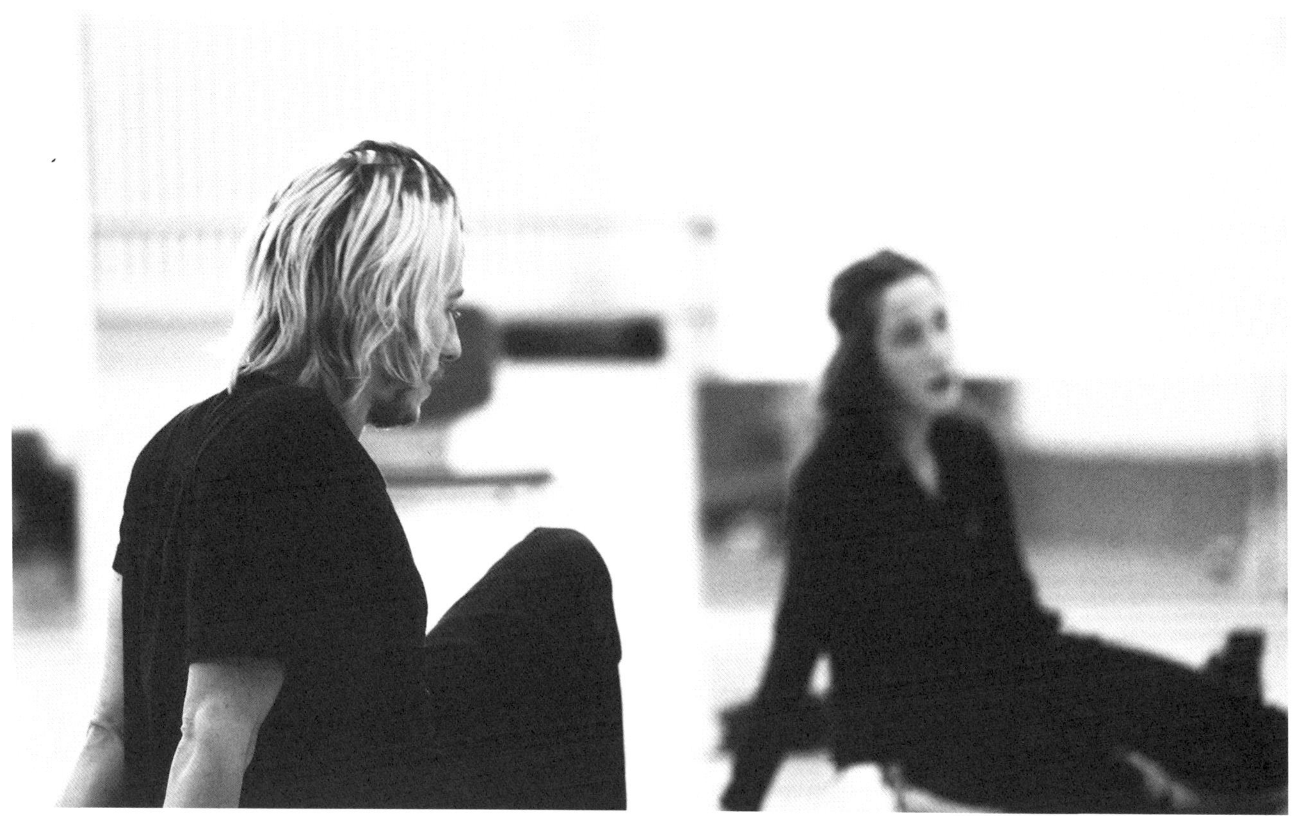

one sentence, but for me it means something else. And then someone else understands it in another way. And then when it has been translated into something else, what does it really mean? In this way it also reflects back on how to direct, how to choreograph, and how to make this kind of piece with five international dancers.

David: **During the rehearsals you've been filmed every day and all the time for the documentation of the process by one camera. Did this change something when you developed the piece?**

Taneli: I was a little bit afraid how it will affect the creation of the piece. But then it was there from the very beginning and I was so surprised how fast we forgot it. I think if it had only happened once a week, it would have felt like a special event. But because it was there all the time, it became normal.

David: **In general, knowledge is transferred from body to body in dance. So the basic mode of working is being in the same space at the same time. How is dance creation affected by this process called digitalization?**

Bojana: Well, nowadays I think all the choreographers are taking advantage of having a camera. Before you would have to remember everything, but now it's easy, we record and go back to the video, in that sense it helps. Sometimes it's difficult because you start to rely on something that is too far away from your body and your mind and feeling.

Milena Wiese: I think you can just never replace the body memory because that's what you will need in the end. You will need to have that relationship with that other person and with the space, feeling physically what you do. I think it's good to use it as a tool, but while dancing you have to be fully there with all your senses in order to make constant decisions.

Honne: For my work digitalization of course has an influence because you see so much, each performance is available to watch because it's recorded. You can google any piece and watch at least parts of it. It's good for knowing how the field is developing as such and what is existing and maybe also getting ideas. But on the other hand, as there is so much, you need to understand better that the quality is that we perform dance in reality and we work with real people. And that each performance needs to be unique and close to the spectators and affect the personal experience, if not even the bodily experience.

TANZ ANNOTATIONEN
DANCE ANNOTATIONS

Online Score
betweenus.motionbank.org

Florian Jenett
Anton Koch
Finn Lakeberg
David Rittershaus
Milena Wiese

„Ich würde sagen, die Dokumentation des Prozesses ist elementar. Sie ist im Grunde ja der Schlüssel zum Wissen über das Stück, und ohne diesen Schlüssel könnten wir mit den Motion-Capture-Daten gar nichts anfangen. Wir würden keinen Sinn darin finden."

Florian Jenett

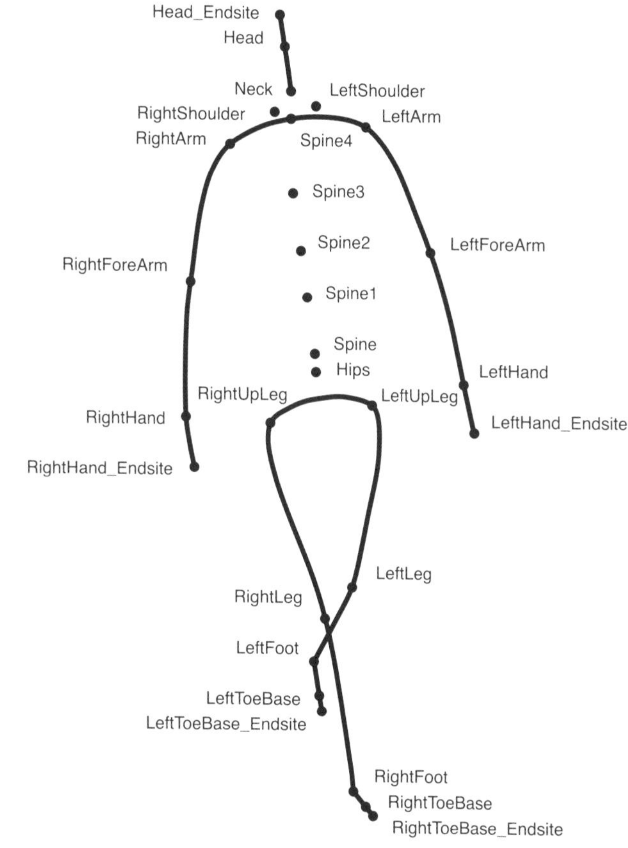

Milena Wiese: **David, wir haben uns gefragt, inwiefern es für eure Arbeit geholfen hat, dass du die ganze Zeit unseren Prozess dokumentiert hast?**

David Rittershaus: Ich würde sagen: sehr, weil ich schon bei den Aufnahmen wusste, durch was für Elemente ihr geht, welche Abschnitte ihr in der Choreografie für euch markiert habt und was diese für eine Struktur hat. Das konnte ich dem Rest des Teams weitergeben, und es hat uns in der Nachbereitung geholfen. Wenn wir die Daten oder die Videoaufzeichnungen betrachtet haben, konnten wir nachvollziehen, was da alles passiert – auch das, was man vielleicht auf den ersten Blick gar nicht sieht.

Florian Jenett: Ich würde sagen, die Dokumentation des Prozesses ist elementar. Sie ist im Grunde ja der Schlüssel zum Wissen über das Stück, und ohne diesen Schlüssel könnten wir mit den Motion-Capture-Daten gar nichts anfangen. Wir würden keinen Sinn darin finden.

David: Ich glaube, es ist zudem etwas Besonderes, was wir mit dieser Mischung von Prozessdokumentation und einer Motion-Capture-Aufzeichnung zusammengestellt haben, weil das selten gemacht wird, dass man eine komplette künstlerische Arbeit auf diese Weise aufnimmt. Es war entscheidend, um sichtbar zu machen, dass hinter den Daten, dass hinter der Bewegung noch mehr steckt, dass es Ideen und Konzepte gibt, die damit verbunden sind.

Finn Lakeberg: **Was hattet ihr für einen wissenschaftlichen Anspruch an dieses Projekt von eurer Perspektive aus? Und/oder wie viel künstlerische Freiheit hattet ihr eigentlich?**

Florian: Wir haben eigentlich fast nie einen künstlerischen Anspruch an die Sachen, die wir machen. Auch in diesem Fall nicht. Das ist nicht unser Feld, sondern wir begleiten künstlerische Prozesse und versuchen, zu verstehen, was dort passiert, und Dinge, die wir dort finden, sichtbar zu machen.

Finn: **Gibt es im Verhältnis zu euren früheren Projekten einen speziellen Aspekt, der euch bei dieser Choreografie von Taneli aufgefallen ist?**

Florian: Es ist ein sehr grafisches Stück, und das war ja auch so von ihm konzipiert. Das spielt uns in diesem

Prozess in die Hände. Wir fanden zudem den Prozess sehr offen, und es hat uns total gefreut und ist super wichtig für unsere Arbeit, dass die Tänzer*innen und der Choreograf auch willens waren, wirklich Einblicke zu gewähren und offen über die Sachen zu reden, ohne groß darüber nachzudenken.

> „Interessant ist der Vergleich von der Datenvisualisierung mittels Strichfigur und dem Video, weil man erst mal einen großen Informationsverlust zwischen Video und dieser Strichfigur feststellt. Nur wenn man eine Frage an diesen Zahlenstrom formuliert, bietet er eigentlich etwas Interessantes an.“
>
> David Rittershaus

Anton Koch: Damit ist es aber auch ein Präzedenzfall, und man kann es im Grunde schlecht vergleichen mit den Aufnahmen vorher. Es ist weniger ein Top-down-Prozess, wo man hingeht und sagt: „Okay, jetzt macht, und dann nehmen wir das irgendwie auf“, sondern der ganze Prozess war verwobener. Dadurch dass es Taneli bewusst war, dass aufgenommen wird, hat dies Einzug in seine choreografische Arbeit genommen, und am Ende hat es uns eine Perspektive gegeben, die es vorher einfach gar nicht gab. Die Bandbreite an Daten, die Tiefe an Einblick in diesen Gesamtentstehungsprozess, das ist nicht vergleichbar.

Milena: **Es war ja auch das erste Mal, dass fünf Tänzer*innen über knapp 60 Minuten außerhalb eines speziellen Studios gleichzeitig aufgenommen werden konnten. Was waren die Herausforderungen?**

Anton: In dieser Form wird Motion Capture normalerweise nicht betrieben. Es wird dafür benutzt, um einzelne kurze Bewegungssequenzen für biomechanische Analysen oder für Spiele und für Filme aufzunehmen. Das sind alles kurze Takes. Keiner macht eine Motion-Capture-Aufzeichnung über eine Stunde ohne Cut. Das ist genauso, wie einen Film in einem Durchlauf zu drehen.

Florian: Unser Ansatz ist eher wie eine klassische Videodokumentation, wo man die Kamera hinstellt und laufen lässt, und dann hat man fünf Stunden Aufnahme, aber alles ist drauf, versus Spielfilm, wo man ganz klare Szenen hat, eine Minute filmt und alles nachher zusammenschneidet. Das war hier gar nicht möglich.

Finn: **Vielleicht könnt ihr noch einmal etwas zu dem Format sagen, wie man sich als Laie dieses voluminöse Datenpaket vorstellen kann und welche Aspekte verloren gehen und welche vielleicht auch erst sichtbar werden?**

Anton: Man kann sich die Motion-Capture-Daten eigentlich ziemlich ähnlich wie ein Video vorstellen. Denkt man an Video, dann ist das einfach nur eine Matrix mit 1920 × 1080 Punkten. Was wir jetzt haben, sind pro Person 29 Schlüsselpunkte am Körper, die Positionen im Raum abbilden. Wir legen das in Standards ab, die jede*r öffnen kann, die oder der sich mit dreidimensionaler Bewegungsaufzeichnung beschäftigt. Durch eigene Abspiel-Software, die wir im Rahmen der Ausstellung anbieten, versuchen wir das aber auch noch ein bisschen zu öffnen. Das richtet sich dann an Leute, die digital gestalten oder digitale Kunst machen.

Florian: Aus unserer Sicht besteht der Datensatz aus mehreren Teilen: den sechs Wochen Prozessdokumentation mit Annotationen, also den Notizen in der Zeit. Dann haben wir natürlich den Motion-Capture-Datensatz selbst. Wir haben aber dazu auch die Videoaufnahmen aus mehreren Perspektiven, und wir haben eine Soundaufnahme. Man muss sich mit allen Teilen beschäftigen. Man muss eine Aufführung oder zumindest mal ein Video vom Stück gesehen haben, um überhaupt zu wissen, was man in den Daten sieht. Man muss wissen, was die Elemente sind, die darin vorkommen, und wie die Struktur der Choreografie funktioniert.

David: Es sind ja erst mal nur Zahlen, und um das verstehen zu können, greift man eigentlich auf etwas zurück, das sich dem Format Video wieder annähert. Man animiert eine Strichfigur, weil man diesen Zahlenstrom als Mensch so roh nicht begreifen kann. Interessant ist der Vergleich von der Datenvisualisierung mittels Strichfigur und dem Video, weil man erst mal einen großen Informationsverlust zwischen Video und dieser Strichfigur feststellt. Nur wenn man eine Frage an diesen Zahlenstrom formuliert, bietet er eigentlich etwas Interessantes an. Diese Fragen kann ich aber nur formulieren, wenn ich mehr darüber weiß, was da passiert. Und durch das Video hat man oft eigentlich ein besseres Bild davon.

Florian: Das ist die klassische Frage des Blicks: Wenn man nicht weiß, wie man auf etwas schaut, dann weiß man auch nicht wirklich, was man sieht. Das ist bei Fotografie ja genauso. Wenn ich keine Haltung habe, dann ist das, was zurückreflektiert, auch unklar. Und so ist es auch hier.

Insofern unterscheidet sich das gar nicht so sehr von dem, was man von anderen Medien gewöhnt ist. Allerdings hat es eine Gefahr: nämlich dass man anfängt, Dinge zu sehen, die gar nicht da sind. Die Gefahr besteht immer bei Daten. Man kann wunderschöne Muster herausarbeiten, die total irrelevant sind. Da muss man sich wirklich sehr stark mit dem Inhalt und der Struktur und der Choreografie und dem Tanzen, dem Physischen, dem Video, am besten in der Aufführung, auseinandersetzen, um zu wissen, womit man arbeitet. Und um die richtigen Fragen zu stellen.

Finn: **Könnte man das Projekt *Between Us* als generelles Plädoyer für Transparenz und Offenlegung von Prozessen sehen?**

Florian: Aus unserer Sicht ist eigentlich das Ziel, das, was wir an Methodik und an Software entwickeln, weitergeben zu können, sodass Tanz grundsätzlich mehr dokumentiert werden kann. Egal, ob diese Dokumentationen dann nachher geöffnet werden oder nicht. Ich finde, die Frage der Öffnung ist dann noch mal eine zweite Frage. Natürlich muss man selber entscheiden, ob man überhaupt dokumentiert, und dann, ob für den internen Bedarf oder um damit an die Öffentlichkeit zu gehen.

David: Nein, nicht generell für Offenlegung. Ich denke, dass es toll ist, wenn eine Öffnung möglich ist. Ich glaube aber auch, dass es für manche Künstler*innen, für bestimmte Projekte wichtig sein kann, den Prozess als einen geschlossenen Raum zu sehen. Es sollte kein Muss geben, und der Raum, in dem diese Prozesse stattfinden, sollte grundsätzlich geschützt sein. Gleichzeitig ist es für die Fragen, die wir an Tanz und Choreografie haben, unglaublich wertvoll, diese Aufzeichnungen zu haben. Auch für Tänzer*innen und Choreograf*innen kann es interessant sein, diesen „unsichtbaren", aber entscheidenden Teil ihrer Arbeit sichtbar zu machen. Deswegen ist es ein Plädoyer dafür, es in dem Maße zu tun, wie das im Einzelfall möglich und gewollt ist.

Dance Annotations

Florian Jenett
Anton Koch
Finn Lakeberg
David Rittershaus
Milena Wiese

Milena Wiese: **David, we were wondering how helpful it was to your work that you documented our entire process?**

David Rittershaus: I would say: very, because I knew even while recording which elements you were walking, which parts of the choreography you had marked out for yourself, and what kind of structure the choreography has. I was able to communicate this to the rest of the team and that helped us in the post-production phase as well. Looking at the data or the video recordings we were able to reconstruct everything that had happened there, even the elements you might not be able to see at first glance.

Florian Jenett: I would say the documentation of the process is elementary. After all, it is essentially the key to our knowledge of the piece—without this key, we would not for example be able to get anything out of the motion capture data, because we wouldn't be able to make any sense of it at all.

David: Also, I do believe that there is something special about what we've put together with this mix of process documentation and motion capture recording. Because it's so rarely done, recording an entire artistic work in this way. It was crucial in visualizing the fact that there are underlying ideas and concepts behind the data, behind the movements.

Finn Lakeberg: **Which kind of scientific aspiration did you have for the project? And/or how great was the range of artistic freedom you enjoyed in this project?**

Florian: We generally almost never have purely artistic aspirations when it comes to the things we do. And this wasn't the case here either, because that's not really our field. Instead we accompany artistic processes and try to understand what is happening there and then render the things we find in them visible.

Finn: **In relation to your earlier projects, was there a special aspect to this choreography by Taneli that caught your attention?**

Florian: It's a very graphic, almost diagrammatical piece and that was after all how he conceived it. Which of course plays into the hands of our process. We also found the process very open and were extremely happy about the fact that the dancers and the choreographer were willing to provide real insights and talk about things openly without overthinking them—that's really important to our work.

Anton Koch: All of that also makes it a precedent which is essentially difficult to compare to the previous recordings. It is less of a top-down process where you go and say: 'Okay, you go ahead and do your thing and we'll record it somehow.' And more of a process that was strongly interwoven. Taneli was aware of the process being recorded and that in turn entered into his choreographic work. In the end this engendered a perspective that hadn't existed beforehand. The bandwidth of data, the depth of insight into the overall process of formation—you can't really compare that to other projects.

'I would say the documentation of the process is elementary. After all, it is essentially the key to our knowledge of the piece—without this key, we would not for example be able to get anything out of the motion capture data, because we wouldn't be able to make any sense of it at all.'

Florian Jenett

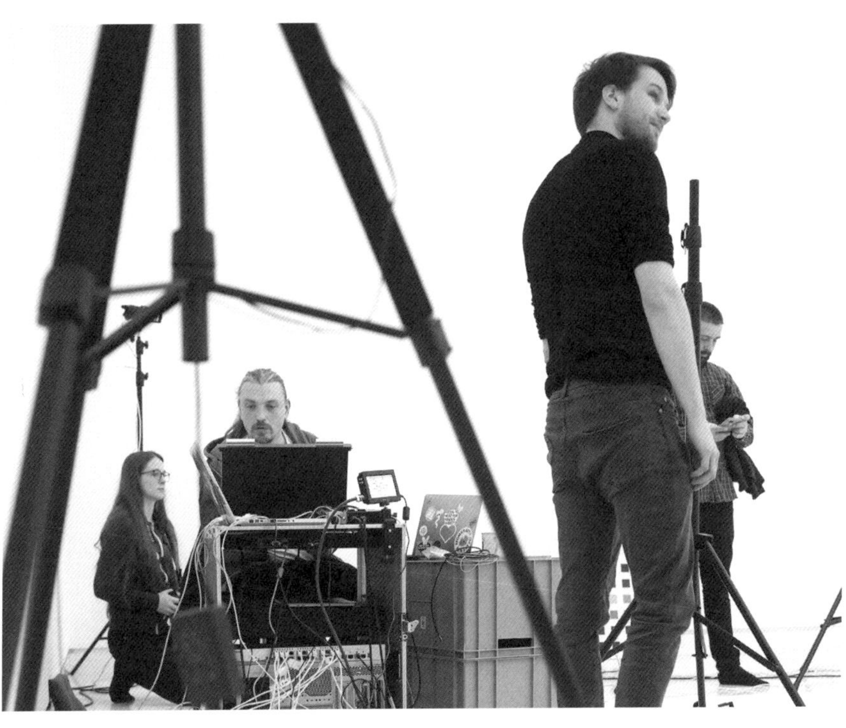

Milena: **It was also the first time that you recorded five dancers for almost 60 minutes outside of a special studio. What challenges did that involve?**

Anton: Motion capture is not usually deployed in this way. It tends to be employed for recording short sequences of movement, for biomechanical analyses, or games, or films. Those are generally short takes. No one does motion capture recordings that last an hour without a cut—that's like filming an entire movie in a single take.

Florian: Our approach is much closer to classic video documentation, where you set up a camera and hit 'record' and then you end up with five hours of recordings, but you've captured everything—in contrast to a feature film, where you have very clear, distinct scenes that are shot by the minute and then pieced together afterwards in the cut. That wasn't possible in this instance.

Finn: **Maybe you could say a little about the format, how a layperson could imagine this huge data package—also which aspects are lost and which may only show up through this recording method?**

Anton: You can imagine motion capture data much in the same way as video. If you think of a video, then that's simply a matrix spanning 1,920 × 1,080 dots. What we have now are 29 key points on the body of each person involved, and those dots represent the positions in space. We save these data in standard formats that anyone working with motion capturing methods can open. But we also try to open things up a bit more by means of a player software we have developed, which we then offer to people in the context of the exhibition. It's geared towards people who, for example, create digital design or art works.

Florian: From our perspective the data set is made up of several parts. Firstly, the six weeks of process documentation with annotations, meaning the notes taken during that time. Secondly of course the motion capture data set itself—but then we also have video recordings from different angles that accompany this, as well as a sound recording. You have to look at all of those parts, to have seen a performance of the piece, or at the very least a video recording of it, in order to gain any idea of what the data shows. You have to know which elements the piece includes and how the structure of the choreography works.

David: After all, to start off with the data simply consists of numbers, and in order to understand them you draw on something that approaches the video format once more. You animate a stick figure, because humans can't comprehend raw streams of numbers like that. Comparing this data visualization using a stick figure with the video is interesting, because the first thing you notice is that a great deal of information is lost in the transition from video to stick figure. It is only once you formulate a question to ask of this stream of numbers that the data provides something interesting. But I can only formulate those questions once I know more about what is happening there. And the video usually gives you a better clue to that.

Florian: That's the classic question of the eye: if you don't really know how you're looking at something then you don't know for sure what it is you're seeing. The same applies to photography of course. If I don't have a clear stance then the things reflected back to me are unclear, too. And the same is true in this case. In this respect it's not so different to what you're used to from other media. However, there is a danger, namely that you start seeing things that aren't there. That danger always exists when it comes to data. Because you can easily start to emphasize patterns that are entirely irrelevant. You really need to analyze the content, and the structure, and the choreography, and the dance very closely and engage with the physical aspects, with the video, or better still the live performance if you want to know what you're working with. And in order to pose the right questions.

'Comparing this data visualization using a stick figure with the video is interesting, because the first thing you notice is that a great deal of information is lost in the transition from video to stick figure. It is only once you formulate a question to ask of this stream of numbers that the data provides something interesting.'

David Rittershaus

Finn: **Could *Between Us* be regarded as a general plea for transparency and the disclosure of processes?**

Florian: From our perspective the goal is to pass on what we develop in terms of methodology and software, in order to make it possible for more to be documented in dance in general, regardless of whether or not that documentation is then disclosed at a later date or not. I think the question of opening things up is a different issue. Of course, you have to decide for yourself whether you want to document at all, and then whether you're documenting for internal use or in order to make this material accessible to the public.

David: No, it's not a general plea for disclosure. I think it's great when opening things up is possible. But I also believe that it can be important to some artists, when it comes to certain projects, to see the process as a closed space. There should be no pressure to do things a certain way and the space in which these processes take place should be protected as a matter of principle. At the same time it is incredibly valuable for us to have these recordings when it comes to addressing the questions we have of dance and choreography. And it can be interesting for dancers and choreographers to render this 'invisible' but crucial part of their work visible. That's why it is a plea for doing things in the dimension that fits the individual case, depending on what's possible and desired.

Im ersten Stock des Turms der Kunsthalle Mainz hat Motion Bank zur Ausstellung einen Raum eingerichtet, in dem man den Prozess des Projekts *Between Us* nachvollziehen kann. An verschiedenen Stationen können dort die Entstehung von *Effect*, die Aufnahme und die Daten betrachtet werden. Arbeitsplätze mit Terminals laden ein zur tiefer gehenden Erforschung des Online Score (http://betweenus.motionbank.org) und dem Experimentieren mit den Daten (http://effect.motionbank.org).

On the first floor of the Kunsthalle Mainz tower, Motion Bank has set up a room accompanying the exhibition in which the process of the Between Us *project can be traced. The creation of* Effect, *the recording, and the data can be viewed at various stations. Workstations with terminals invite visitors to delve deeper into the online score (http://betweenus.motionbank.org) and experiment with the data (http://effect.motionbank.org).*

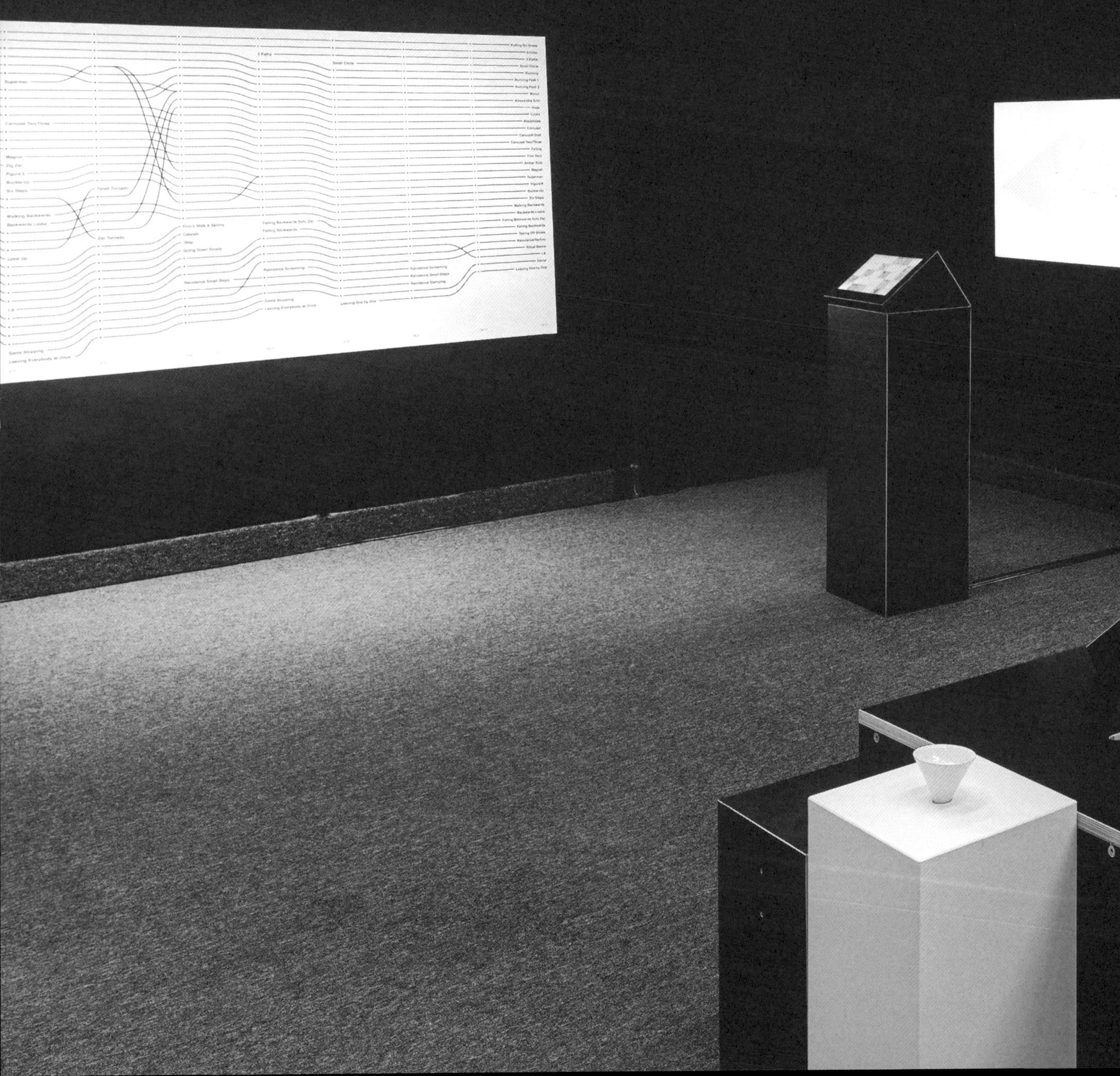

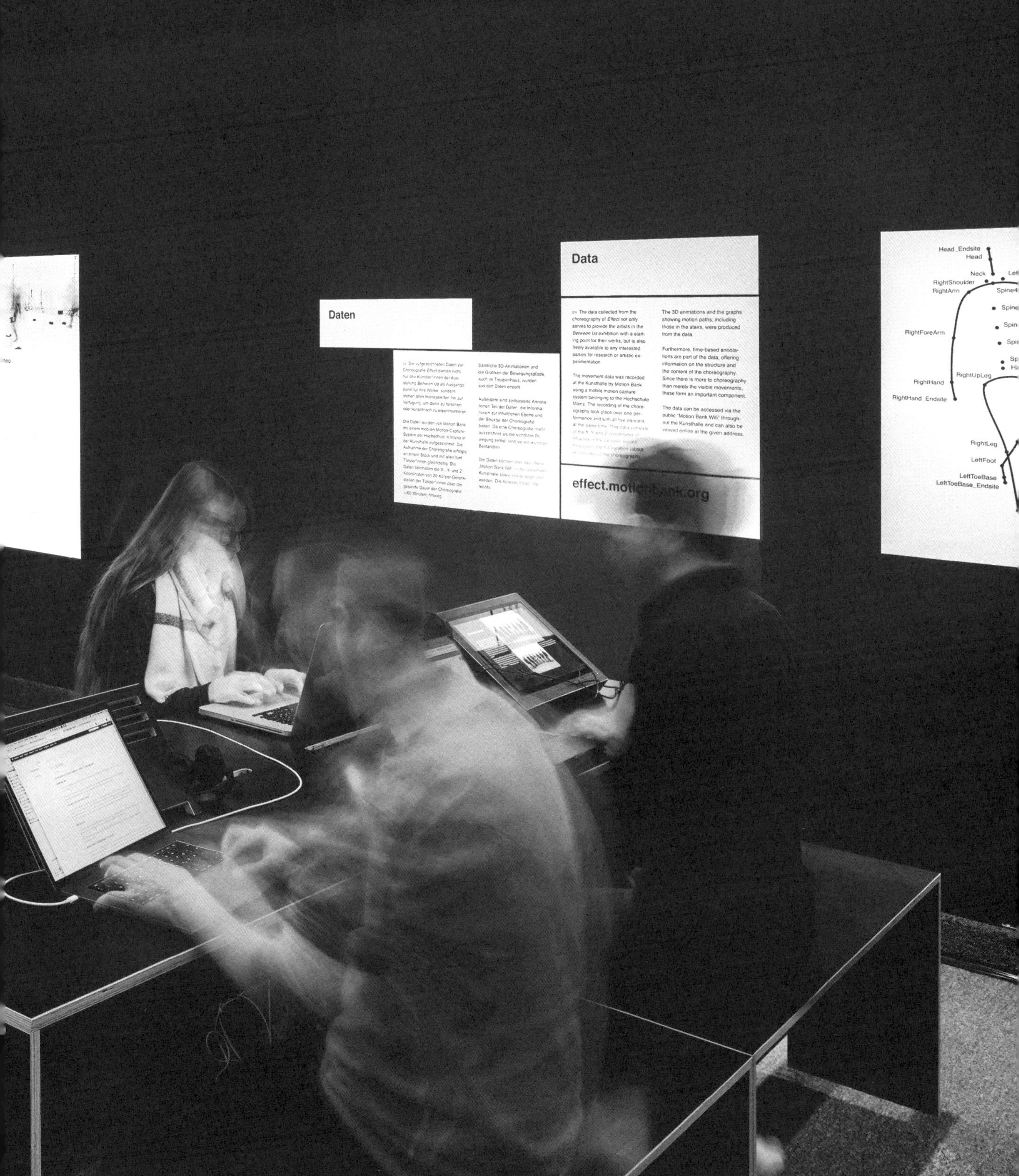
Daten
Sämtliche 3D-Animationen und die Grafiken der Bewegungspfade, auch im Treppenhaus, wurden aus den Daten erstellt.
Data
The data collected from the choreography of Effect not only serves to provide the artists in the Between Us exhibition with a starting point for their works, but is also freely available to any interested parties for research or artistic experimentation.
The movement data was recorded at the Kunsthalle by Motion Bank using a mobile motion capture system belonging to the Hochschule Mainz. The recording of the choreography took place over one performance and with all five dancers
The 3D animations and the graphs showing motion paths, including those in the stairs, were produced from the data.
Furthermore, time-based annotations are part of the data, offering information on the structure and the content of the choreography. Since there is more to choreography than merely the visible movements, these form an important component.
The data can be accessed via the public "Motion Bank Wifi" throughout the Kunsthalle and can also be viewed online at the given address.
Head_Endsite
Head
Neck
RightShoulder
RightArm
RightForeArm
RightHand
RightHand_Endsite
RightUpLeg
RightLeg
LeftFoot
LeftToeBase
LeftToeBase_Endsite

Motion Bank
Motion Capturing

Start

0:00
Putting On Shoes

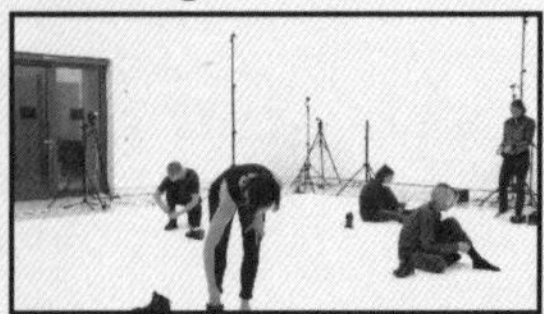

3:12
Circles

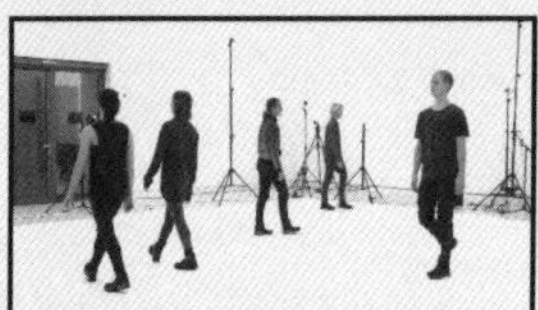

12:34
Small Circle

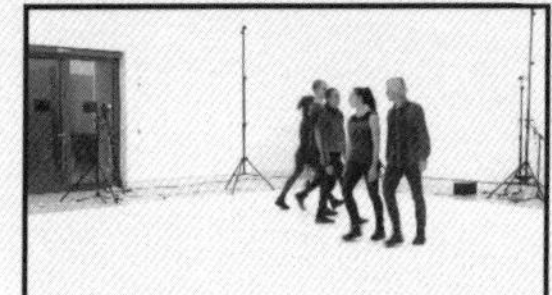

14:04
Running

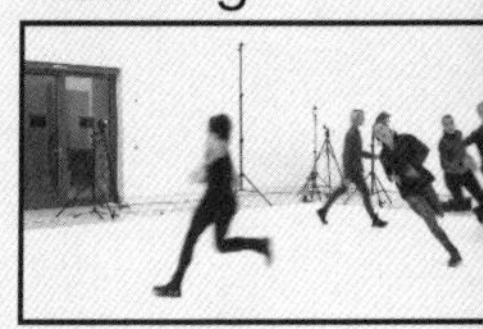

21:10
Blackholes

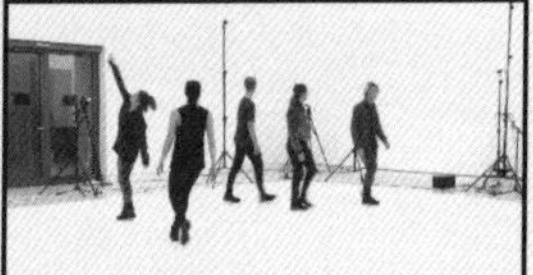

24:31
Carousel

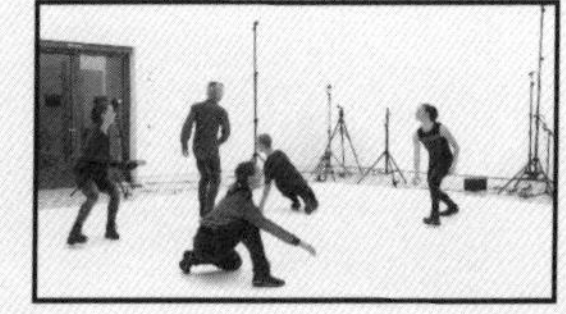

30:37
Superman

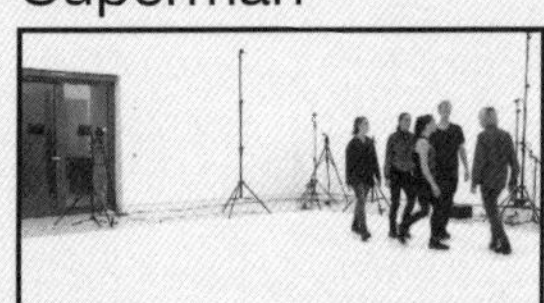

32:19
Figure 8

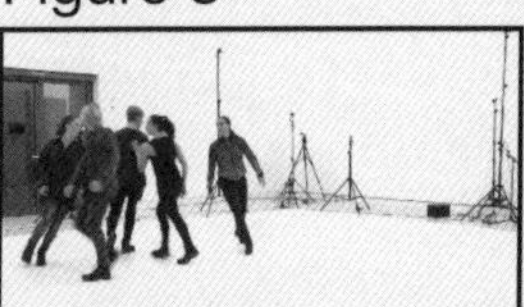

34:06
Buckle-Up

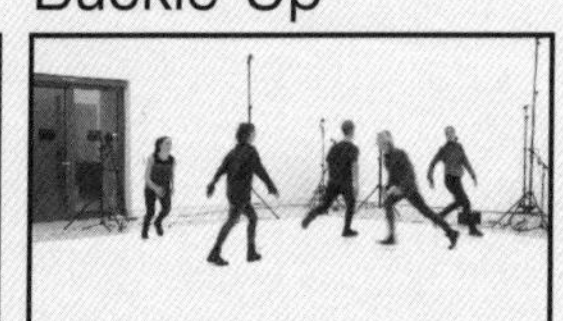

34:21
Six Steps

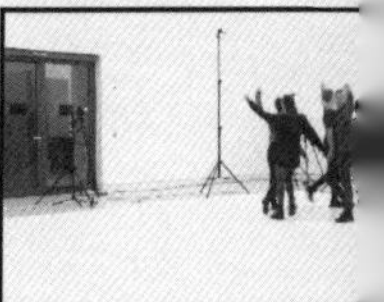

40:25
Falling Backwards

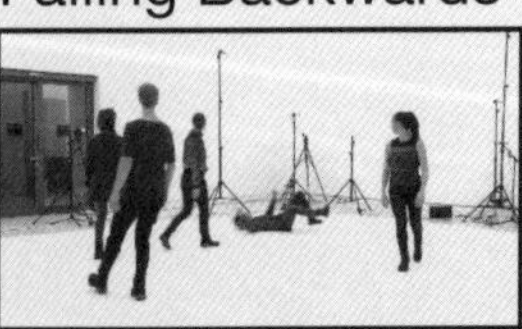

41:01
Taking Off Shoes

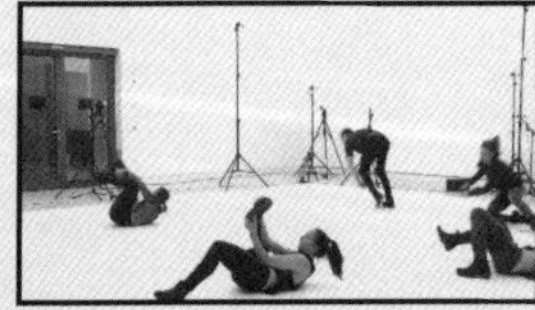

41:27
Raindance/Techno

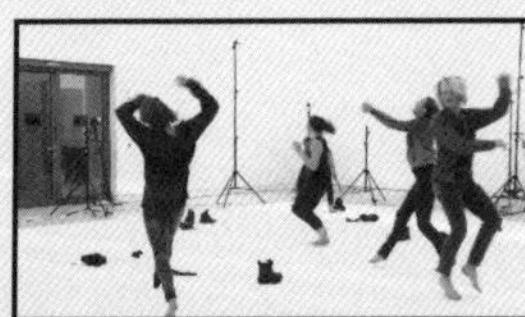

42:44
Ritual Dance

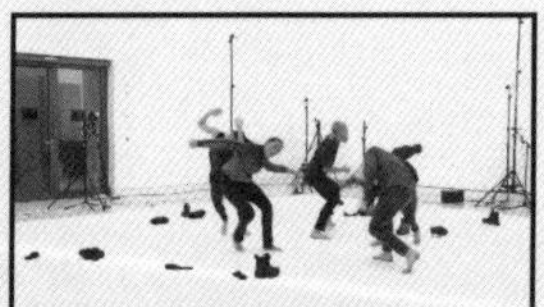

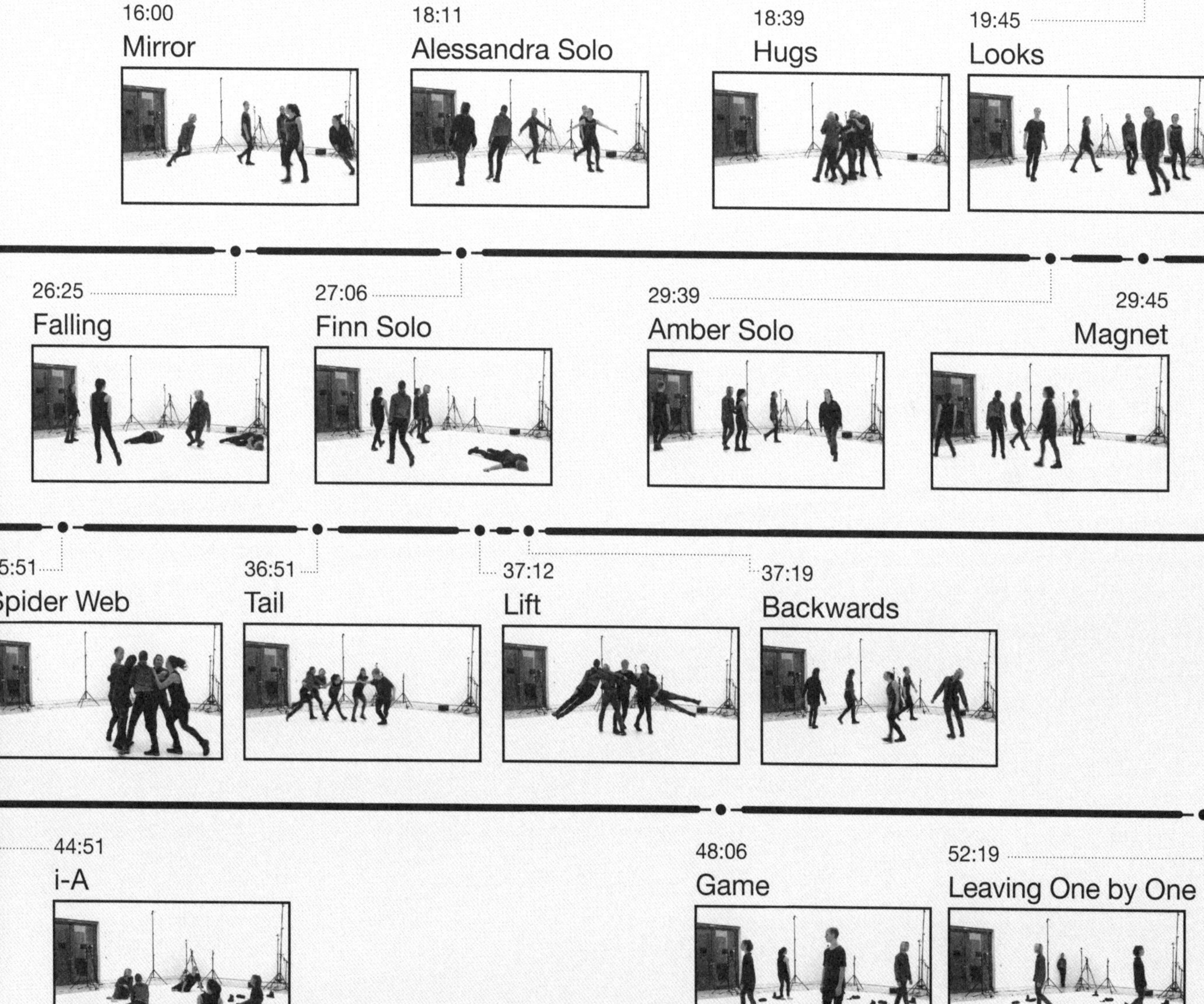
16:00
Mirror
18:11
Alessandra Solo
18:39
Hugs
19:45
Looks
26:25
Falling
27:06
Finn Solo
29:39
Amber Solo
29:45
Magnet
35:51
Spider Web
36:51
Tail
37:12
Lift
37:19
Backwards
44:51
i-A
48:06
Game
52:19
Leaving One by One
End

Bewegungsdaten
Motion data

Amber
Amber Pansters

Zac
Zachary Chant

Bojana
Bojana Mitrović

Finn
Finn Lakeberg

Mila
Milena Wiese

Die abgebildeten Graphen wurden aus den Bewegungsdaten der Aufzeichnungen von *Effect* erstellt. Dargestellt sind die Bewegungspfade der Tänzer*innen über ausgewählte Zeiträume des Stücks hinweg, die anhand der Bewegung des Kopfes oder der Füße ermittelt wurden. Sie zeigen die sonst unsichtbaren Spuren, die für den jeweiligen Abschnitt charakteristisch sind.

The charts illustrated were compiled using motion data from the recording of *Effect*. The display the paths taken by the dancers' heads or feet selected periods of time during the piece. The charts reveal otherwise invisible tracks that are characteristic of the particular section.

Putting On Shoes

00:00

Die Tänzer*innen betreten zu Beginn des Stücks einzeln die Bühne und ziehen ihre Schuhe an. Damit bereiten sie sich auf das nachfolgende Gehen im Kreis vor. Sie müssen sicherstellen, dass die Schuhe für die Aufführung gut sitzen, wie vor einer Bergwanderung. Da noch keine Musik läuft, lassen sich die Geräusche der Schuhe, wie das Festzurren der Schnürsenkel, gut hören. Ein Detail, auf das Choreograf Taneli Törmä Wert gelegt hat.

The dancers enter the stage one after the other at the beginning of the piece and put on their shoes. This prepares them for the following walk in a circle. They make sure that the shoes fit well for the performance like one would do before a mountain hike. Since no music is playing yet, the noises of the shoes and the lashing of the laces can be heard well. This is a detail choreographer Taneli Törmä has put a lot of emphasis on.

Diese Abbildung zeigt die Bühne von oben. Die Linien sind Bewegungspfade der Füße der Tänzer*innen.

This image shows the stage as seen from above. The lines are the movements of the feet of the dancers.

Diese Graphen zeigen die Bewegungspfade der Köpfe der fünf Tänzer*innen.

These lines show the movement of the five dancers' heads.

Circles

03:12

„Ihr bewegt euch um einen Mittelpunkt herum, in die gleiche Richtung im Kreis. Ihr könnt den Abstand zum Mittelpunkt ändern. Die Bewegung ist reduziert auf Gehen und Laufen. Selbst wenn ihr mal stehen bleibt, behaltet ihr das Gefühl, vorwärtszugehen. Das ist die Aufgabe: Es geht die ganze Zeit vorwärts. Und noch eine Aufgabe: Diese Reise, die macht ihr allein. Wir gehen in der Gruppe, aber wir sind immer allein. Ihr könnt Impulse aufnehmen oder mit der Spannung spielen, ihr könnt Effekte auf die anderen haben, aber ihr seid immer noch auf eurer eigenen Reise. Letzte Sache: Wenn ihr vorwärtsgeht – geht ihr irgendwohin, geht ihr fort?"

Gekürzte Anweisung von Choreograf Taneli Törmä bei der ersten Probe mit den Tänzer*innen.

Das Grundprinzip der Szene wurde bis zum Ende beibehalten, jedoch wurde viel an Details gearbeitet. In den ersten Minuten sind die fünf Kreisbahnen, auf denen die Tänzer*innen gehen, und die Bahnwechsel festgelegt, später löst sich die Struktur auf. Vieles davon ist in den Graphen zu erkennen.

'You move around a center point, in the same direction in a circle. You can change the distance from that center. Movement is restricted to walking and running. Even if you stop now and again you will still feel as if you are moving forwards. That is the task: Moving forwards all the time. And another task: this journey, you're on it on your own. We walk in a group, but we are always alone. You can take in impetus or play with the tension, you can have effects on the others, but you are still on a journey of your own. One more thing: when you go forwards, are you going somewhere, or leaving?'

Abridged instructions by choreographer Taneli Törmä at the first rehearsal with the dancers.

The basic principle of the scene was retained until the end, but a lot of work was done on the details. For the first few minutes the five circular strips on which the dancers walk, and when they change strips, are specified, later on the structure dissolves. A lot of that is recognizable in the charts.

Mirror

16:00

Im Element „Mirror" spiegeln sich die Tänzer*innen gegenseitig, während sie weiter im Kreis gehen. Es gibt mehrere klar definierte Bewegungen, die in einer festgelegten Reihenfolge erscheinen sollen, die Tänzer*innen müssen einander konzentriert ansehen, weil sie herausfinden müssen, wer die Bewegung einleitet und wer sie dann spiegelt. Es ist nicht beabsichtigt, dass das Publikum alle Bewegungen bemerkt. Einige von ihnen wirken sehr beiläufig und alltäglich, wie das Zurückstreichen der Haare oder das Ausstrecken eines Arms. Ab einem bestimmten Zeitpunkt wird nur noch gespiegelt, was Amber vorgibt („Alessandra Solo").

In the element 'Mirror' the dancers mirror each other as they continue to walk in circles. There are several clearly defined movements to appear in a fixed order, but the dancers need to watch at each other closely because they need to find out who is initiating the movement and who is mirroring it. It is not the intention that the audience will notice all the movements. Some of them seem very casual and everyday, like stroking back one's hair or stretching out an arm. From a certain point onwards, only what Amber does is being mirrored ('Alessandra Solo').

Hugs

18:39

Dies ist der erste Moment des Stücks, in dem sich die Tänzer*innen gegenseitig berühren. Die Bezeichnung „Hug" (Umarmung) wurde im Laufe der Proben für alle möglichen Varianten der gemeinsamen Berührung im Zentrum der Bühne eingeführt, während die Tänzer*innen weiter im Kreis gehen. An dieser Stelle des Stücks gibt es drei Umarmungen, wobei die erste nicht richtig zustande kommt: eine Umarmung ohne Berührung.

It is the first moment of the piece in which the dancers touch each other. The term 'Hug' was introduced during the rehearsals for all possible variations of the common touch in the center of the stage, during which the dancers continue to walk in circles. At this point of the play there are three embraces, the first of which does not come about properly: a touchless embrace.

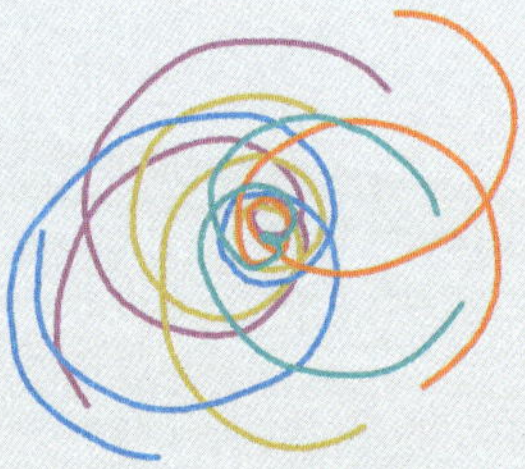

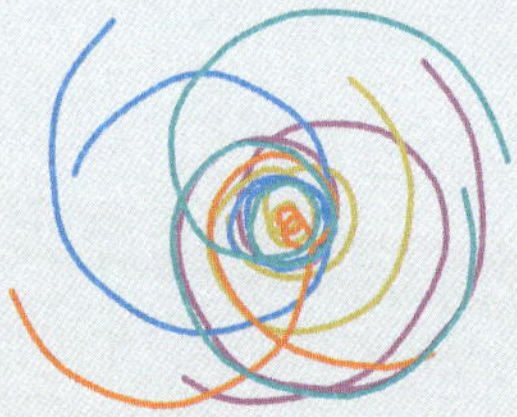

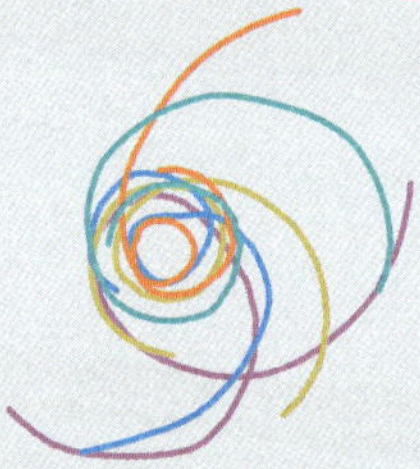

Looks

19:45

Im Abschnitt „Looks" ändert sich der Blickfokus der Tänzer*innen. Anstatt geradeaus zu schauen oder einander anzusehen, blicken sie nun nach außen in den Raum. Nach und nach beginnen sie dabei, in die gleiche Richtung zu schauen. Rennt eine*r der Tänzer*innen eine Runde, ist dies das Zeichen für die ganze Gruppe, den gemeinsamen Fokuspunkt zu wechseln.
Die Blickrichtung der Tänzer*innen ist über das ganze Stück hinweg festgelegt und Teil der Choreografie. Die Zuschauer*innen neigen dazu, der Verschiebung der Blicke zu folgen, damit ändert sich auch die gesamte Körperwahrnehmung.

For the section 'Looks' the focus of the dancers' gaze changes. Instead of looking straight ahead or looking at each other, they now look outwards into the room. Gradually they begin to look in the same direction. If one of the dancers runs a round, this is the sign for the whole group to change the common focus point.
The direction of the dancers' gaze is fixed throughout the whole piece and is part of the choreography. The perception of the whole body movement changes due to the shift of the gaze, because the spectator tends to follow the gaze.

Carousel

24:31

Der Abschnitt wird „Carousel“ genannt, weil die Gesamtbewegung der Gruppe an ein Karussell oder, besser gesagt, an ein „Breakdancer“-Karussell erinnert. Das „Carousel“ ist durch eine bestimmte Schrittbewegung geprägt, die „Triangle Steps“ genannt wird. Grundsätzlich gehen die Tänzer*innen dabei in einem Dreieck und kreuzen die Beine nur selten. Die Beinstellung ist immer offen und erfordert ein leichtes Plié, also gebeugte Knie. Der Oberkörper folgt der Bewegung der Füße, während der Blick und der Kopf unabhängig davon umherwandern.

The section is called 'Carousel' because the overall movement of the group is reminiscent of a merry-go-round, or rather a 'breakdancer' merry-go-round. The 'Carousel' is characterized by a certain step movement called 'triangle steps.' Basically the dancers walk in a triangle and rarely cross their legs. The leg position is always open and requires a slight plié, i.e. bent knees. The upper body follows the movement of the feet, while the gaze and the head wander around independently.

Diese Darstellung zeigt die Spuren der Füße der Tänzer*innen.

This image shows the traces of the dancers' feet.

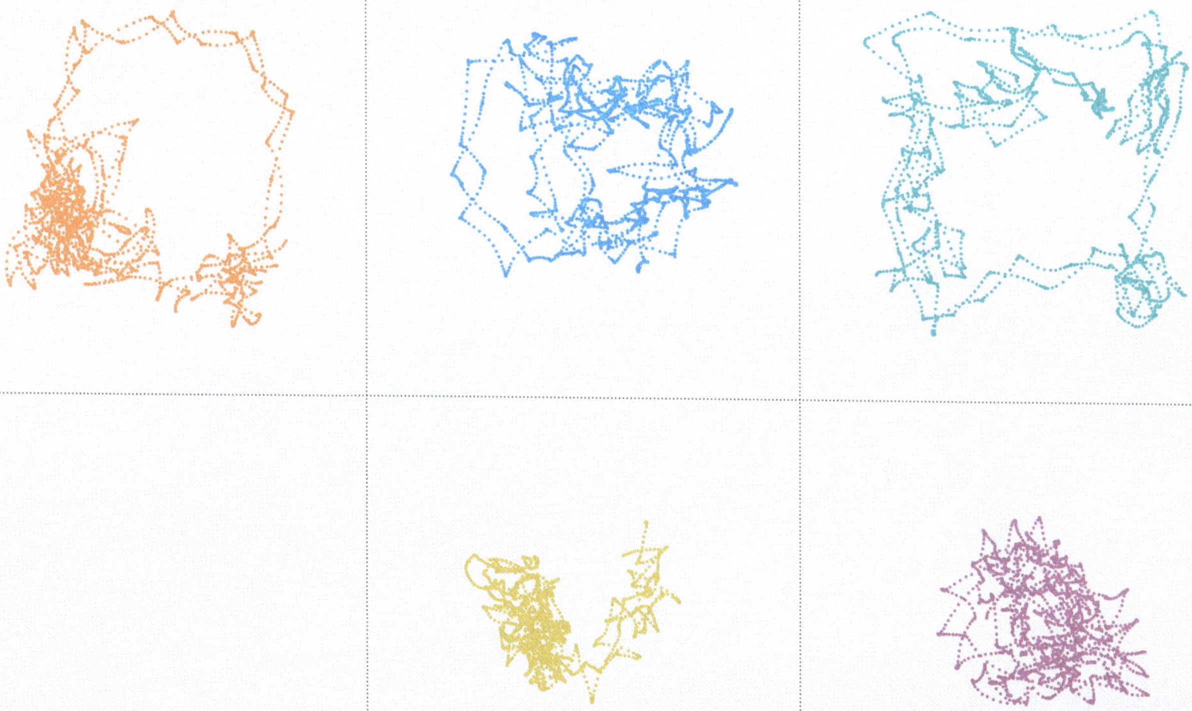

Falling

26:25

Regel für das Fallen: Nur wenn jemand fällt, kann ein anderer aufstehen.

Rule for falling: only when someone falls can someone else stand up.

Finn Solo

27:06

Finns Solo ist ein Teil, in dem es für das Publikum womöglich einfacher ist als in anderen Abschnitten, eine Geschichte im Tanz zu sehen. Nachdem alle Tänzer*innen immer wieder gefallen und aufgestanden sind, bleibt Finn als Einziger am Boden liegen, während die anderen um ihn herum unbeirrt im Kreis gehen. Schließlich rollen und ziehen sie ihn durch die Gegend, bis er wieder aufsteht. Choreograf Taneli Törmä ist bei dieser Szene daran gelegen, keine eindeutige Geschichte zu erzählen, um den Moment für verschiedene Lesarten offenzuhalten. Die innere Haltung, die Finn daher einnehmen soll, ist einfach die eines „müden Tänzers", der noch einen Moment verweilen will. Alles andere geschieht in den Köpfen der Zuschauer*innen.

In comparison to the other parts Finn's Solo might be looked at as a story by the audience. After all the dancers have fallen and got up again and again, Finn is the only one who remains on the floor, while the others around him walk in circles. Finally they roll and pull him along until he gets up again. In this scene choreographer Taneli Törmä is not trying to tell a clear story but rather to keep it open for different readings. Finn's inner attitude is simply that of a 'tired dancer' who wants to linger for a moment. Everything else happens in the heads of the audience.

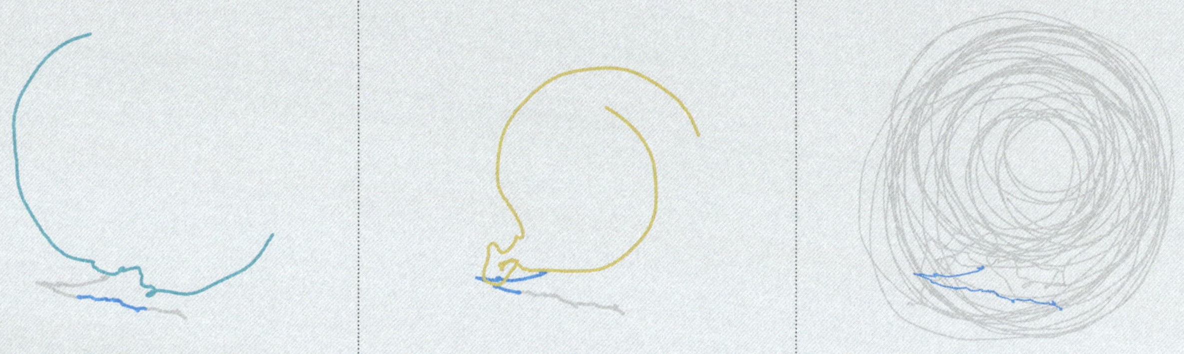

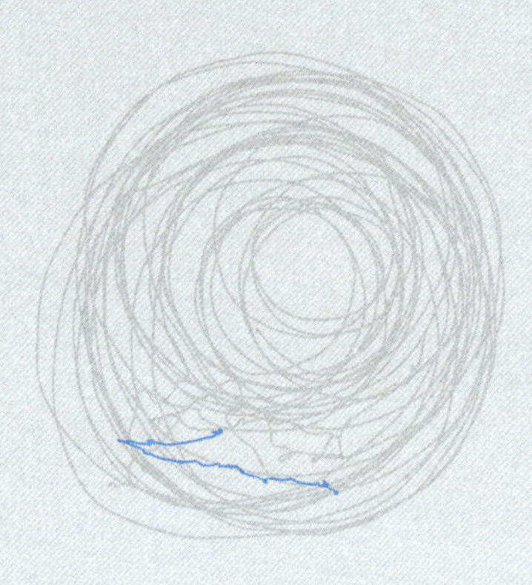

Magnet

29:45

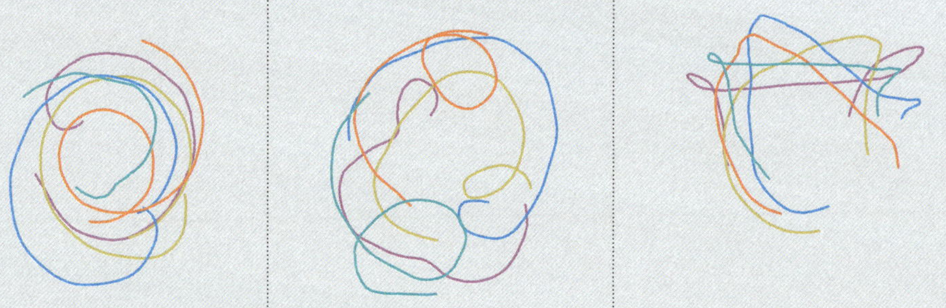

Für „Magnet" stellen sich die Tänzer*innen ein Gravitationszentrum in der Mitte der Bühne vor, das eine anziehende Kraft hat, während sie sich gegenseitig abstoßen. Gleichzeitig versuchen sie, auf ihren Bahnen weiter im Kreis zu gehen.

For 'Magnet,' the dancers imagine a gravitational center in the middle of the stage that has an attracting force on them while they repel each other. At the same time, they try to keep going in circles on their orbits.

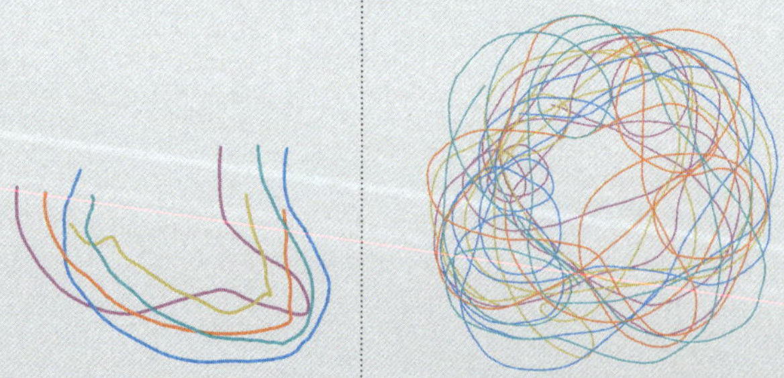

Figure 8

32:19

Die Figur Nr. 8 war das achte Knotenmuster auf einem Blatt mit mehreren Abbildungen von Seilknoten. In den Proben diente es als erste Vorlage für dieses choreografische Element. Außerdem ist die Grundform des Knotens, die von den Tänzer*innen räumlich adaptiert wurde, eine Acht. Das Muster lässt sich in den abgebildeten Graphen der Bewegungspfade besonders gut wiedererkennen. Außer der Knoten-Figur mit der Nummer 8 wurden noch andere Formen in das Element eingearbeitet. Die choreografische Arbeit folgt hier besonders deutlich der Idee des Körpers als Zeichenstift im Raum.

Figure no. 8 was the eighth knot pattern on a sheet with several illustrations of rope knots. In the rehearsals it served as the first model for this choreographic element. In addition, the basic shape of the knot, which was spatially adapted by the dancers, is an eight. The pattern can be seen particularly well in the graphs of the movement paths. In addition to the knot figure with the number 8, other shapes have been incorporated into the element. The choreographic work here clearly follows the idea of the body as a pencil in space.

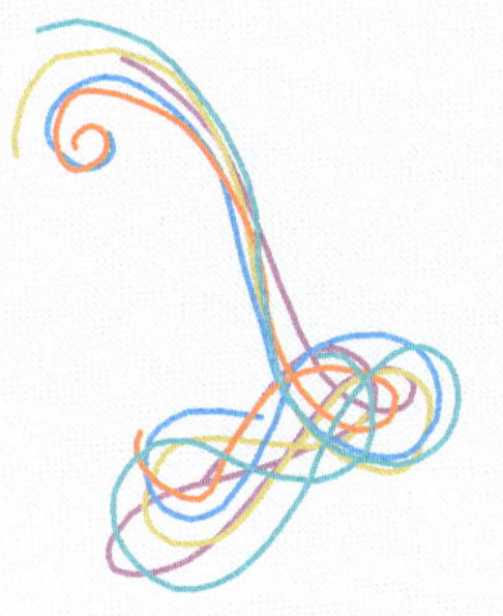

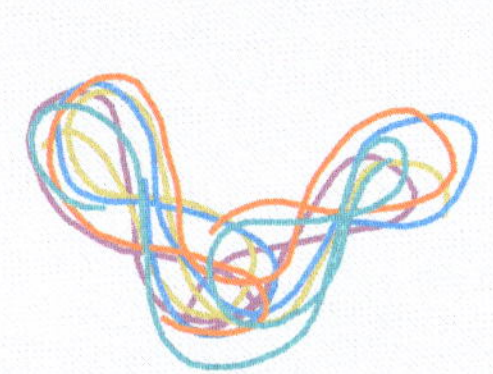

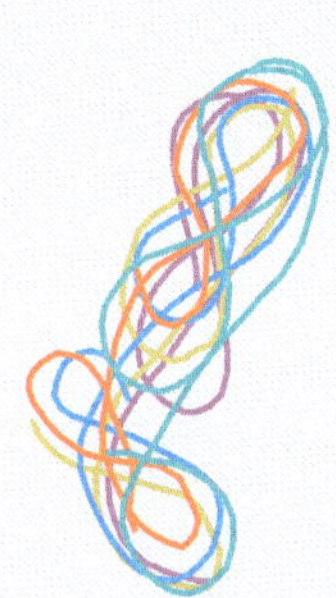

Buckle-Up

34:06

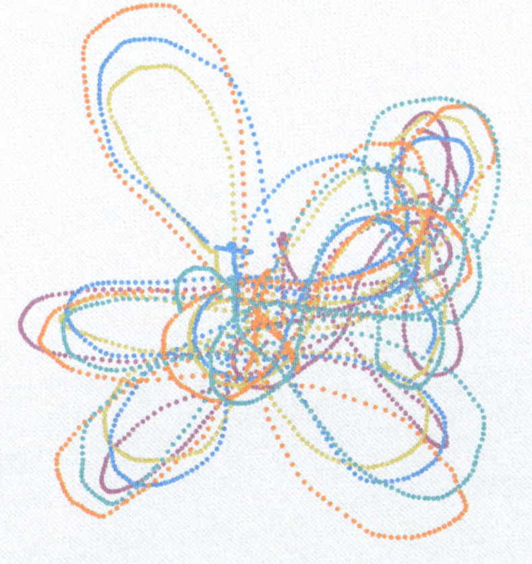

Spider Web

35:51

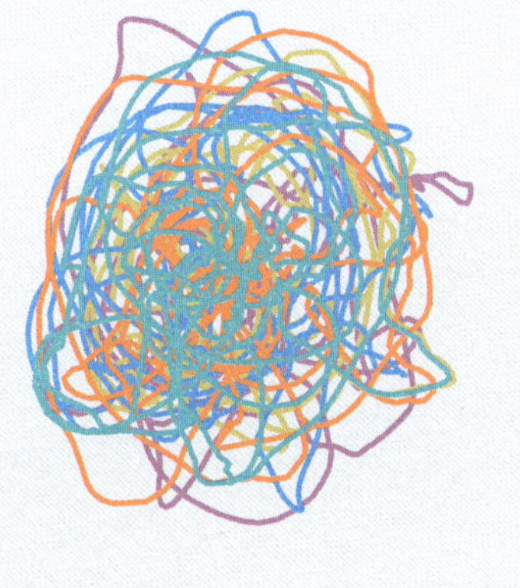

Der Name „Spinnennetz“ deutet bereits an, was passiert: Die Tänzer*innen verhaken sich in einem selbst geschaffenen Netz ihrer Körper, gleichzeitig versuchen sie, in der Gruppe immer etwas Platz für sich selbst zu erhalten. Zuerst setzten sie dafür vor allem die Hände und Arme ein, jedoch zunehmend ihren gesamten Körper, sodass der zweite Teil davon auch als „Wrestling“ bezeichnet wird. Gerade im Vergleich zur sonstigen Berührung im Stück erhält die Szene durch die aggressivere Körperlichkeit eine andere Konnotation.

The name already indicates what happens: the dancers get caught in a web of their own bodies, but at the same time they always try to make some space for themselves in the group. First they use their hands and arms, but in the course of the sequence more and more their whole body, so that the second part of it is also called 'Wrestling.' Especially in comparison to other moments of touching this scene has a different connotation because of the more aggressive physicality.

Backwards

37:19

In diesem Abschnitt des Stücks gehen die Tänzer*innen rückwärts und finden dabei zurück auf die Kreisbahnen vom Anfang, die sich in den vorigen Elementen immer mehr aufgelöst haben. Beim Rückwärtsgehen sollten die Tänzer*innen das Bild des ersten Teils des Stückes im Hinterkopf haben. Elemente wie das Rennen und der Blick nach außen tauchen wieder auf.

In this section of the piece, the dancers go backwards and find their way back to the circular paths from the beginning, which have dissolved more and more in the previous sections. When walking backwards, the dancers should imagine the image of the first part of the piece. Elements like the race and looking to the outside reappear.

Raindance/Techno

41:27

Der Tanz in diesem Teil wurde während des Entstehungsprozesses häufig als „Regentanz“ bezeichnet, manchmal aber auch als „Techno“. Ähnlich wie beim Gehen entspringt der Techno-Aspekt einer Bewegungsrecherche im Laufe der Proben, die sich mit alltäglicher Bewegung beschäftigte. Es geht um Bewegung, die kein Publikum adressiert, wie das ekstatische Tanzen in einem Club. Außerdem stecken in diesem Element einige Bewegungsformen, die ihren Ursprung in einer Recherche zu Volkstänzen und religiösen Gruppenritualen mit kreisförmig choreografierter Bewegung haben. Insbesondere der letzte Teil des Abschnitts erinnert mit seiner klar festgelegten ornamentalen Struktur an ein Ritual.

The dance in this part was often called 'Raindance' during the creation process, but sometimes also 'Techno.' Similar to walking, the Techno aspect arises from an exploration of everyday movements in the course of the rehearsals. It makes use of movement that doesn't address an audience, like ecstatic dancing in a club. In addition, there are some movement forms in this element that have their origin in research on folk dances and religious group rituals with circularly choreographed elements. The last part of the section in particular, with its clearly defined ornamental structure, is reminiscent of a ritual.

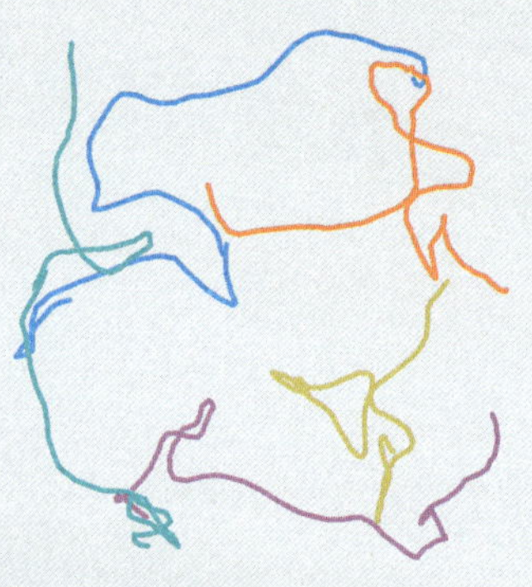

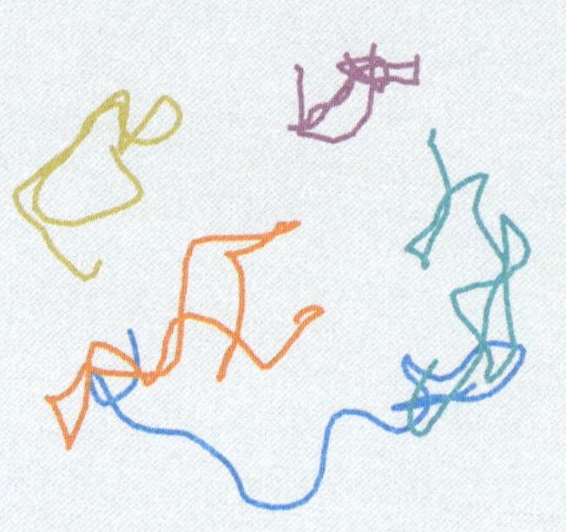

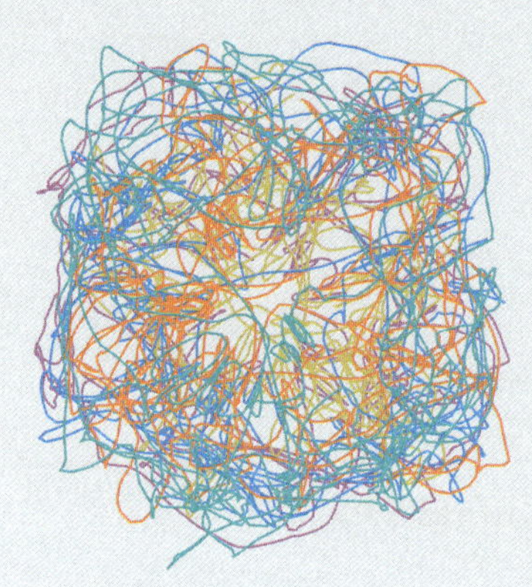

Ritual Dance

42:44

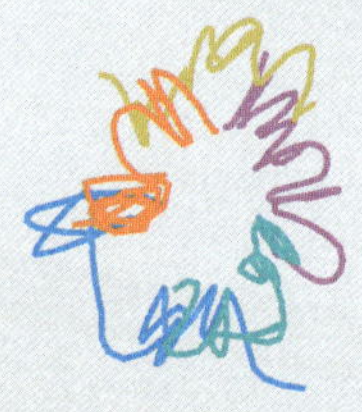

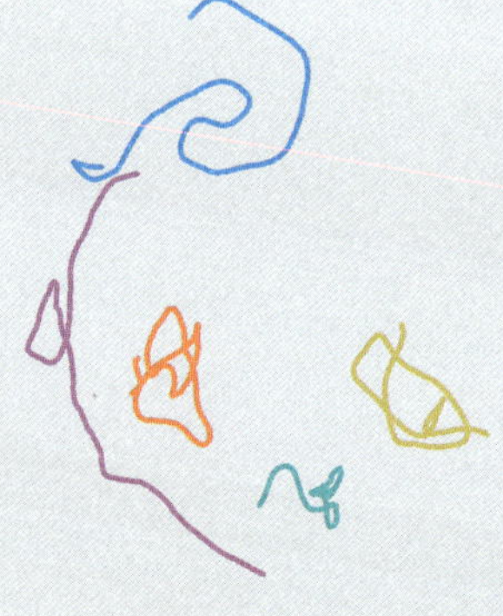

i-A

44:51

Die stimmlichen „i-A“-Klänge, welche die Tänzer*innen hier gemeinsam von sich geben, kommen von „in“ und „out“ („o“ wurde zu „A“) und beschreiben die Bewegung ihrer Brust, die sie, auf dem Boden sitzend, einziehen oder rausschieben. Zu Beginn und am Schluss bewegen sie sich im gleichen Rhythmus, dazwischen etablieren einzelne Tänzer*innen ein anderes Muster, dem sich manche anschließen, andere nicht. Auch dieses Element der Choreografie hat, wie das vorausgehende, seinen Ursprung in einer Recherche zu Ritualen. Das thematische Motiv des Verhältnisses von Individuum und Gruppe, das für das ganze Stück eine Rolle spielt, ist auch hier präsent.

The vocal 'i-A' sounds, which the dancers speak together, come from 'in' and 'out' ('o' became 'A') and describe the movement of their chest, which they pull in or push out sitting on the floor. At the beginning and at the end they move in the same rhythm, in between some dancers establish a different pattern, which some follow, others do not. This element of the choreography, like the previous one, also has its origin in a research into rituals. The thematic motif of the relationship between individual and group, which plays a role for the whole piece, is also present here.

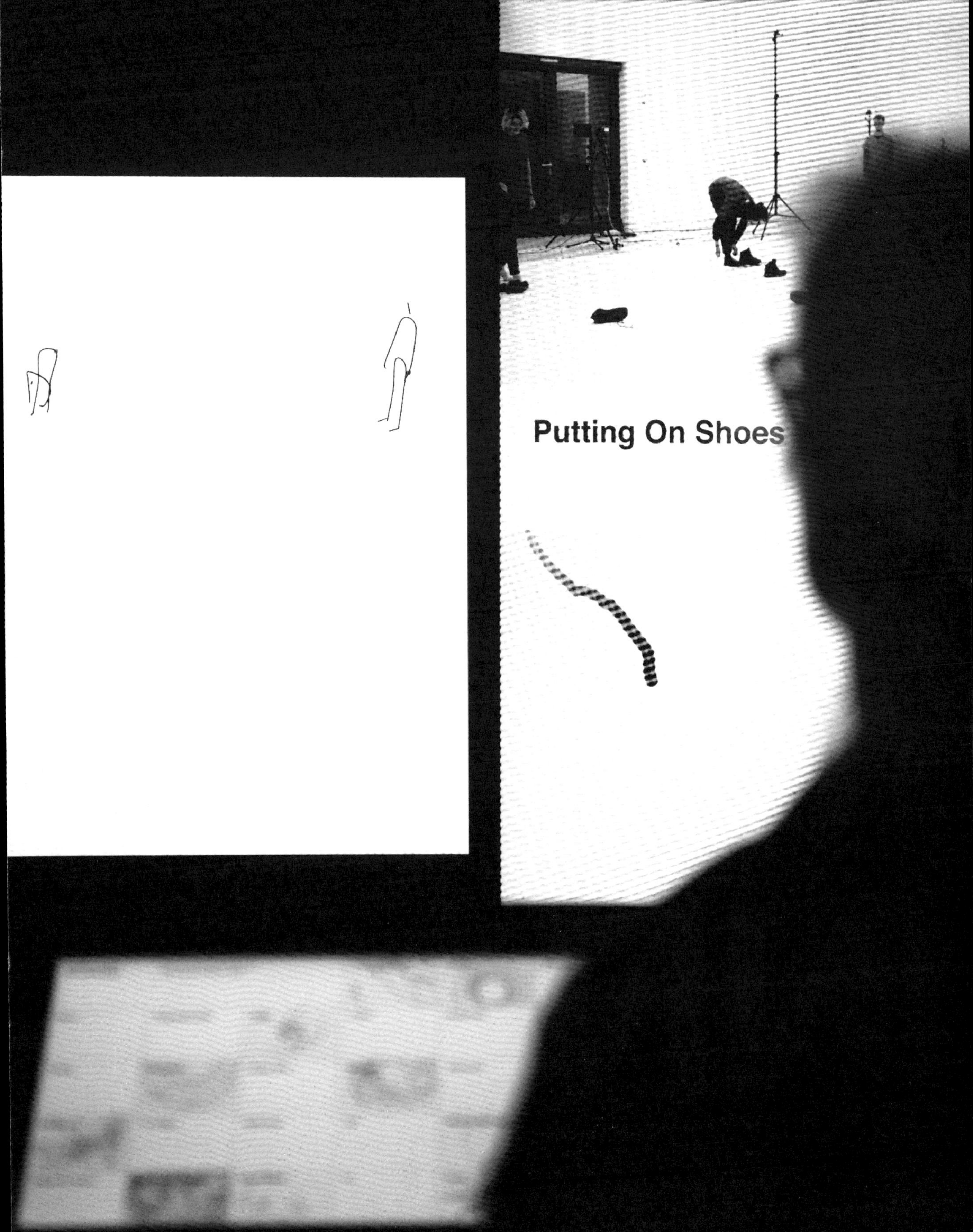

Putting On Shoes

KÜNSTLERINNEN

Tim Etchells
TRY, PUSH, LOOK, STAND, NO REASON, ONE PLACE TO ANOTHER

Tamara Grcic
movements

AR TI STS

Žilvinas Kempinas
SPIN

Isabel Lewis
Social Dances as Cultural Storage Systems

Søren Lyngsø Knudsen
Figure Eight

Sissel Tolaas
In_Between Us—SmellCoding / Air Movement

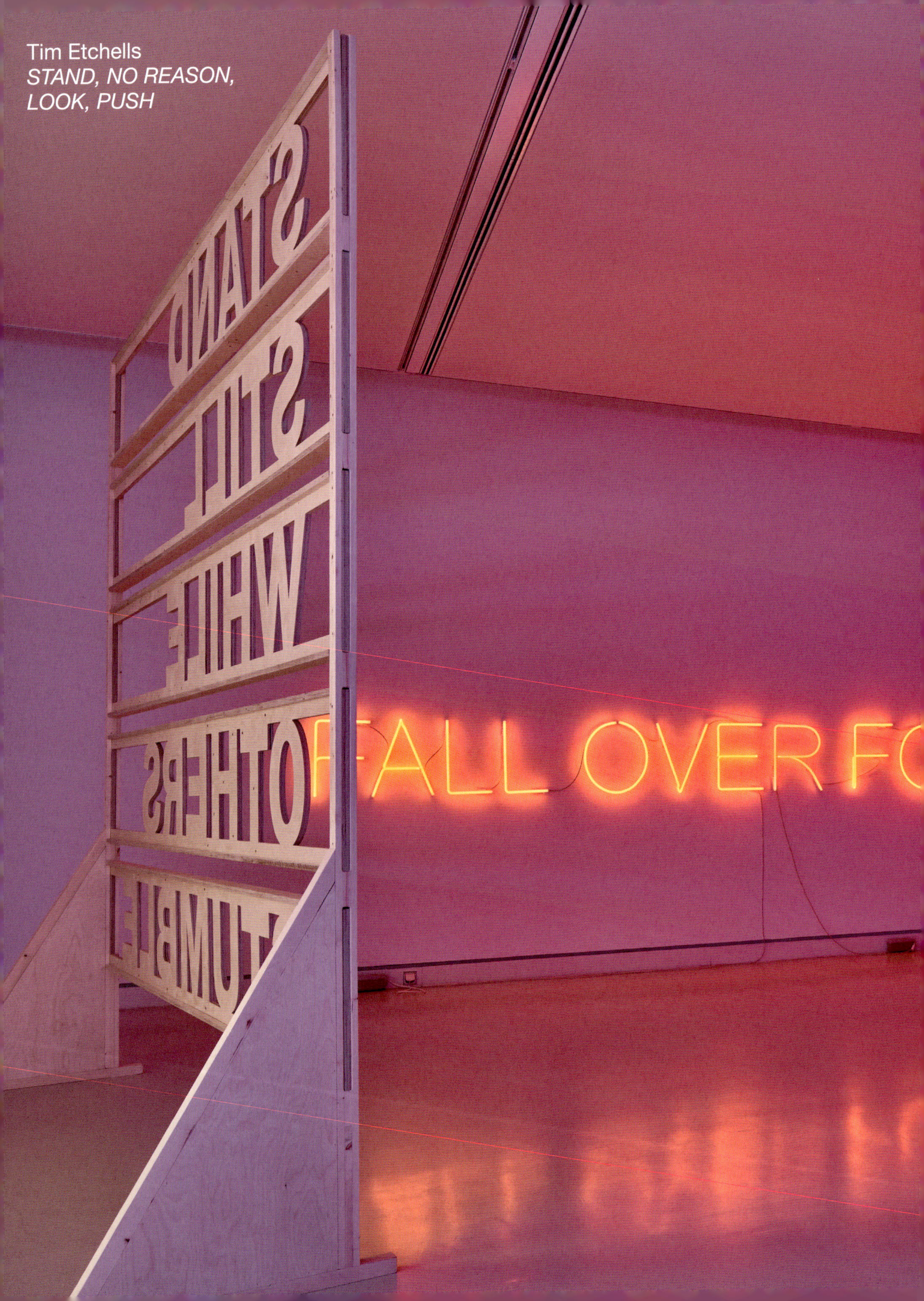

Tim Etchells
STAND, NO REASON, LOOK, PUSH

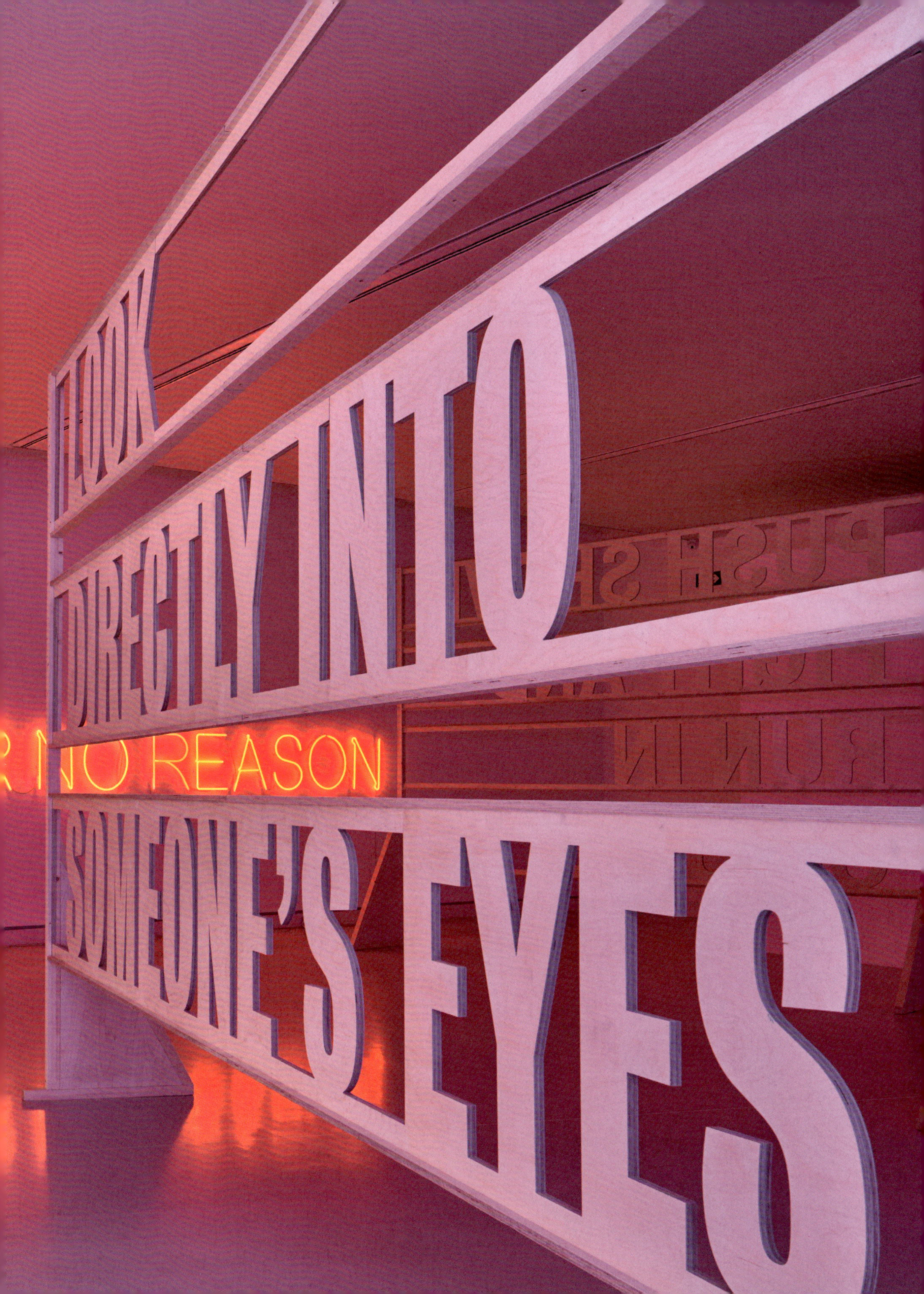
I LOOK
DIRECTLY INTO
SOMEONE'S EYES
NO REASON

Sissel Tolaas

In_Between Us—SmellCoding/
Air Movement

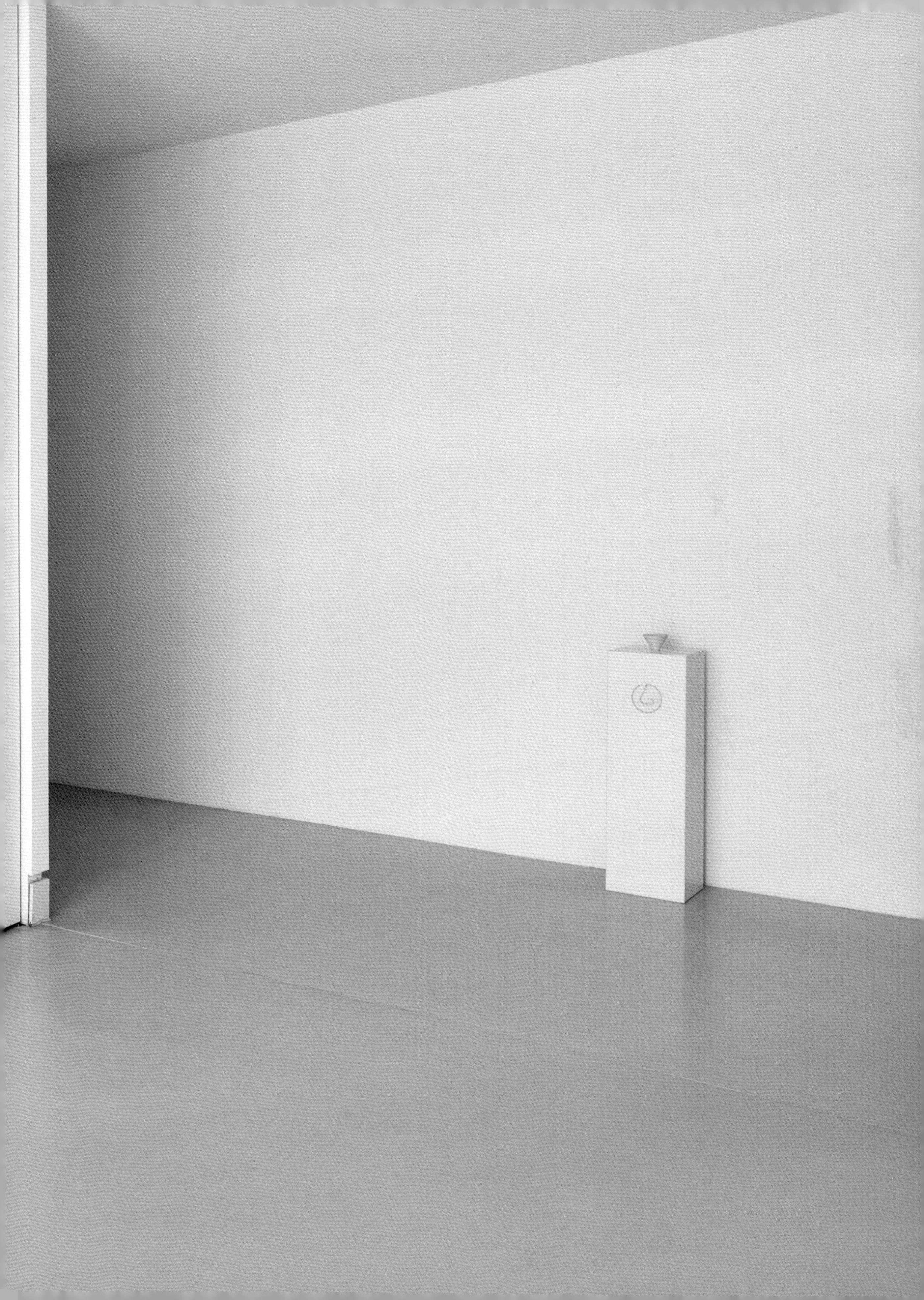

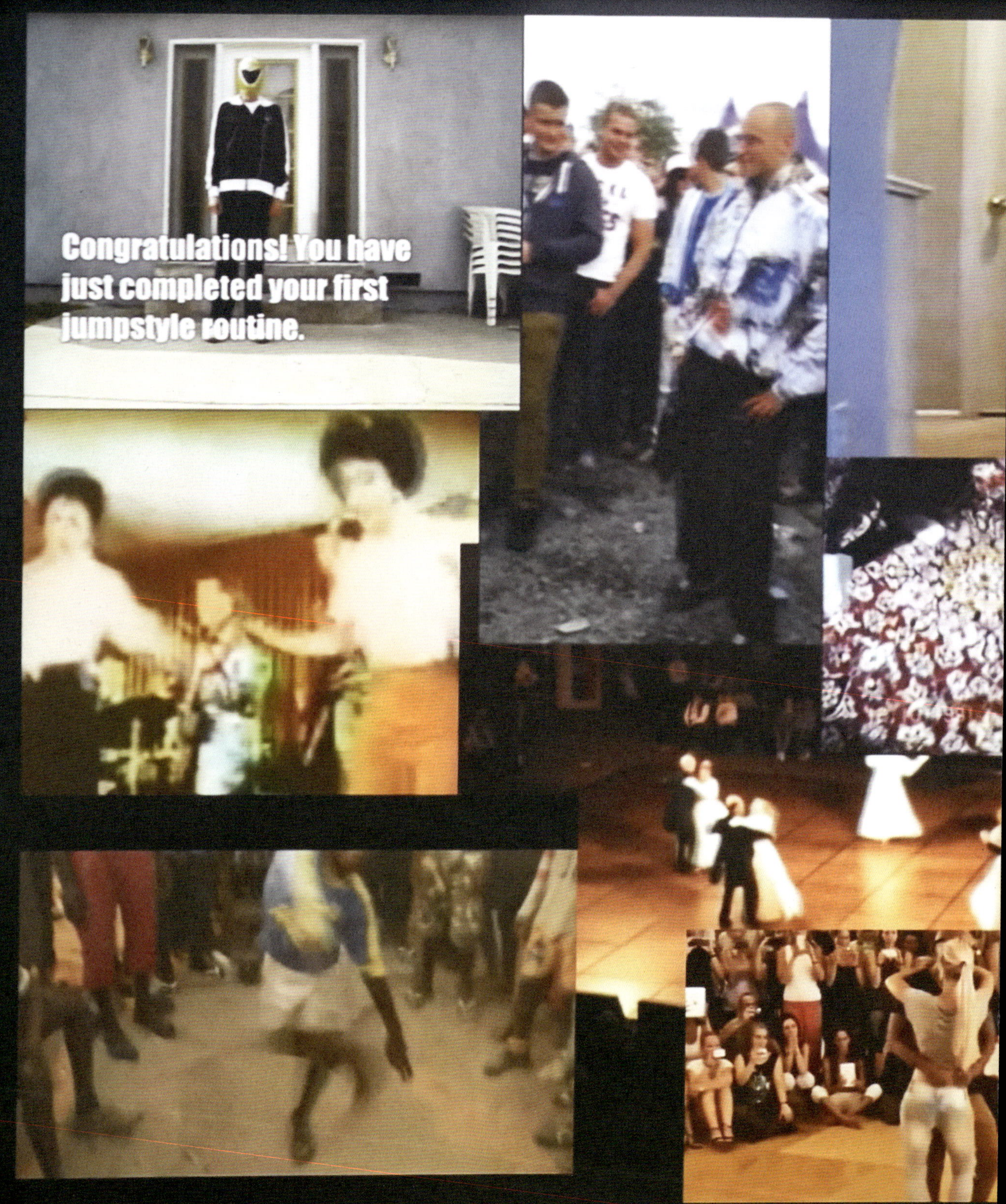
Congratulations! You have
just completed your first
jumpstyle routine.

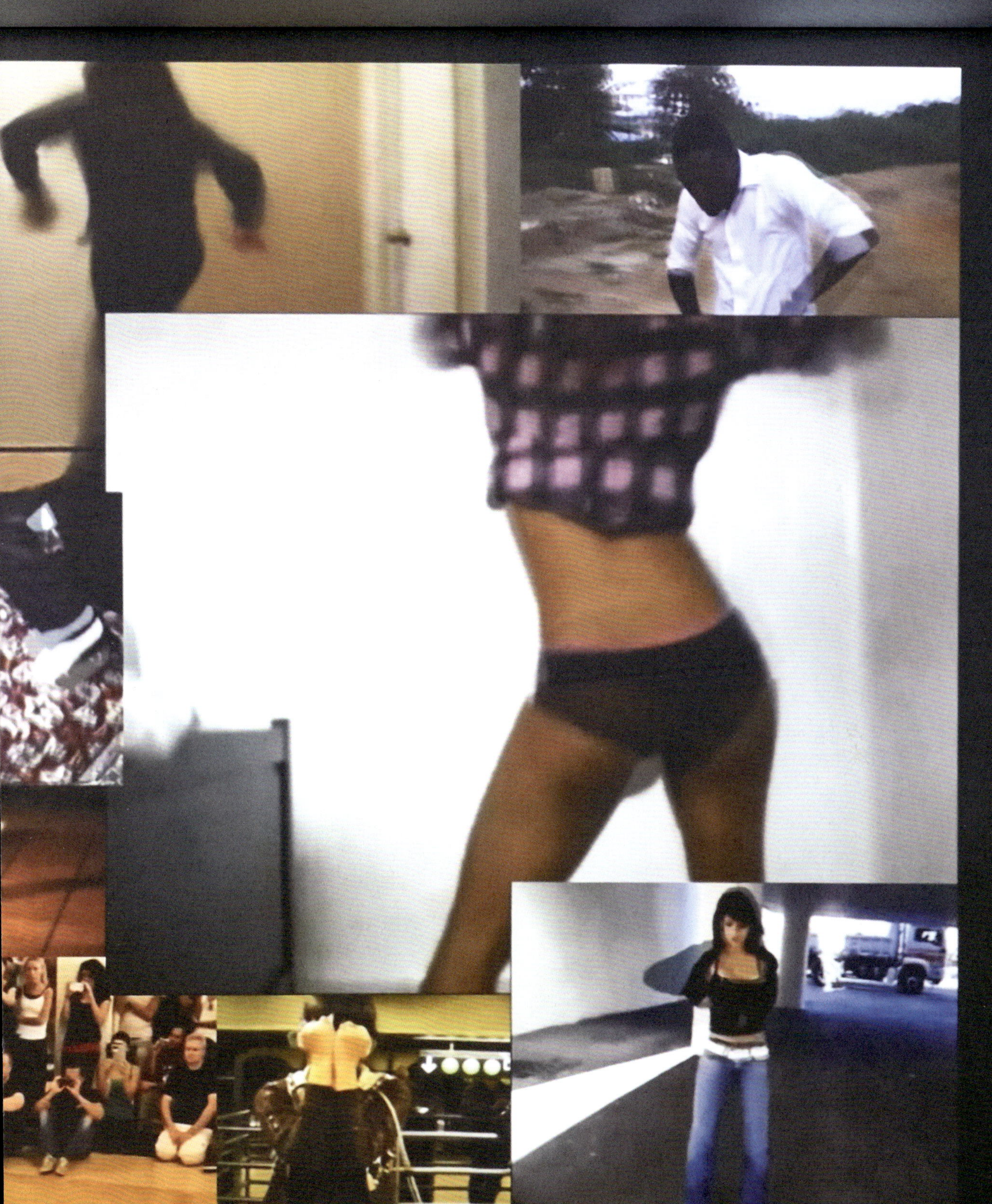

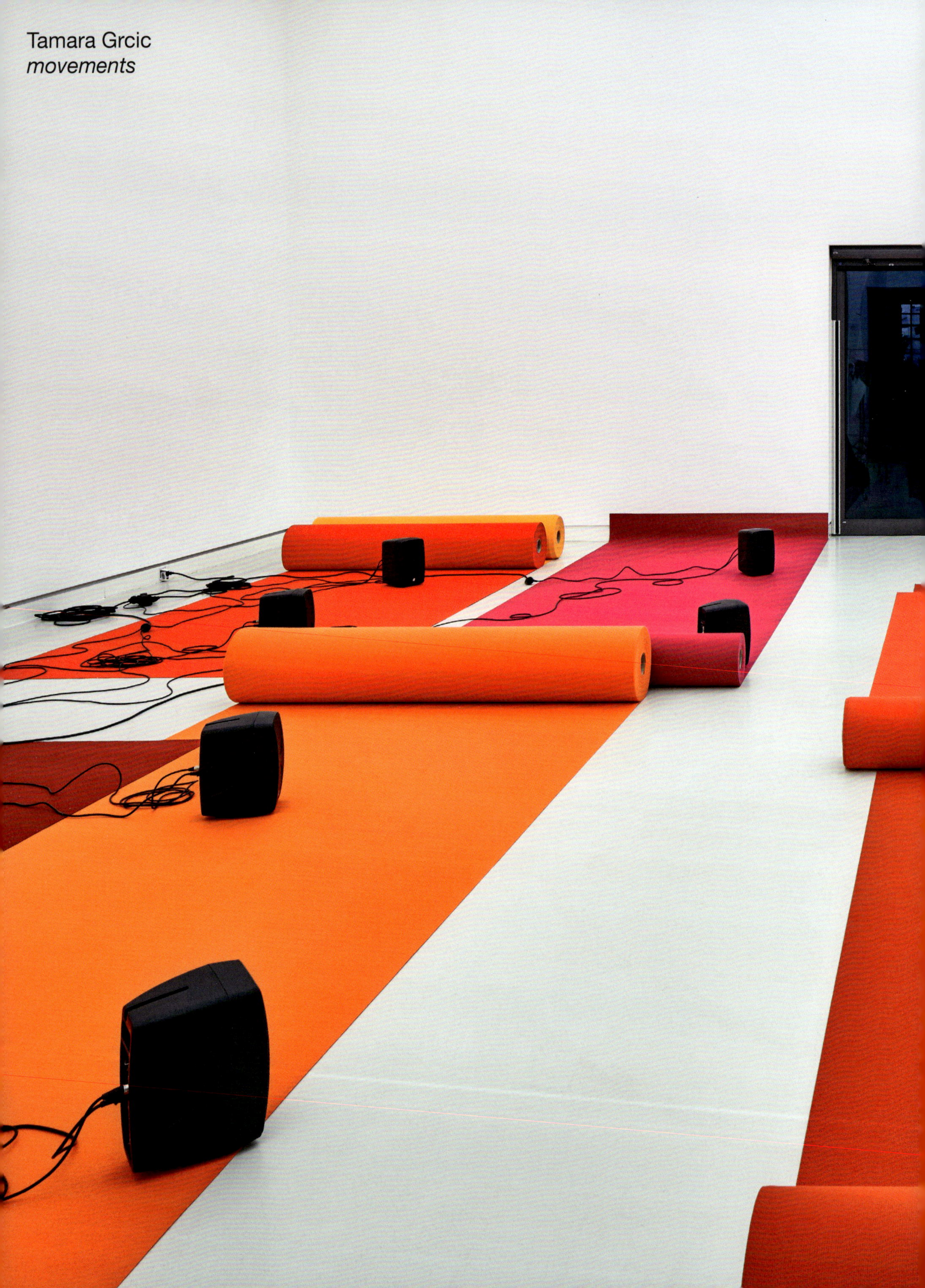
Tamara Grcic
movements

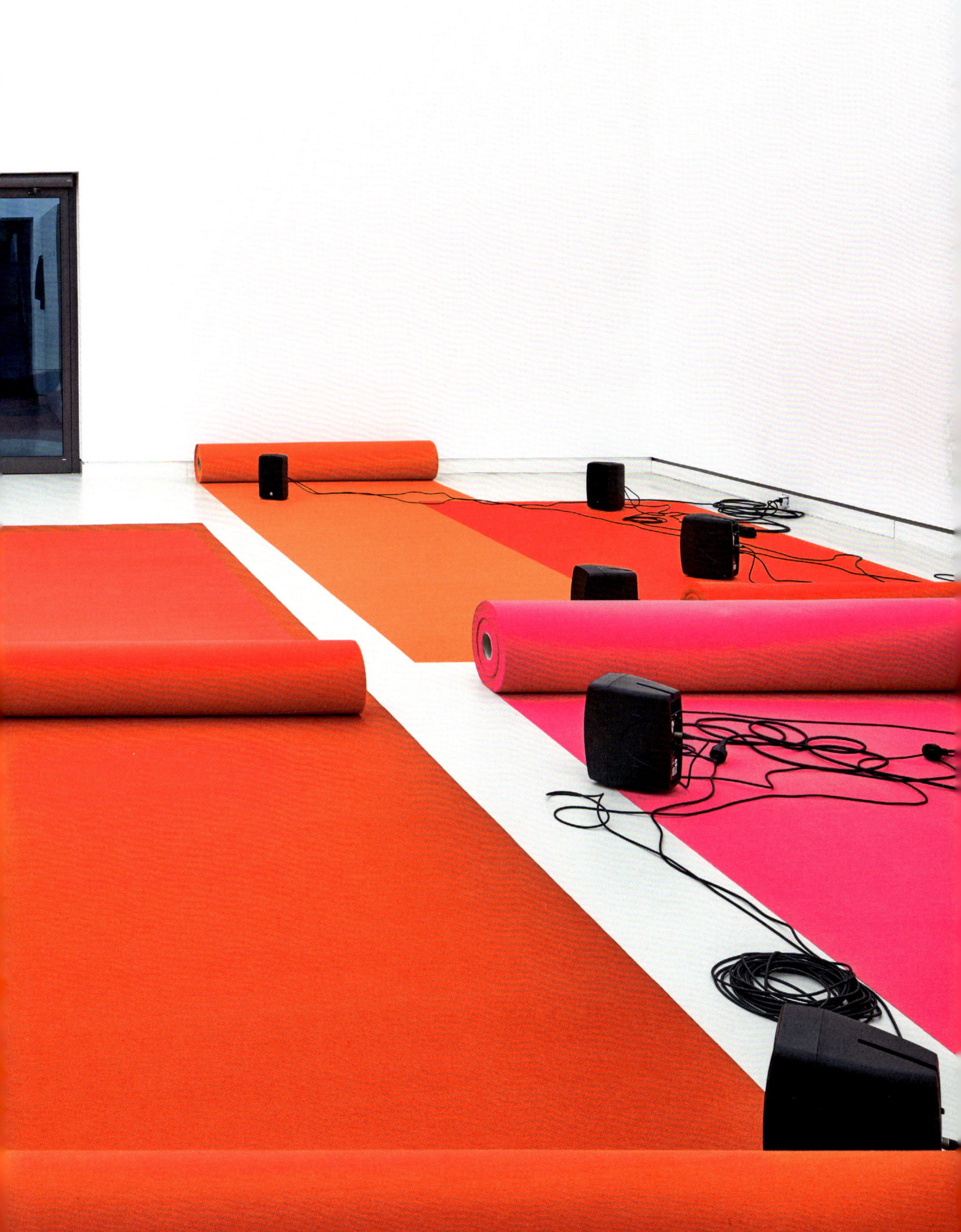

Søren Lyngsø Knudsen
Figure Eight

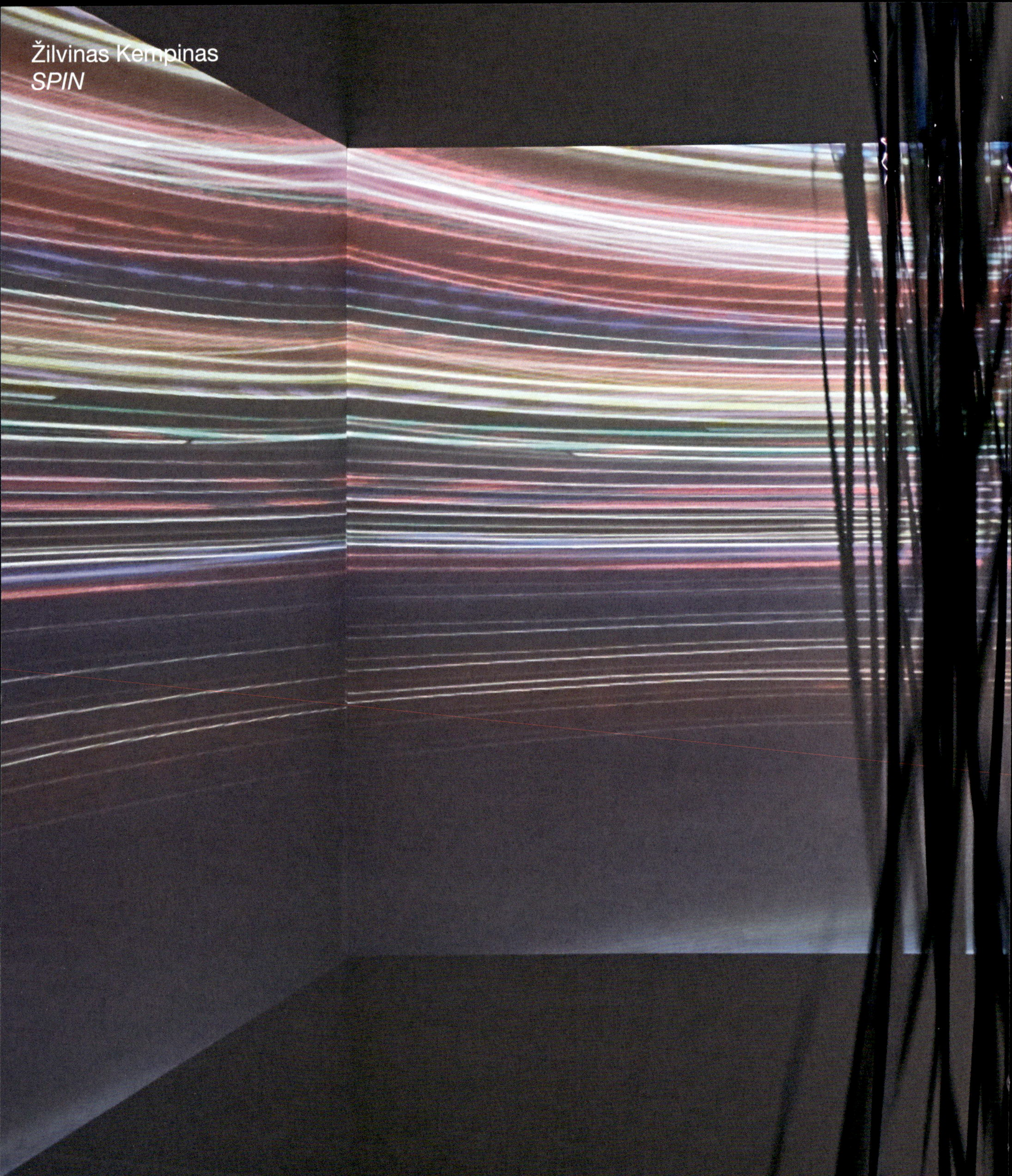
Žilvinas Kempinas
SPIN

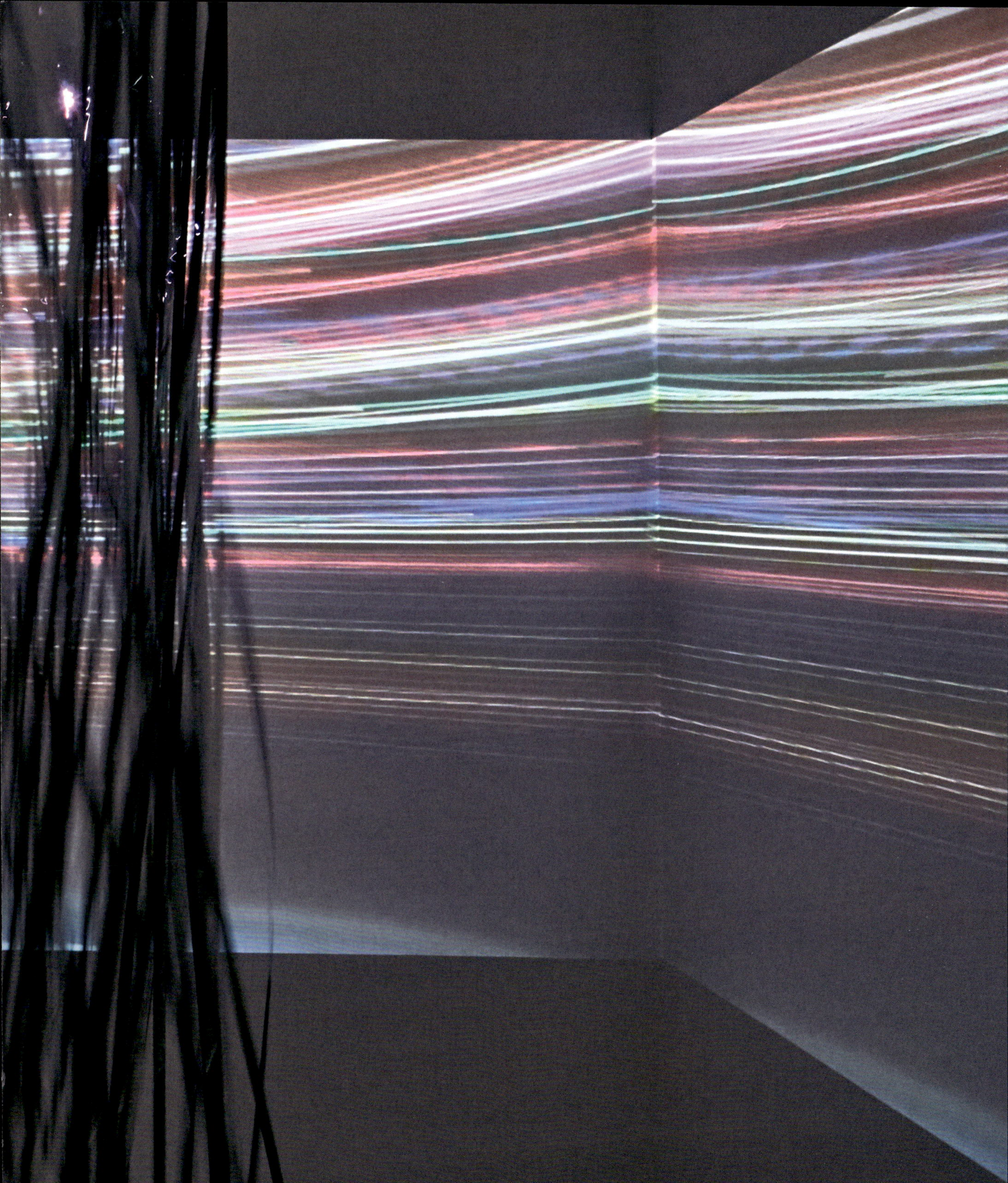

Tim Etchells

TRY, PUSH, LOOK, STAND, NO REASON, ONE PLACE TO ANOTHER

Sperrholz, CNC-Zuschnitt,
Neon-Schriftzug
Plywood, CNC cutting,
NEON sign

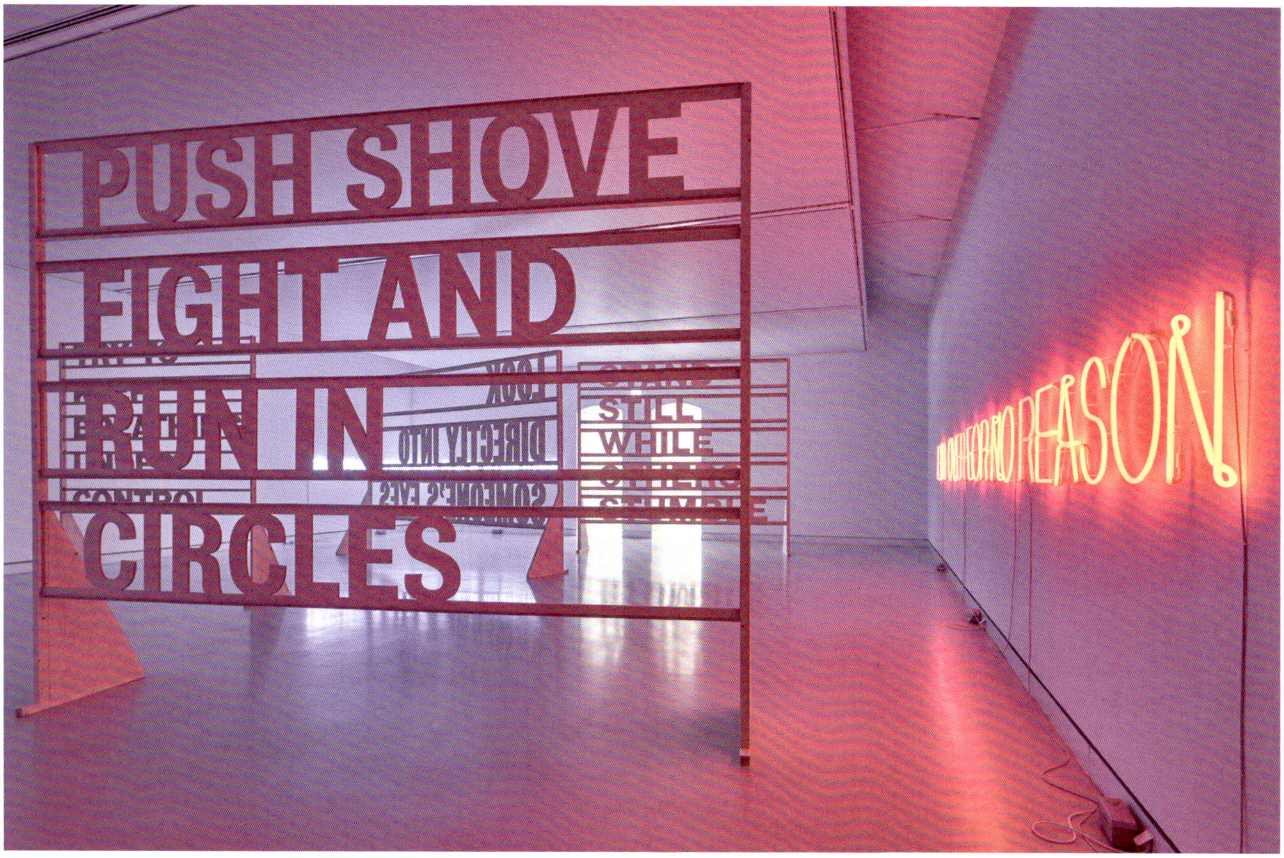
PUSH SHOVE
FIGHT AND
RUN IN
CIRCLES
STAND
STILL
WHILE
REASON!

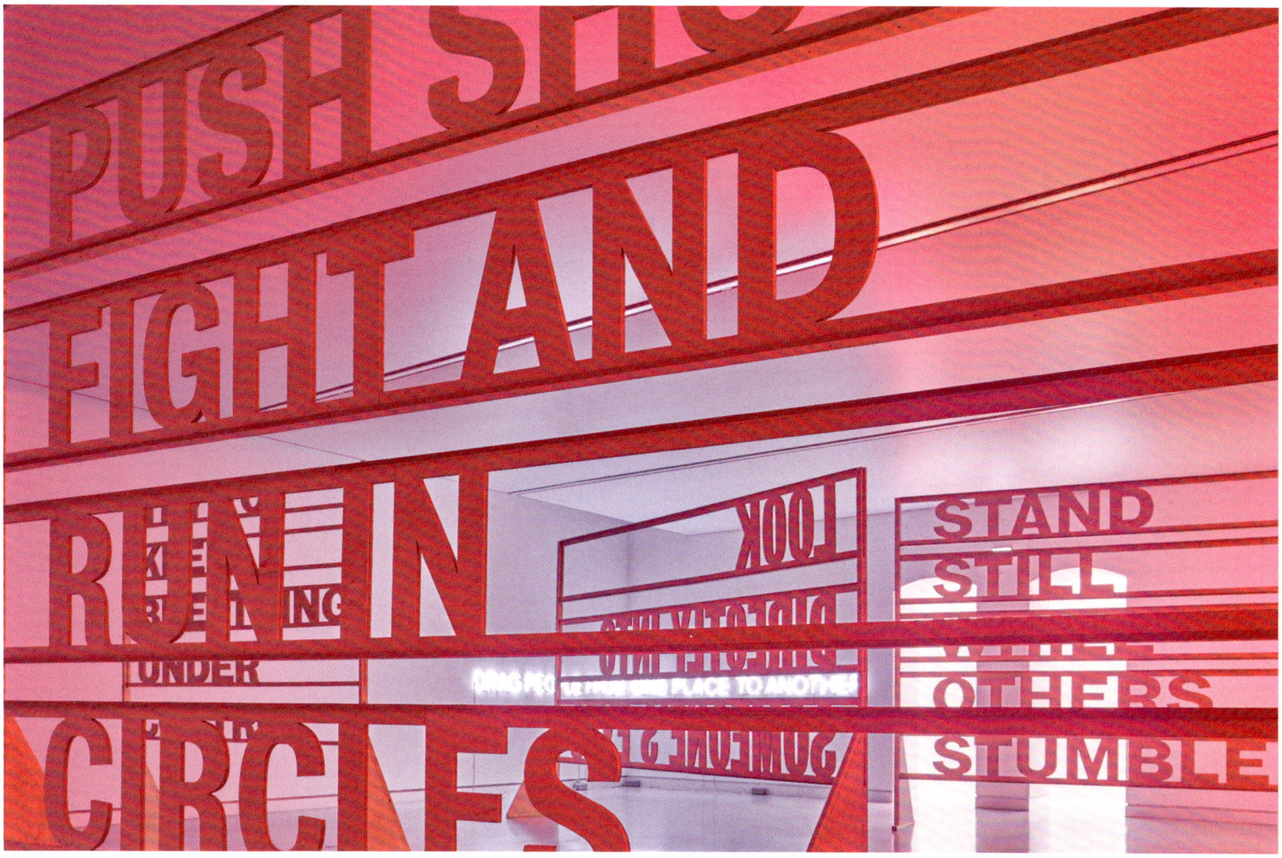
FIGHT AND
RUN IN
LOOK
STAND
STILL
OTHERS
STUMBLE

Stefanie Böttcher: ***Between Us* stellt Fragen nach Einflüssen, Konstellationen, Beziehungen zueinander. Du arbeitest als bildender Künstler, als Performer, du bist künstlerischer Leiter von Forced Entertainment, hast mit anderen Künstler*innen, Musiker*innen und Tänzer*innen kollaboriert. Interdisziplinärer Austausch und Kollaborationen sind nichts Neues für dich. Warum hast du die Einladung zum Projekt angenommen? Was hat dich daran angesprochen?**

Tim Etchells: Ich interessiere mich allgemein für die Frage, wie ich Beziehungen zu anderen Werken und Künstler*innen herstellen, wie ich auf Werke oder Artefakte reagieren kann – die Idee eines Dialogs war also definitiv etwas, was mich angesprochen hat. Ich denke, gerade weil sich meine Arbeit so oft mit Antwort und Reaktion, Interpretation und Fehlinterpretation beschäftigt, schien dies ein Projekt zu sein, in dem man diese Dinge auf eine ganz bestimmte Art und Weise erkunden kann.

Stefanie: **Trotzdem war dir deine „Bewegungsfreiheit" ungemein wichtig. Das war eine meiner Befürchtungen, als wir dieses Projekt starteten. Ich habe viel mit den anderen Projektpartnern darüber diskutiert, dass es schwierig ist, den Künstler*innen eine derartige Aufgabe zu geben. Sie könnte sich wie eine Einschränkung oder etwas, mit dem sie sich nicht arrangieren können, anfühlen.**

Tim: Ja! Ich weiß aus anderen Projekten, an denen ich beteiligt war, dass ich nicht gerne die Verantwortung habe, etwas Bestimmtes vertreten zu müssen. Wenn also ein Projekt diesen Prozess umfasst, auf etwas zu reagieren, versuche ich immer, direkt klarzustellen, dass ich nicht die Auflage haben möchte, etwas genau zu erklären oder eine „gute, ehrliche und wahre" Übersetzung bzw. Wiedergabe einer Recherche einzureichen. Das ist nicht interessant für mich. Ich war an einigen Projekten beteiligt, habe zum Beispiel Texte geschrieben, bei denen ich mit anderen Künstler*innen zusammengearbeitet habe – mit Taus Makhacheva, Elmgreen & Dragset oder mit FormContent. In jedem dieser Fälle lag bereits viel Material auf dem Tisch, als ich ankam – Recherchen oder erfolgte kreative Arbeit –, aber ich machte immer deutlich, dass ich es möglicherweise nicht in der erwarteten Weise verwenden würde. Der Prozess ist für mich wie das Betrachten eines Objekts und das Nachdenken darüber, was ich einbringen kann. Welche neue Version dieses Objekts gerät in den Fokus, wenn es aus meiner Perspektive betrachtet wird? Oder wie kann ich auf interessante Weise von ihm wegführen? Bei *Between Us* befürchtete ich anfangs, etwas zu machen, was scheinbar nur wieder zurück zum Tanz zu lenken schien, wie eine Wiederholung oder ein Kurzschluss. Ich wollte einen Weg finden, mich auf den Tanz zu beziehen, auf ihn zu verweisen, aber gleichzeitig in einen anderen Bereich vordringen, zu einer anderen Denkweise führen.

Stefanie: **War es für dich wichtig, bei den Proben dabei zu sein?**

Tim: Ja, das war für mich wichtig, aber es war auch gut, Zugang zu den anderen Materialien zu haben. Wie du weißt, lehnte ich es ab, irgendwelche Ideen zu entwickeln, bevor ich nicht das Stück gesehen und die Leute getroffen hatte! Manchmal wird man zu Projekten eingeladen, die auf der Idee der Reaktion basieren, aber aus pragmatischen Gründen müssen die Verantwortlichen im Voraus wissen, was du wahrscheinlich tun wirst! Wir haben das hier vermieden, und ich war froh darüber. Ich kam nach Mainz als eine Art Schwamm, als ein Paar Augen und Ohren, um zu schauen und zu hören, alles aufzusaugen und dann wieder zu fahren und nachzudenken. Beim Nachdenken habe ich viele verschiedene Möglichkeiten durchgespielt, von denen wir einige besprochen haben. Ich ging viele Möglichkeiten durch, bevor ich zu der Lösung kam. Ich habe die ganze Zeit darüber nachgedacht, was ich tun könnte, um die Situation auf sinnvolle Weise für mich zu öffnen.

Stefanie: **Was hast du für *Between Us* entwickelt?**

Tim: Die erste Entscheidung, die ich traf, war, dass ich mit Text in Bezug auf die Choreografie arbeiten würde. Ich hatte während und nach der Probe Notizen gemacht – das ist etwas, was in vielen verschiedenen Bereichen meiner Arbeitspraxis eine Rolle spielt, nämlich die wörtliche Beschreibung einer Handlung. Ich war schon immer fasziniert von der Idee, das, was als Bewegung oder als physisches Ereignis stattfindet, in die gesprochene oder geschriebene Sprache zu übersetzen, weil es irgendwie unmöglich ist. Das ist das, was mich wirklich interessiert, denke ich: was Sprache erfassen und nicht erfassen kann von einer Handlung. In gewisser Weise dreht sich das gesamte Projekt *Between Us* um diese Frage: Was kann Motion Capture erfassen?

„Ich war schon immer fasziniert von der Idee, das, was als Bewegung oder als physisches Ereignis stattfindet, in die gesprochene oder geschriebene Sprache zu übersetzen, weil es irgendwie unmöglich ist.“

Tim Etchells

Was kann ein Video erfassen? Was kann eine Tonaufnahme erfassen? Was kann Sprache erfassen? Eines der besten Dinge beim Arbeiten mit Sprache – gesprochen oder geschrieben – ist die Möglichkeit, sehr präzise, aber auch sehr offen zu bleiben. Also nahm ich meine Notizen über die Choreografie, meine Reaktionen, meine Interpretationen und fing an, mit ihnen zu arbeiten, um eine Sammlung von Sätzen zu generieren, die als Anweisungen zu verstehen sind. Das ist im Grunde das Werk: zwei Neonschriftzüge und vier Textskulpturen aus Holz, die frei im Raum stehen. Jeder Schriftzug verwendet eine einzelne Phrase, die ein Bild oder eine Aktion abruft. Die Handlungen stammen ursprünglich aus der Choreografie, aber ich habe alles auf eine sehr offene Art und Weise artikuliert – die Texte schlagen andere Dinge, andere Möglichkeiten, andere Erzählungen und andere Begegnungen zwischen Menschen vor. Ich versuchte, nichts zu sehr herunterzubrechen, nicht auf den Tanz zu verweisen, sondern den Tanz über die Sprache zu nutzen, um zu anderen Ideen und Erfahrungen zu gelangen.

In den Texten heißt es etwa: „Ziehe Menschen von einem Ort zum anderen“ oder „Stehe still, während andere um dich herum ins Stolpern geraten“. Das Lesen dieser Texte erinnert an Ereignisse, die in den Nachrichten zu sehen sind, oder an Fälle von sozialer und politischer Gewalt. Ich habe das wahre Leben im Sinn – Situationen der Intimität oder Konflikte. Es gibt eine performative dynamische Kraft in der Arbeit, durch die du dich direkt angesprochen fühlst, wenn man diese Bilder kreativ ausgestaltet und sich vorstellt, diese Anweisungen auszuführen. Natürlich ist die Choreografie augenscheinlich sehr physisch, sehr körperlich, aber wenn man diese Bewegungen erfasst, in Ton oder Video übersetzt, besteht die Gefahr, dass die Materialität und die physische Beanspruchung verschwinden. Die Werke, die ich entwickelt habe, sind skulpturale Objekte, die auf Text beruhen, aber ihre Ansprache an den*die Betrachter*in – die Kraft des Imperativs – zieht sie*ihn in den Bann und fordert auf, sich physisch einzubringen. Eine physische Aussagekraft, ein Gefahrenpotenzial liegt den artikulierten Anregungen zugrunde. Es interessiert mich, eine Art innerer Hitze oder das Gefühl körperlicher Nähe zu entfesseln.

Stefanie: **Man muss sich als Betrachter*in tatsächlich körperlich mit diesen Textskulpturen auseinandersetzen. Denn ob ihres enormen Maßstabs ist man gezwungen, um sie herumzugehen, Kurven zu drehen oder einen Schritt zurückzutreten, um sie erfassen zu können.**

Tim: Stimmt. Es liegt eine Körperlichkeit in dem, was der Text als Aktionen vorschlägt, aber auch darin, wie die Schriftzüge den Raum zerteilen, in ihn eingreifen und den Besucher*innen einen anderen Weg aufzwingen. Der Maßstab der Werke und ihre Positionierung schaffen eine andere Art von Choreografie. In gewissem Sinne reagierte ich auf den Raum, aber es war auch eine Entscheidung, die Werke in einer einschüchternden Größe zu produzieren. Sie berühren gerade noch nicht die Decke, sind aber nahe daran, und so, wie sie positioniert sind, ist man als Besucher*in sofort beim Eintritt in den Ausstellungsraum mit den ersten Textskulpturen konfrontiert. Man ist ihnen augenblicklich zu nahe und muss zurücktreten, um sie lesen zu können. Es ist eine ziemlich intensive Umgebung, in die man hineingerät. Und die verschiedenen Werke sind noch dazu chaotisch angeordnet – sie weisen in unterschiedliche Richtungen, überlappen sich zum Teil. Insgesamt ergibt sich so eine Art Collage, die ein Durcheinander an Textmaterial erzeugt. Es sind Erscheinungsform und Positionierung der Schriftzüge, die deren Beziehung zu den Betrachter*innen überhaupt erst verändern. Danach suche ich.

In meiner künstlerischen Praxis arbeite ich oft zweidimensional – als sei das der Standard, einen Text zu produzieren, den man an eine Wand bringt. Die Wand wird damit zur Seite. Ich denke allerdings schon eine ganze Weile verstärkt über Dreidimensionalität nach. Natürlich gab es die auch bereits ansatzweise in anderen Projekten – meine Installation *Red Sky at Night* in Bremen (2011) oder meine

Arbeiten für Frieze (2018), meine Soundinstallationen *Together/Apart* (2017) in Braunschweig und *Stand Off* (2015) im Plymouth Arts Centre verfügen alle über eine dynamische 360-Grad-Raumqualität.

Stefanie: **Es ist das erste Mal, dass du mit hölzernen Textskulpturen arbeitest, und du bringst auch erstmals unterschiedliche Materialien zusammen: hölzerne Textskulpturen und Neonschriftzüge. Du hast mal davon gesprochen, der extrem minimalistischen Choreografie etwas entgegensetzen zu wollen, diesen Ansatz aufzuhebeln, anstatt ihn aufzugreifen.**

Tim: Ja. Ich habe definitiv den Minimalismus und die Abstraktion der Choreografie wahrgenommen. Das sind Dinge, die mir gefallen und auch für meine Arbeit wichtig sind, aber ich fragte mich, welcher Gegensatz fruchtbar sein könnte. Ein Ansatzpunkt war, zu überlegen, wie es der Text ermöglichen könnte, auf andere soziale und politische Situationen zu verweisen. Und der andere Weg bestand darin, über die formale Eigentümlichkeit der Choreografie nachzudenken und auszuloten, wie man eine etwas unregelmäßigere oder gestörtere Ästhetik in die Ausstellungsräume bringen könnte. Daraus resultierte meine Entscheidung, Neonarbeiten mit Holzskulpturen zu kombinieren, anstatt alles in demselben Material, mit derselben Sprache zu erschaffen.

Stefanie: **Der knifflige Teil des Projekts besteht möglicherweise darin, dass du nicht einfach eingeladen wurdest, mit einem bestimmten Material zu arbeiten, sondern mit dem Werk eines anderen, mit etwas, das einem künstlerischen Prozess entsprang. Man kann schnell das Gefühl haben, mit diesem Material besonders vorsichtig umgehen zu müssen. War das für dich ein Thema?**

Tim: Das ist interessant. Ich hatte nicht das Gefühl, dass ich höflich sein musste. Ich habe es auf jeden Fall versucht, zu vermeiden, zu einfühlsam zu sein. Ich wollte für mich selbst stehen, in dem Verständnis, dass ich mich auf einer weitestgehend getrennten, aber dennoch parallelen Mission befinde. Vielleicht kommt meine Vorgehensweise – der Unhöflichkeit – daher, weil ich es gewöhnt bin, in Kollaborationen zu arbeiten. In diesem Zusammenhang denke ich immer, dass eine Art kreative Unhöflichkeit ein wichtiger Teil des Prozesses sein kann. Denn wenn alle nur vorsichtig in Bezug auf die Sachen aller sind, wird es langweilig. Man muss die Dinge auch unordentlich und unhöflich sein lassen! Es gibt eine großartige Dokumentation über Warhol und Basquiat, die sie während ihrer Zusammenarbeit an den gemeinsamen Gemälden zeigt: Basquiat malt gerade mitten in einer der Warhol-Arbeiten herum, und Warhol befindet sich in einem Lagerkollaps-Horror-Modus: „O nein – er malt darauf?! Michel, Michel, du übermalst die besten Stellen." Es ist diese großartige, sehr verspielte und echte Störung, die für mich Teil des Dialogs sein muss, ein Bestandteil der Zusammenarbeit.

Die andere Sache hier in *Between Us* ist natürlich, dass alle Werke der Künstler*innen unabhängig voneinander in separaten Räumen ausgestellt werden und existieren. Wir sind durch die Ausstellung miteinander verbunden, aber ansonsten bestehen wir getrennt. Die choreografische Arbeit ist eine Art erste Geste, aber ich wusste immer, dass ich in eine andere Richtung würde gehen müssen. Ich musste etwas aus dem Tanz mitnehmen, um an einen anderen Ort zu gelangen. Es ist mir wichtig, dass der*die Betrachter*in auf sich selbst blickt und sich in Bezug auf die Arbeit und die Welt sieht.

‘I’ve always been fascinated with the idea of translating what is taking place as movement or as physical event into spoken or written language, because it is sort of impossible to do that.’

Tim Etchells

Stefanie Böttcher: ***Between Us*** **is based on questions of influences, constellations, relationships. You work as a visual artist, a performer, as artistic director of Forced Entertainment, you collaborate with other artists, musicians, dancers. So interdisciplinary exchanges and collaborations are nothing new to you. Why did you accept the invitation to this project? What attracted you?**

Tim Etchells: I’m interested generally in this question of finding or making relations with other artists and responding to other works or to artifacts—so the idea of a dialog was definitely something that connected. I think because my work is so often concerned with response and reaction, interpretation and misinterpretation—this seemed like a project where one could explore those things in a very specific way.

Stefanie: **But nevertheless it was really important to you that you had your freedom. That was one of my worries when we started this project. I often discussed the fact that it’s tricky to give the artists such a task with the other project partners. It could all feel like a restriction or something to which they would not be able to adapt.**

Tim: Yes! I know from other projects I’ve been involved in that I don’t like to have the responsibility to represent something! So, if a project involves this process of responding to something I always try to make it clear I don’t want the burden of explaining or handing in a ‘good, honest and true’ translation or rendition of the research. That doesn’t interest me. I’ve done some projects, writing texts for example, where I’ve worked with other artists—producing things with Taus Makhacheva, Elmgreen & Dragset or with FormContent. In each of those cases there was a lot of material on the table when I arrived, research or existing creative work, but I made it clear I might not use it in the way that was expected. The process, for me, is like looking at an object and thinking: what can I bring to this? What new version of this comes into focus if it’s looked at from my perspective? Or how can I fade away from this in an interesting way? The thing I was worried about in *Between Us* was making something that seemed to circle back to the dance—a repetition or a short circuit. I wanted to find a way to refer to the dance or to gesture towards it, but at the same time to propel things forwards into another kind of space, another way of thinking.

Stefanie: **Was it important to you to see the rehearsals?**

Tim: Yes, that was important to me and it was good to have access to the other materials, too. As you know, I basically resisted having any ideas until I’d seen something of the piece and met people! Sometimes you get invited into projects notionally based on the idea of response but for pragmatic reasons people need to know in advance what you’re thinking you might do! We avoided that here, and I was glad of that. I came on the first trip as a kind of sponge or as a set of eyes and ears—to look and listen, and then go away and think. In thinking I did go through a lot of different possibilities, some of which we talked about. But I went all around the houses before coming to a solution. I was thinking all the time about what I could do that would open the situation out in a useful way for me.

Stefanie: **Could you please describe what you created for *Between Us*?**

Tim: The first decision I came to was that I would work with text in relation to the choreography. I’d made notes during and after the rehearsal I saw, and I was thinking about something that comes from many different areas of my practice, which is the literal description of action. I’ve always been fascinated with the idea of translating what is taking place as movement or as physical event into spoken or written language, because it is sort of impossible to do that. This is what’s interesting to me, I guess—what language can and can't capture of what's happening? In any circumstances! In some ways the whole *Between Us* project is about this question—what can motion capture itself capture? What can video capture? What can sound recording capture? What can language capture? Of course for me one of the great things about working with language—spoken or written—is the ability it affords you to be very precise, but also very open. So I took my notes on the choreography, my reactions, my interpretations, and I began to work from those to create a set of phrases which appeared to be instructions. That's the final work basically—two neon signs and four wooden text sculptures that stand on their own in the room using those texts. Each work uses a single phrase which summons an image or an action. The actions come from the choreography initially but I've articulated everything in a way that's also very open—the texts suggest other things, other possibilities, other narratives, other encounters between human beings. I was trying not to close down, not to point back to the dance, but instead to use the dance, via language, to jump to other kinds of ideas and experiences.

The texts say things like 'drag people from one place to another' or 'stand still while others stumble.' Reading those texts brings to mind things one might see in the news or instances of social and political violence. I'm thinking about real life—situations of intimacy or situations of conflict. There's a performative, dynamic force to the work in that you feel addressed and implicated in that very direct way as you make those images, imaginatively and as you might imagine enacting those instructions. Of course in the first place the choreography is very physical, very body-based, but, when you translate that into motion capture, sound or video there's a danger that the materiality and physical risk disappears. The text pieces I've made are sculptural objects of course, but the way they address the viewer—the force of the imperative—pulls you in and makes a gesture towards reinscribing the physical. There's a physical proposition, a potential of danger in what the works suggest. I was interested to reach for that kind of heat or viscerality.

Stefanie: **You really have to deal physically with these text sculptures, because you are forced to go around them, to walk in curves or step back to get a clear view, and also because of their enormous scale.**

Tim: That's right. There's physicality in what the text works propose as actions, but also in how they carve up and create an intervention in the space which forces the visitors to take another route. The scale of the works and their position create another kind of choreography. In one sense I was responding to the room, but it was also a choice to make the pieces quite intimidating in scale. They don't touch the ceiling but they're close to it and the way they're positioned when you first enter the gallery you're immediately confronted by the first pieces. You're really already too close and you're forced to step back in order to read. It's a pretty intense environment you're in. And the different works are arranged chaotically as we discussed—some facing one way and some another, overlapping. So, on a total level there is a sort of collaging that creates a jumble of textual material. It's the manifestation of them and the arrangement that create the different kind of relation to the viewer I am looking for.

In my practice more broadly I'm often working very 2-D—as if there's a default of making a text work and it's going on a wall—then the wall becomes the page. So it's been on my mind for a while now to think harder about 3-dimensionality! I've been there a bit of course, in other projects—my *Red Sky at Night* installation in Bremen (2011), or my Frieze work (2018), my sound installations *Together/Apart* (2017) too in Braunschweig, and *Stand Off* (2015) in Plymouth Arts Centre all have this more dynamic 360-degree spatial quality.

Stefanie: **It's the first time that you've worked with wooden text sculptures and the first time that you are mixing these very different materials up: wooden text sculptures and neons. You told me before that to some extent it was a reaction to the super-minimalist choreography, too, that you somehow had the feeling that you have put something against it, rather than just adjusted to it.**

Tim: Yes. I definitely felt the minimalism and abstraction of the choreography. Those are things I like and are important to my work, too. But I did wonder what kind of counterpoint might be generative. One impulse was to think how the text might allow me to reach to other kinds of social and political situations. And the other impulse was to think about the formal singularity of the choreography and to wonder about putting a slightly more irregular or disrupted aesthetic into the gallery. So that informed my decision to combine neons with the wooden sculptures rather than to do everything in one language.

Stefanie: **The tricky part of the project might not be that you were invited to work with a specific material, but to work with a piece of somebody else, with something artificially created. You might feel the need to be sensitive with this kind of material. Was this an issue for you?**

Tim: That's interesting. I didn't feel I had to be polite. I tried to avoid being too sensitive in any case. I tried to insist for myself, on the understanding that I am here on some quite separate though parallel mission. Maybe my approach—of impoliteness—stems from the fact that I'm actually quite used to working in collaborations. And in that context I always think a kind of creative impoliteness can be an important part of the process. Because if everybody's going around being super-careful about everybody's stuff, it's not interesting. You have to let things be messy and impolite! There's a great documentary with Warhol and Basquiat, during their collaboration, where they're working on the shared paintings. Basquiat is busy painting over the middle of one of the Warhol pieces and Warhol is in this camp mock-horror mode—'Oh no, he's drawing on that?! Michel, Michel you're drawing on all of the best bits.' It's this great, very playful and real disruption, and for me that's got to be part of dialog, part of collaboration.

The other thing here in *Between Us* of course is that all the artists' work exists independently, in separate space. We're linked in the frame of the exhibition, but otherwise we are separated. The choreographic work is a kind of first gesture but my thought was always I need to be moving in another direction. I need to be taking something from the dance in order to get to somewhere else. I want the viewers looking at themselves in relation to the work and the world.

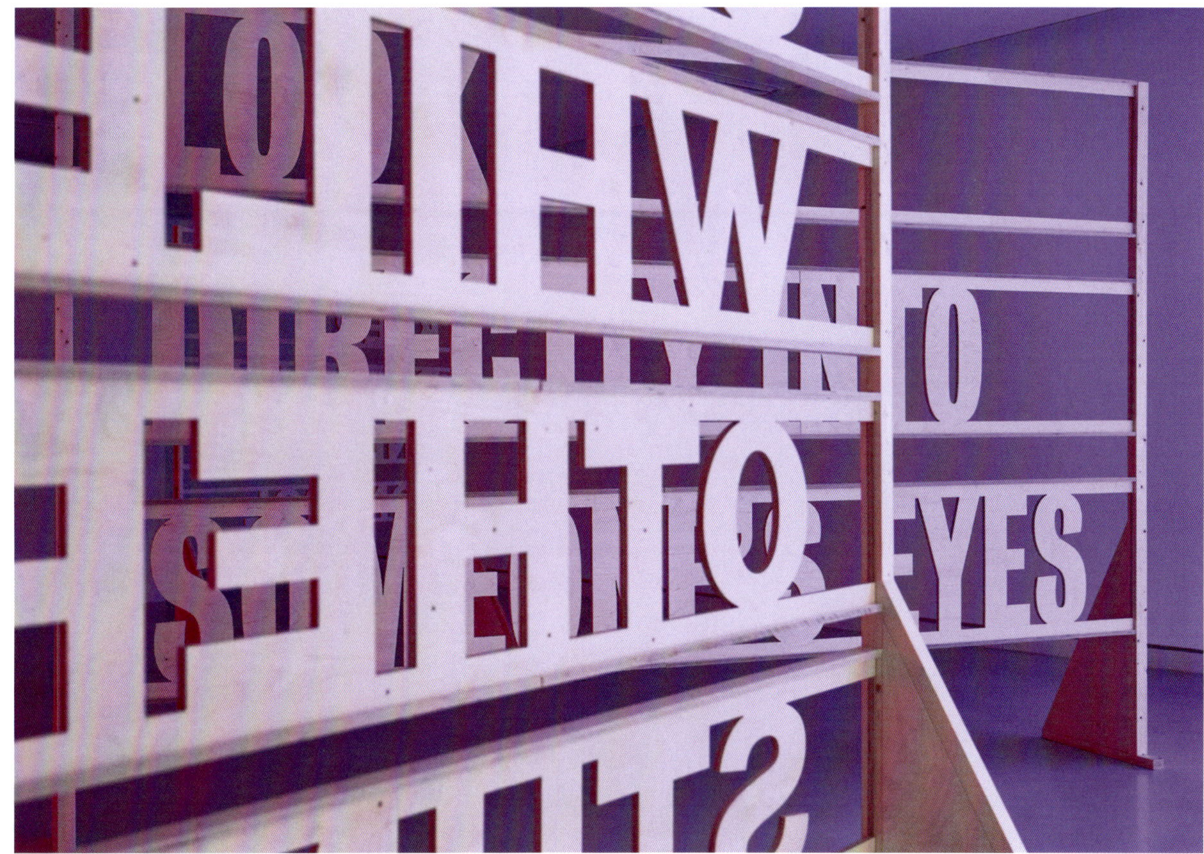

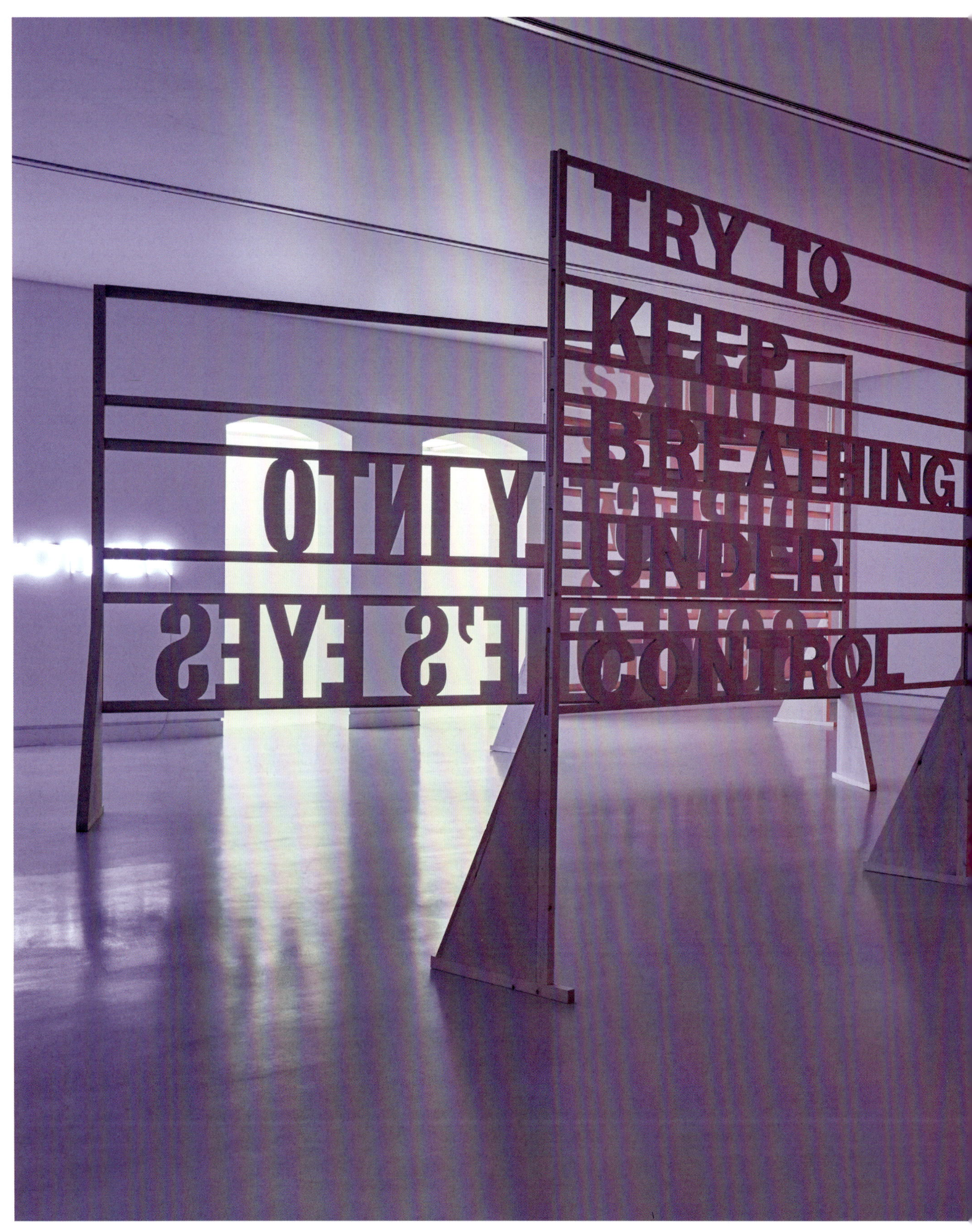
TRY TO
KEEP
BREATHING
UNDER
CONTROL

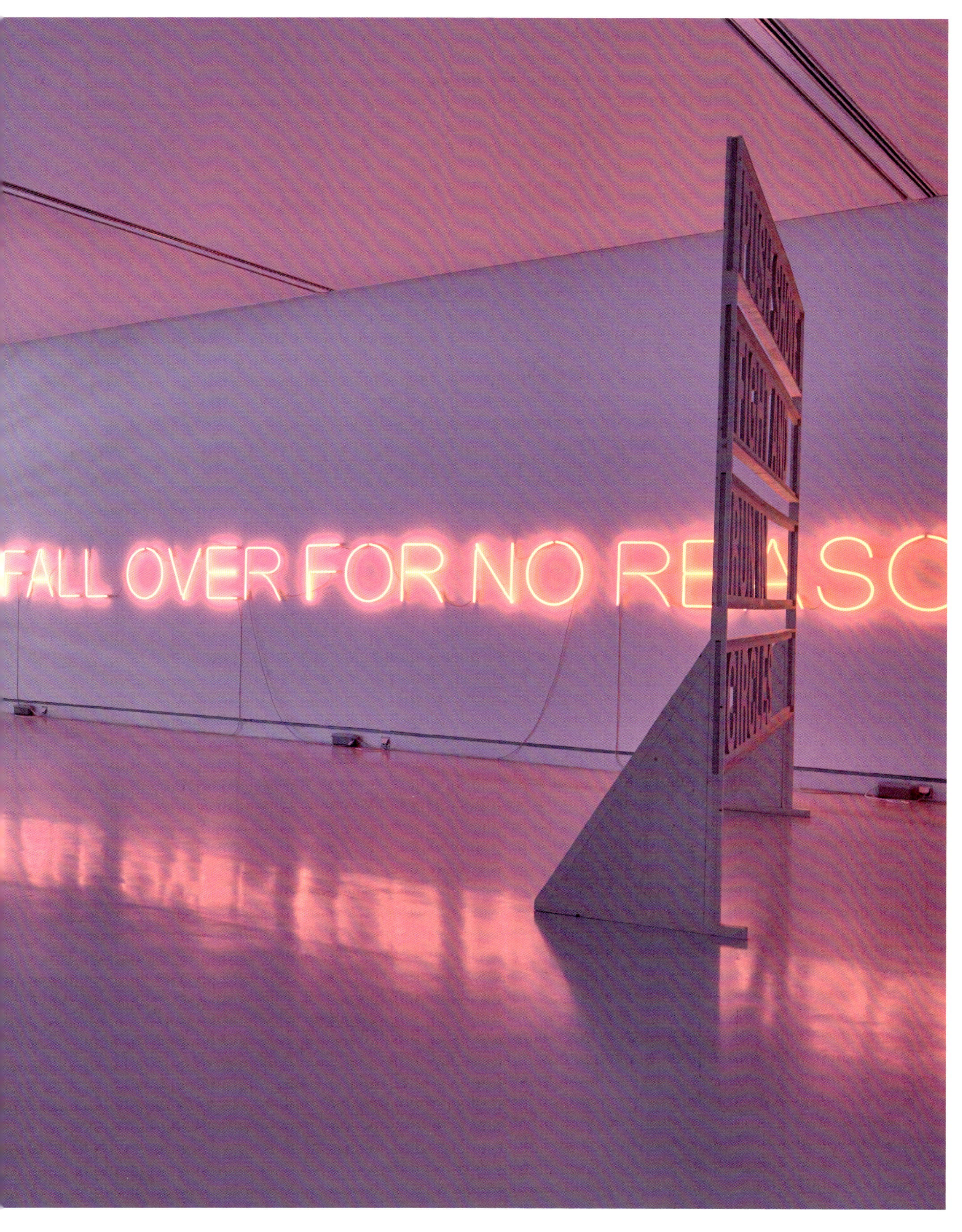
FALL OVER FOR NO

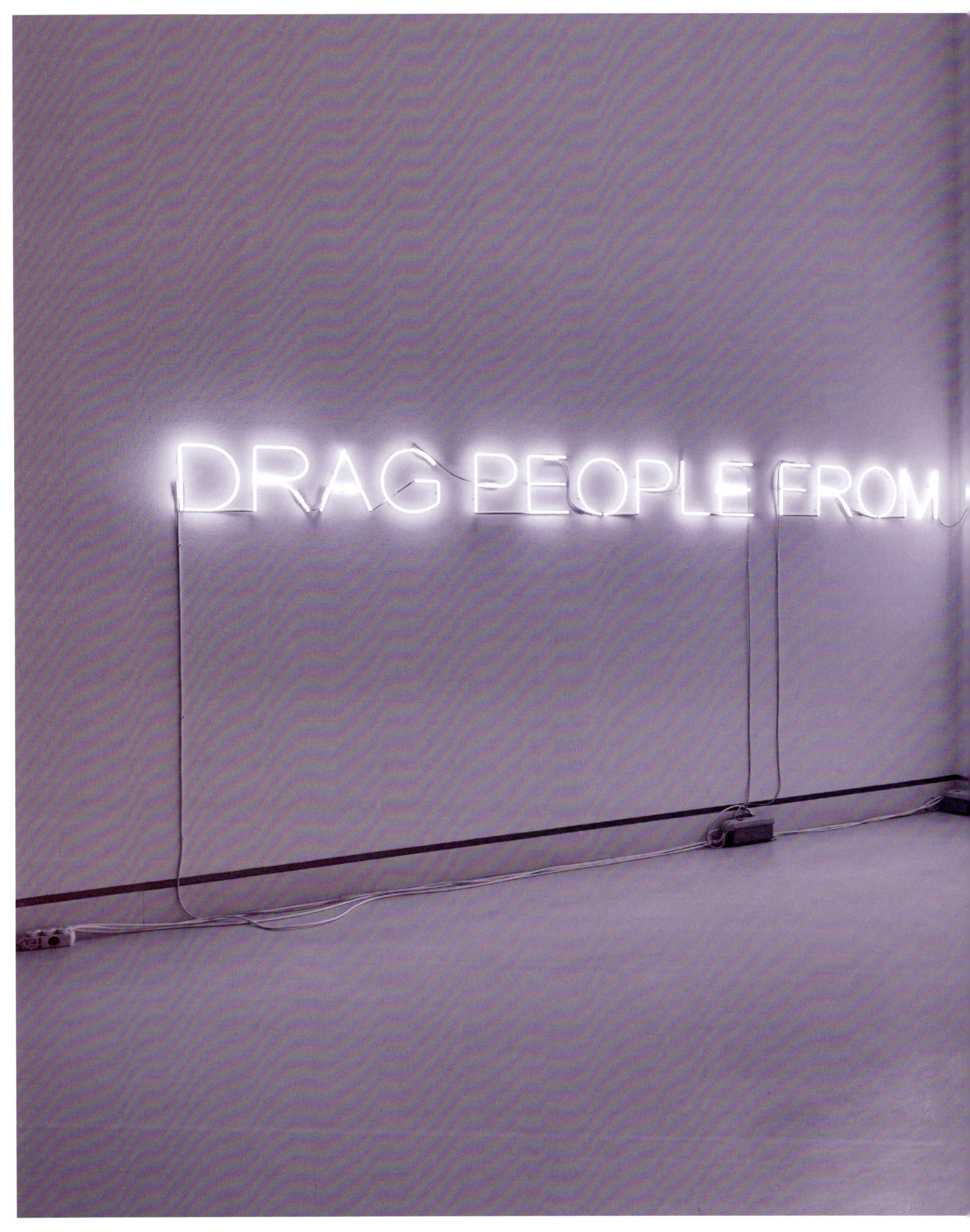
DRAG PEOPLE FROM

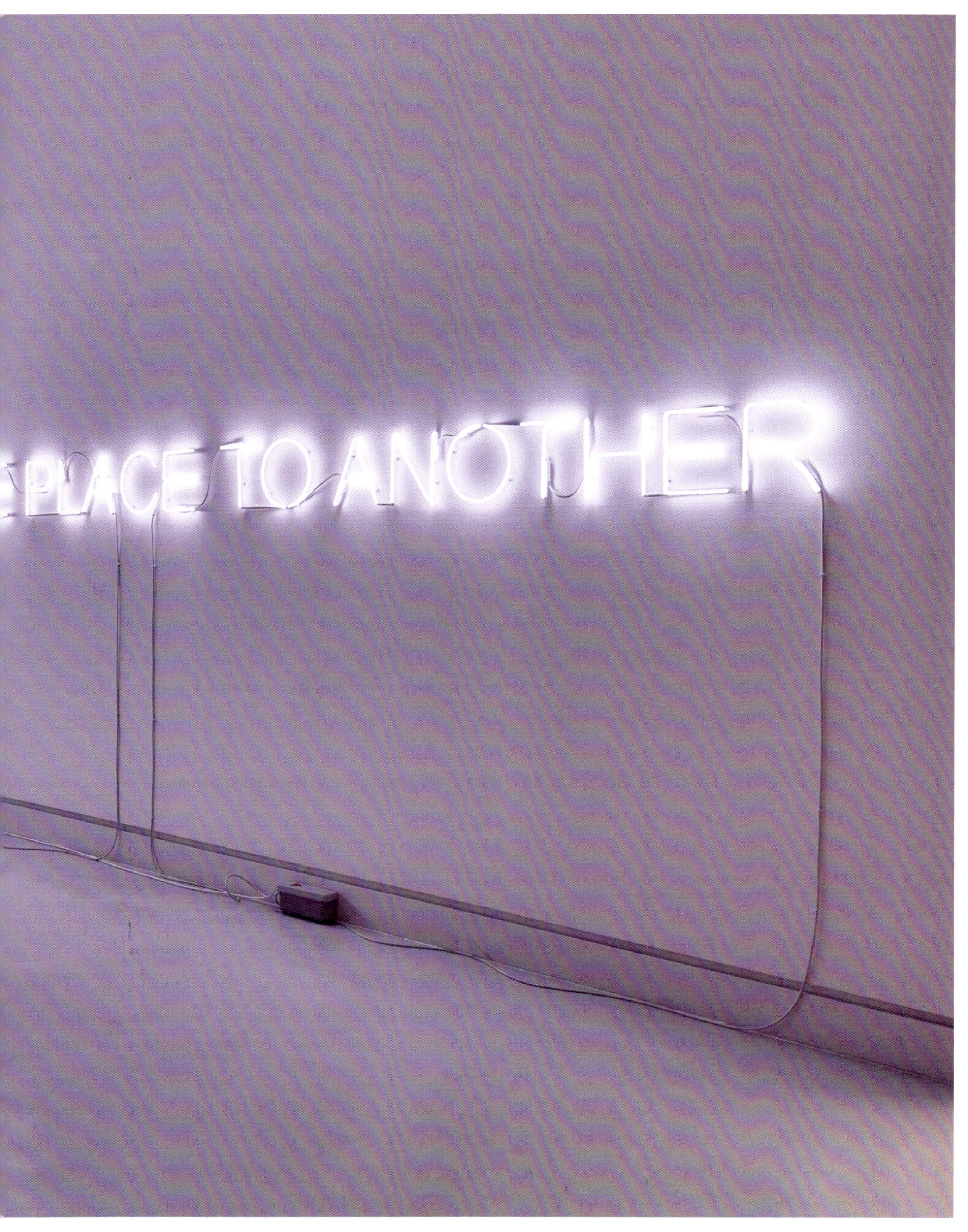
PLACE TO ANOTHER

Tamara Grcic

movements

16-Kanal-Soundinstallation,
16 Lautsprecher, Kabel, Player, 11 Teppichrollen
16-channel-sound-installation,
16 speakers, cables, player, 11 rolled carpets

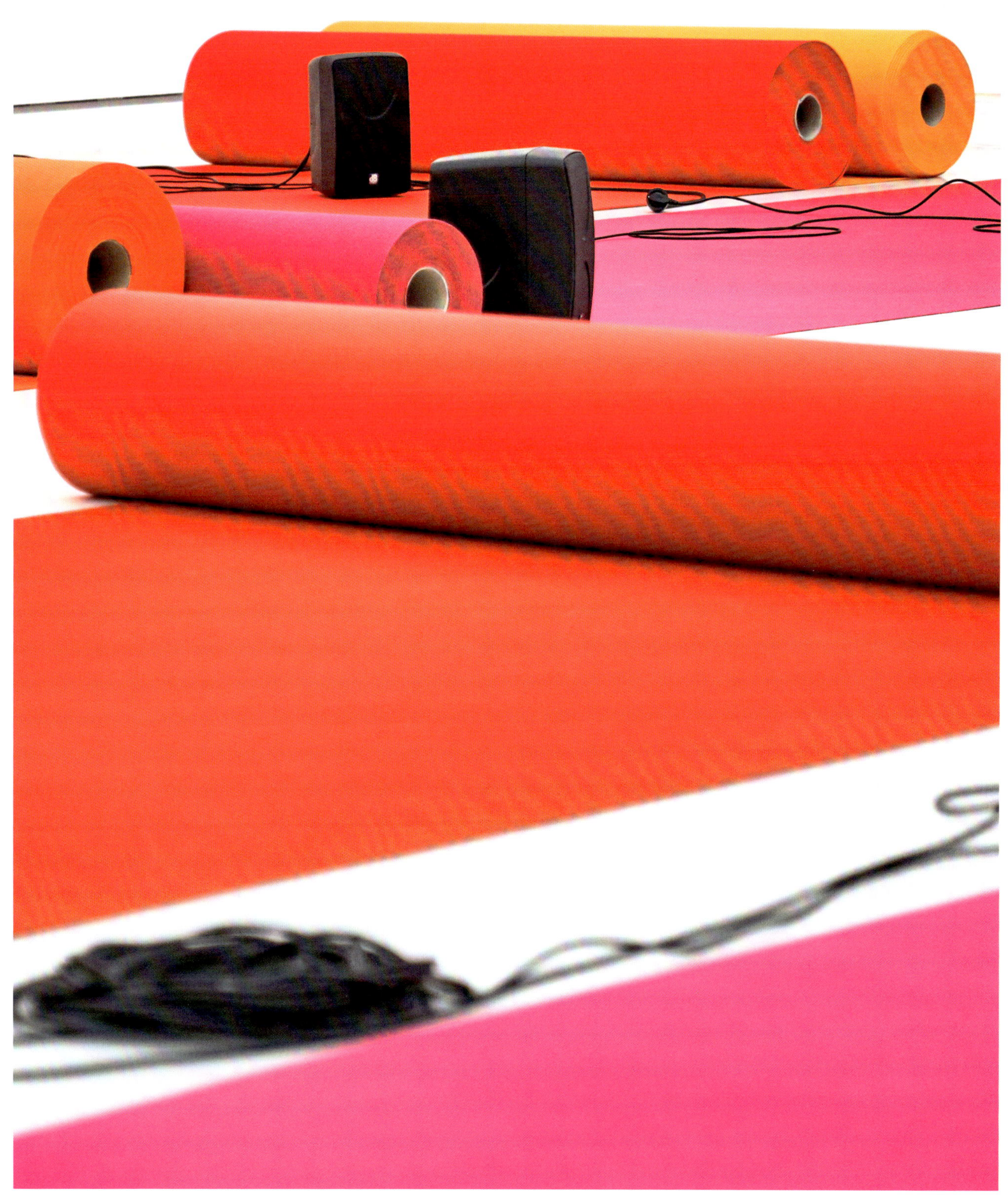

Stefanie Böttcher: **Unsere Vorgaben für die bildenden Künstler*innen bei *Between Us* waren sehr klar und hätten als restriktiv empfunden werden können. Ich habe euch gebeten, Werke zu entwickeln, die auf Taneli Törmäs Choreografie *Effect* oder deren Aufzeichnung und Weiterverarbeitung durch Motion Bank beruhen. Du hast meine Einladung sofort angenommen – worin lag für dich der Reiz an *Between Us*?**

Tamara Grcic: Tanz ist eine Ausdrucksform, die mich schon immer fasziniert hat. Die real stattfindende, unmittelbar körperliche Energie und die Bewegungen von Tänzer*innen im Raum erlebe ich sehr gerne. Damit zu arbeiten, diese Energie weiterzutransportieren, dafür eine neue, eigene Form zu entwickeln fand ich spannend. Ich hatte sofort Lust, mich auf diese Berührung mit Choreografie und Tänzer*innen einzulassen.

Stefanie: **Du hast dich auch schon in früheren Arbeiten mit Tanz auseinandergesetzt.**

Tamara: Ja, das ist schon lange her. 1999 habe ich für die Kunsthalle Sankt Gallen eine Arbeit mit Jone San Martin, einer Tänzerin der damaligen Forsythe Company, gemacht. Ich habe versucht, mit verschiedenen Kameras in der Hand mich sehr nah zu ihr und mit ihr zu bewegen. Aus diesen verschiedenen Bewegungen ist am Ende ein kurzer 16-mm-Film entstanden, der als Loop im Raum lief. Man sieht die nackte Körperstelle zwischen Schlüsselbein und Brustansatz, die sich zusammenzieht und dehnt im Rhythmus der Atmung. Ein schnelles, aufgeregtes Atmen, das sich beruhigt und wieder beschleunigt wird. Der Film hat keinen Ton. Der Motor des 16-mm-Projektors, der das Bild in Bewegung bringt, produziert den Ton. Dazu hört man den Motor einer Industrie-Nähmaschine, die auch im Raum steht und deren Nadel sich ständig auf und ab bewegt. Zwei gegeneinander laufende Maschinen treffen auf Bilder dieser sehr fragilen Stelle des Körpers und die Bewegungen des Atmens.

Florian Jenett: **Du warst vor Ort und hast die Choreografie *Effect* live gesehen. Wie wichtig war das für dich, für deine Arbeit, sie in persona sehen zu können?**

Tamara: Ich habe mir die Choreografie sogar öfters angesehen. Es war wichtig, die Tänzer*innen direkt zu erleben, ihre Präsenz im Raum über die eigenen Sinne wahrzunehmen, um Momente zu finden, von denen aus ich etwas Eigenes entwickeln kann.

> „Man muss sich auf etwas von außen Gesetztes einlassen, verstehen, was daran interessant ist, zunächst sehr offen sein, und am Ende verbindet es sich natürlich immer mit etwas Eigenem."
>
> Tamara Grcic

Florian: **Wir haben für euch Künstler*innen ein Datenpaket bereitgestellt. Hast du dort Elemente wiedergefunden, die du vorher quasi live entdeckt hast? Oder gab es für dich Bezüge zwischen diesem Live-Sehen und dem Datensatz, oder sind das zwei Teile?**

Tamara: Für mich waren das zwei verschiedene Teile. Aus dem Motion-Bank-Material haben mich die genauen Aufzeichnungen der Proben am meisten interessiert. Das war gut, um zu verstehen, wie sich das Stück entwickelt hat. Der erzählerische Durchlauf bei euch war auch wichtig, da er die Struktur des Stücks offengelegt hat. Am allerwichtigsten war dennoch, die Choreografie direkt wahrzunehmen, zu sehen und zu hören.

Stefanie: **Welche Elemente oder Aspekte der Choreografie, der Weiterverarbeitung des Datenmaterials haben dich zu deinem Beitrag für *Between Us* inspiriert?**

Tamara: Von Anfang an gab es zwei Dinge, die mich interessiert haben. Das Gehen, diese sehr alltägliche Bewegung, die bei *Effect* auf verschiedene Weise durchgespielt wird. Und zweitens, dass sich die Tänzer*innen in Wanderschuhen bewegen. Der Ton der gehenden, rennenden, sich bewegenden Tänzer*innen in den Wanderschuhen auf dem Tanzboden hat mich sofort infiziert. So war schnell klar, dass der Ton der Tänzer*innen, ihre Energie im Raum ohne Musik der Ausgangspunkt für die Arbeit sein würde. Es war dann gar nicht so einfach, diesen Ton aufzunehmen, da für die Tänzer*innen die Musik ein wichtiger Orientierungspunkt im Stück ist. Wir konnten erst sehr spät, am 23. Februar 2019, einen solchen Durchlauf machen. Gleichzeitig habe ich bereits mit ein paar jungen Tänzer*innen der Hochschule in Frankfurt Aufnahmen gemacht, auch mit Wanderschuhen, gehend, rennend, fallend – Bewegungselemente, die in der Choreografie vorkommen. Wir hatten hier mehr Zeit und Spielräume, verschiedene Bewegungen mit unterschiedlichen Mikrofonen aufzunehmen. Das eigentliche Ausgangsmaterial ist aber der Sound der Tänzer*innen von *Effect*. Dieses Tonmaterial weiterzutransportieren, zu bearbeiten, zu schneiden, zu verdichten, um damit ein ganz eigenes Ereignis für den Ausstellungsraum zu bauen, hat mich interessiert.

Stefanie: **Ich finde es interessant und total nachvollziehbar, dass du die Choreografie physisch wahrnehmen musstest. Für *Between Us* hast du dich für eine Soundinstallation entschieden. Diese bezieht sich gerade auf das Physische, suggeriert durch Klang und Rhythmus Nähe oder Ferne und choreografiert gewissermaßen die Bewegungen der Besucher*innen durch den Raum.**

Tamara: Wenn ich das Tonmaterial schneide, löse ich es von den realen Bewegungen der Tänzer*innen im Raum. Ich kann Tonspuren übereinanderlegen und auseinanderziehen. Ich kann sie in genaue Klangeinheiten unterteilen und ganz unterschiedlich zusammenfügen und anordnen. Mich interessiert dieses Material mit seinem realen Bezug zum Körper und gleichzeitig seinem abstrakten Klang in der Verdichtung. In der Arbeit *movements* ist es für mich wichtig, eine Balance zwischen beidem zu finden und damit einen ganz eigenen Zustand von Bewegungen im Raum zu erzeugen. 16 Lautsprecher sind im Raum verteilt. Der Klang bewegt sich zwischen den Lautsprechern. Die Besucher*innen bewegen sich zwischen den Lautsprechern mit und gegen den Klang. So entsteht eine maximale Bewegung im Raum.

Stefanie: **Zusätzlich zum Sound bringst du eine physische oder eine Objektebene ein, indem du Teppiche integrierst. Die Teppiche sind farbig – das ist ein großer ästhetischer Eingriff, den du in dieser supercleanen weißen Halle durchführst.**

Tamara: Bei dieser Arbeit wollte ich zu dem Tonereignis zusätzlich ein Bild setzen. Ein Bild, das auch einen Zustand von Bewegung zeigt. Gehen hat für mich mit Linienverläufen und einer Richtung zu tun, so sind die Teppichrollen aufgetaucht. Die Teppichbahnen sind in verschiedenen Farben und verschiedenen Zuständen, mal mehr oder weniger ausgerollt. Sie ergeben mit ihren Flächen und Farben einen weiteren Rhythmus im Raum. Sie erinnern in ihren unterschiedlichen Längen an die verschieden langen, zueinander montierten Tonspuren. Man kann sich auch auf ihnen niederlassen. Damit verändert sich wieder der Eindruck des Klangs, denn man befindet sich auf gleicher Höhe mit den Lautsprechern. Außerdem verbessern sie die Akustik im Raum.

Florian: **Wenn du in zehn Jahren auf das Projekt zurückblickst, würde dein Beitrag für *Between Us* herausfallen aus deinen anderen Arbeiten? Oder würdest du sagen, dass die Entwicklung eines Werks im Grunde immer auch fremden Einflüssen unterliegt und man Teile aufnimmt, die man sich entweder selbst sucht oder die gegeben sind, und schaut, wie man damit umgeht? Und wäre dann unsere Vorgabe vielleicht gar nicht so anders?**

Tamara: Eine Vorgabe eröffnet immer wieder neue Möglichkeiten. Natürlich hat man selbst gewisse Interessen, bestimmte Themen, Visionen, an die man anschließt. Dennoch hätte ich diese Arbeit ohne die Einladung so nicht gemacht. Ich war mit anderem beschäftigt, hatte einen Film in Kopf. Das ist jetzt etwas zur Seite gerutscht. Ich mag solche konkreten Einladungen. Man muss sich auf etwas von außen Gesetztes einlassen, verstehen, was daran interessant ist, zunächst sehr offen sein, und am Ende verbindet es sich natürlich immer mit etwas Eigenem. Manchmal verbindet es sich mit etwas, was für einen selbst gerade gar nicht so greifbar an der Oberfläche liegt. Ich verstehe solche konkreten Anlässe als Zündungspunkte für Arbeiten. Man muss sich mit etwas Konkretem auseinandersetzen, um darin einen eigenen Ansatz zu finden. Dafür war es wichtig, bei mehreren Durchgängen von *Effect* dabei zu sein und herauszufinden: Was ist das? Was passiert da? Was interessiert mich daran? Die Vorgabe ist eine Schwierigkeit und gleichzeitig eine Stärke des Projekts. In diesem Fall arbeitet man mit etwas bereits Verdichtetem, mit einer Kunstform, einer künstlich gestalteten Choreografie. Das ist viel schwieriger, als mit etwas Realem im Sinne von alltäglich, natürlich „ungekünstelt“ zu arbeiten. Deshalb war ich sehr froh, dass es in der Choreografie das „reale Gehen“ und die Wanderschuhe gab.

Stefanie Böttcher: **Our task for the fine artists taking part in *Between Us* was very clear and could have been regarded as restrictive. I asked those taking part to develop works based on Taneli Törmä's choreography *Effect*, or on its recording and the further processing supplied by Motion Bank. You accepted my invitation immediately—what was the appeal of *Between Us* to you?**

Tamara Grcic: Dance is a form of expression that has always fascinated me. I very much enjoy experiencing the immediate, physical energy, the dancers' movements in the space you share with them. I found working with that, transporting that energy, and finding a new, idiosyncratic form for it really exciting. I immediately felt like getting involved and engaging with choreography and the dancers.

Stefanie: **You had already dealt with dance in some of your earlier works.**

Tamara: Yes, a long time ago. Back in 1999 I created a piece in collaboration with Jone San Martin, who was a dancer at the Forsythe Company at the time. Using various hand-held cameras, I tried to move alongside her, close-up and in harmony with her as she danced. These various movements finally resulted in a short 16 mm film that was shown as a loop in the space. You see the naked part of the body between the collarbone and the top of the breast, which contracts and expands in rhythm with the breath. A fast, excited breath that becomes calmer, slower and then speeds up again. The film doesn't have sound—the motor drive in the 16 mm projector setting the image in motion is what produces the sound. Alongside this you hear the motor of an industrial sewing machine also set up in the space, with its needle constantly moving up and down. Two machines running against each other are juxtaposed with images of this very fragile part of the body and the movement of the breath.

Florian Jenett: **You were on site and saw the *Effect* choreography live. Was it important to you for your work, to see the piece in person?**

Tamara: I actually watched the choreography several times. I found it crucial to experience the dancers in a direct way, to perceive their presence in space with my own senses. This allowed me to find moments, which I could use for developing my own ideas.

Florian: **We compiled a data package for you artists. Did you rediscover elements here that you had previously encountered live? Were there links between seeing the live performance and the data packet, or did you consider these two separate components?**

Tamara: For me they were two distinct components. In terms of the Motion Bank material, what interested me the most were the precise recordings of the rehearsals. They helped me understand how the piece was developed. The narrative run-through you carried out was also important to see, it reveals the structure of the piece. But experiencing the choreography directly and live, seeing and hearing it, that was the most important part.

Stefanie: **Which elements or aspects of the choreography or of the further processing of the data inspired your contribution to *Between Us*?**

Tamara: From the very start there were two things that interested me: walking, this everyday movement which is acted out in various ways in *Effect*. And secondly the fact that the dancers move in hiking boots. The sound of the dancers walking and moving about on the dance floor in these boots immediately infected me. It quickly became clear to me that the sound the dancers were making, this energy in the space, would be the starting point for my work—but that I would be using it without the music. It wasn't at all easy to record the sound by itself, because the music is an important point of orientation for the dancers in the piece. We were only able to carry out a run-through like that at a very late point, on February 23. Parallel to this, I also made some recordings with a couple of young dancers at the academy in Frankfurt, where they were walking, running and falling also in hiking boots—all of these elements are part of the choreography. We had more time and wriggle room to record different movements with a range of microphones there. But the actual source material is the sound of the *Effect* dancers. Transporting this material, working on it, cutting it, making it denser, in order to build a distinct event for the exhibition space: that was what interested me.

Stefanie: **I find it interesting and entirely relatable that you needed to physically experience the choreography. You opted for a sound installation in your contribution to *Between Us*. This is specifically related to the physical, it alludes to**

‘You have to engage with something that has been stipulated by someone else, and that means understanding what is interesting about it. In order to do this, you need to start off by being very open, and of course in the end you naturally connect it to something that is personal and specific to you.’

Tamara Grcic

proximity or distance through sound and rhythm, and in a way choreographs the movement of the visitors through the space.

Tamara: When I’m cutting the sound material I detach it from the dancers’ actual movement in space. I can layer the audio tracks or spread them out. I can divide them into precise sound units and piece them together or arrange them in very different ways. I am interested in this material in terms of its genuine connection to the body, but at the same time also in the abstract sound that is produced as it is condensed. In *movements* it has been important to me to strike a balance between the two—and in doing so, creating an entirely distinct state of movements in space. 16 loudspeakers are spread throughout the space. The sound moves between those loudspeakers. The viewers move between the loudspeakers, with and against the sound. This achieves a maximum degree of movement in the space.

Stefanie: **In addition to the sound you have introduced a physical or object-related level by integrating carpets. The carpets are multi-colored—that’s a considerable aesthetic intervention you’re implementing in the super-clean white hall.**

Tamara: In this piece I wanted to offer viewers an image to sit alongside the sound experience. An image that also shows a state of movement. For me, walking is related to lines and direction, and that led me to the rolls of carpet. The lengths of carpet appear in various colors and conditions, more or less rolled out. Their surfaces and colors create a further rhythm in the space. With their different lengths they remind me of the audio tracks: when those are placed alongside each other some are longer and some are shorter. You can also sit or lie down on them. That in turn also changes the impression you’ll get of the sound, as you are then at the height of the loudspeakers. And the carpets also make the acoustics of the space better.

Florian: **When you look back on the project in ten years’ time, do you think your contribution to *Between Us* will stand out from your other works? Or would you say that the development of a piece is always fundamentally subject to external influences—with you incorporating parts that you either search out yourself or are given, then figuring out how to approach these in a second step? And might our briefing not be so very different then?**

Tamara: Guidelines or briefings always open up new possibilities. Of course you bring to the table your own interests, themes, and the visions that your draw on. Nevertheless: I wouldn’t have made this work in quite the same way without having been invited. I was working on something else; I had a film in mind. That’s fallen to the side a little for now. But I like these kinds of specific invitations. You have to engage with something that has been stipulated by someone else, and that means understanding what is interesting about it. In order to do this, you need to start off by being very open, and of course in the end you naturally connect it to something that is personal and specific to you. Sometimes you even connect it to something that isn’t quite so tangible for you at the time or that may not lie close to the surface. I see such concrete specifications as points of ignition for my work. You have to engage with something specific in order to find your own approach to the issue. That’s why it was important to me to witness several run-throughs of *Effect*, in order to find out: What is it? What’s happening there? What is it that interests me about it? The specification is a difficulty, but at the same time it’s were the strength of the project lies. In this case you’re working with something that is already condensed, with an art form, and artificially arranged choreography. That’s much more difficult than working with something real in the sense of its being mundane, natural, and ‘uncontrived.’ That’s why I was happy that the choreography included ‘real walking’ and the hiking boots.

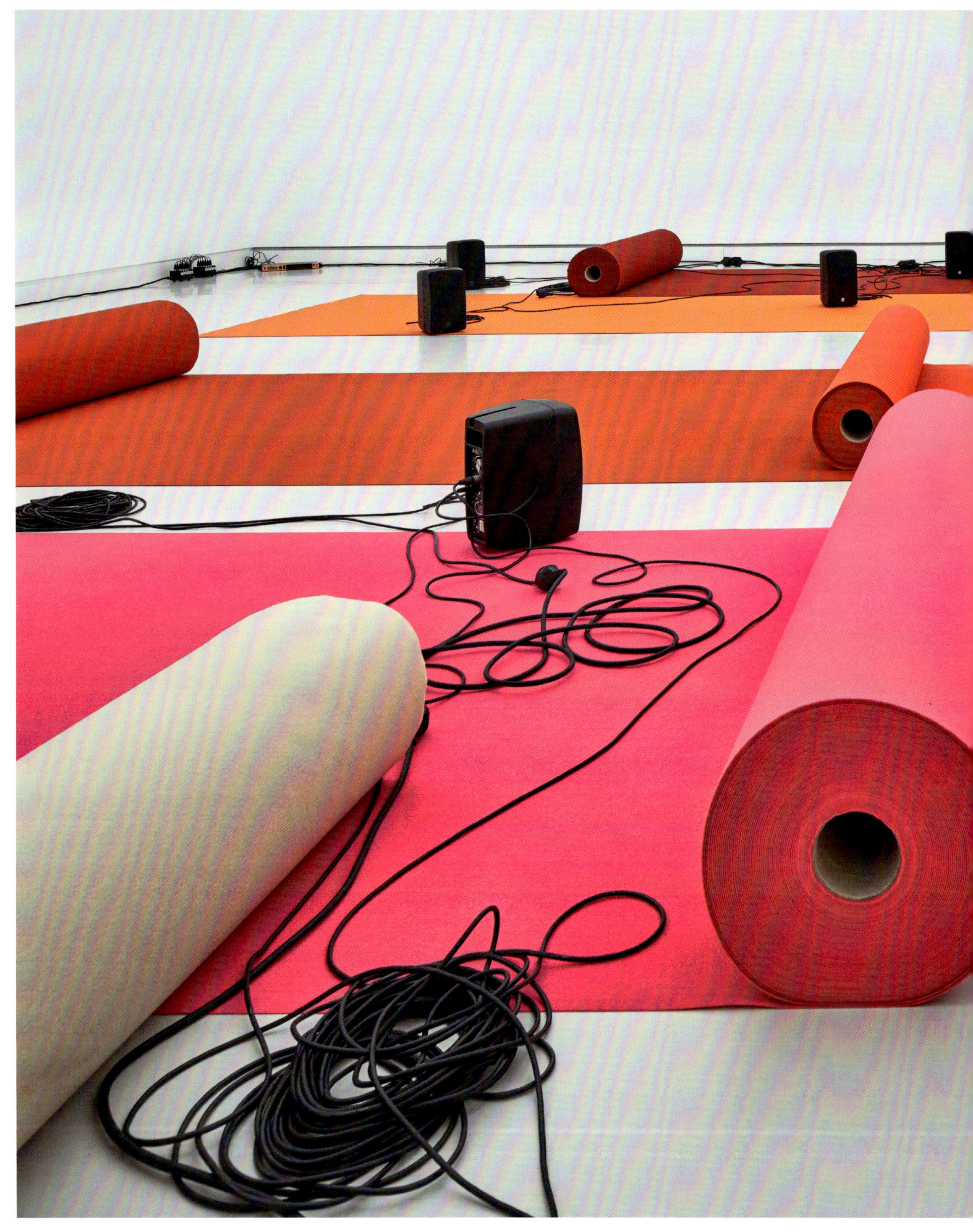

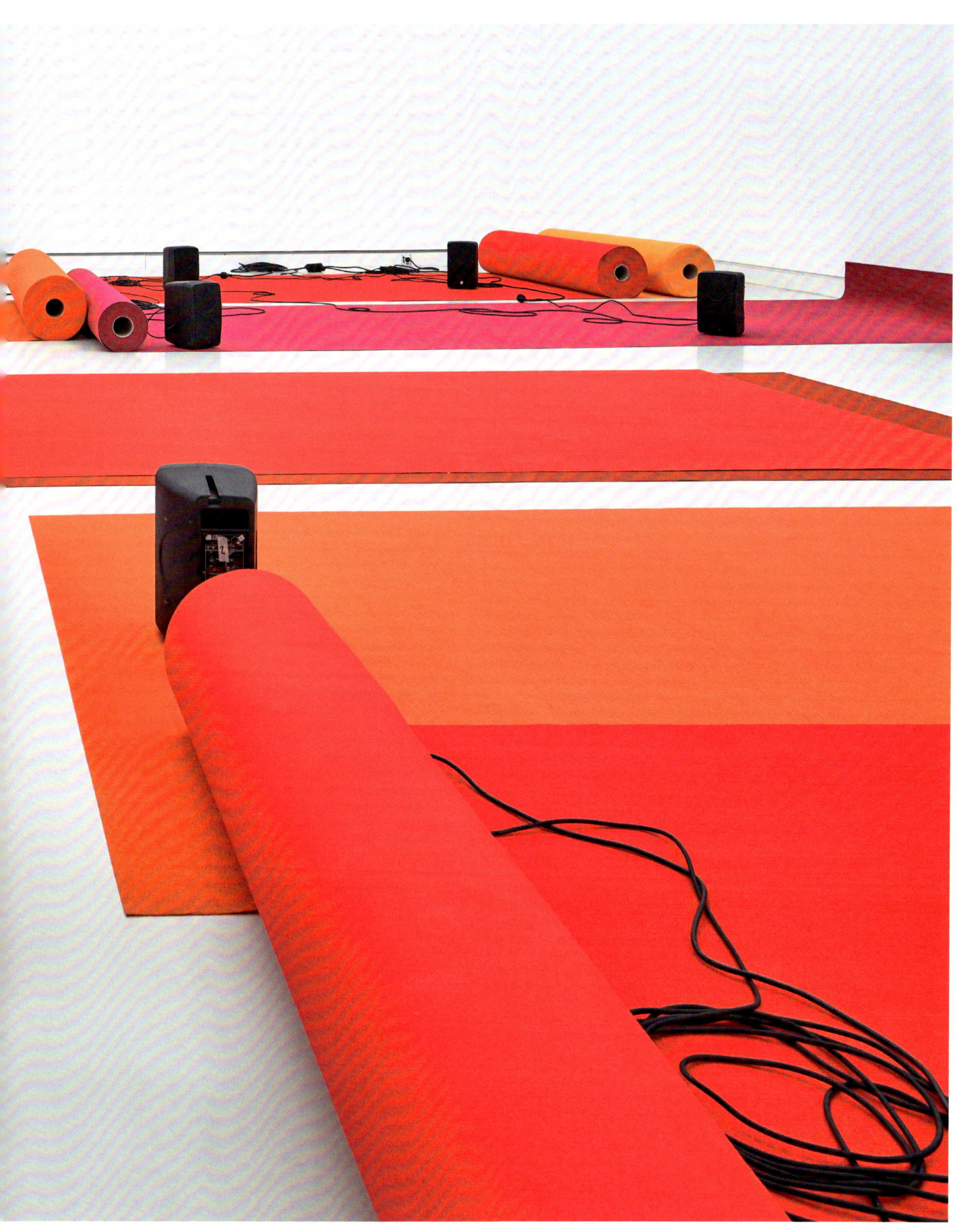

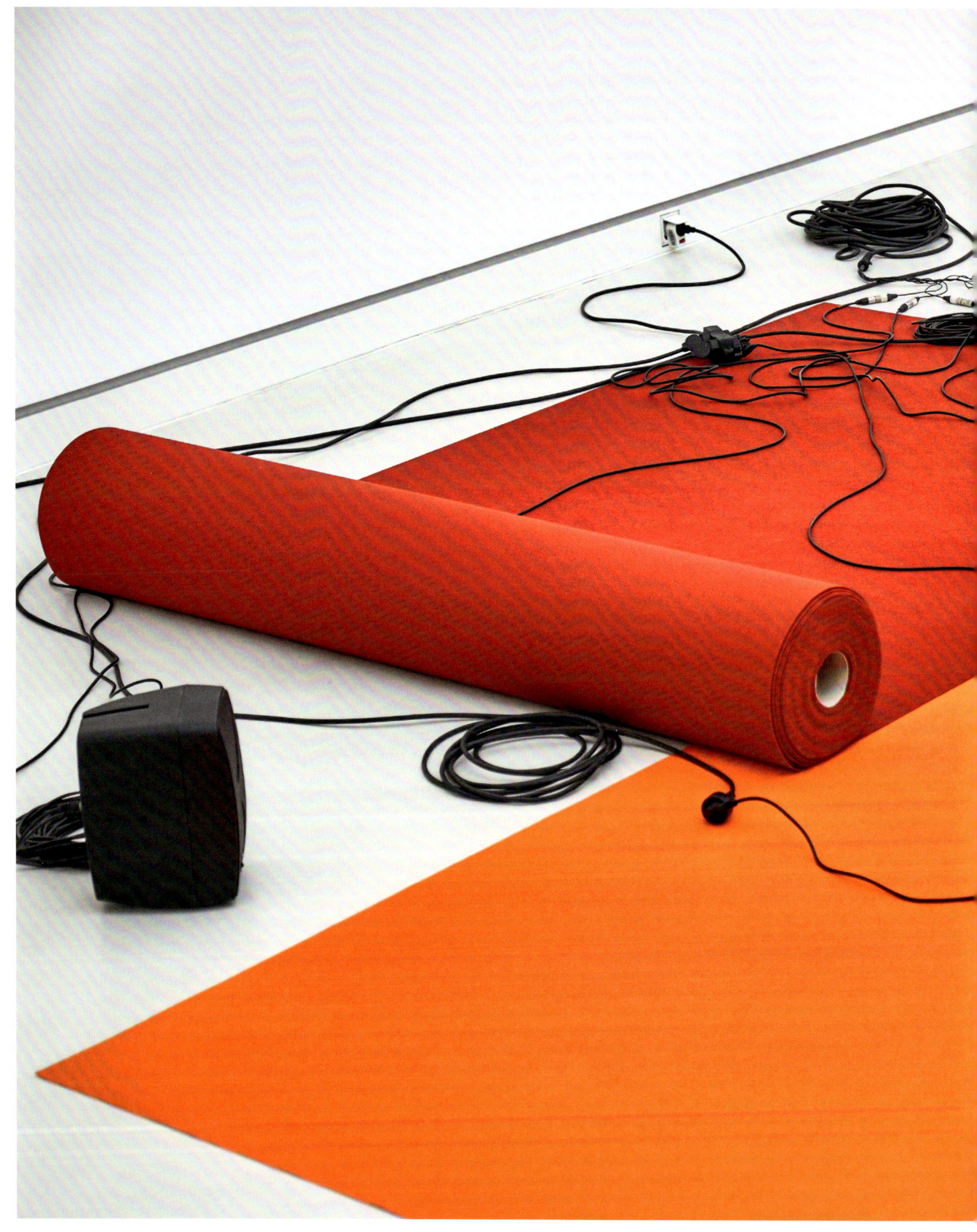

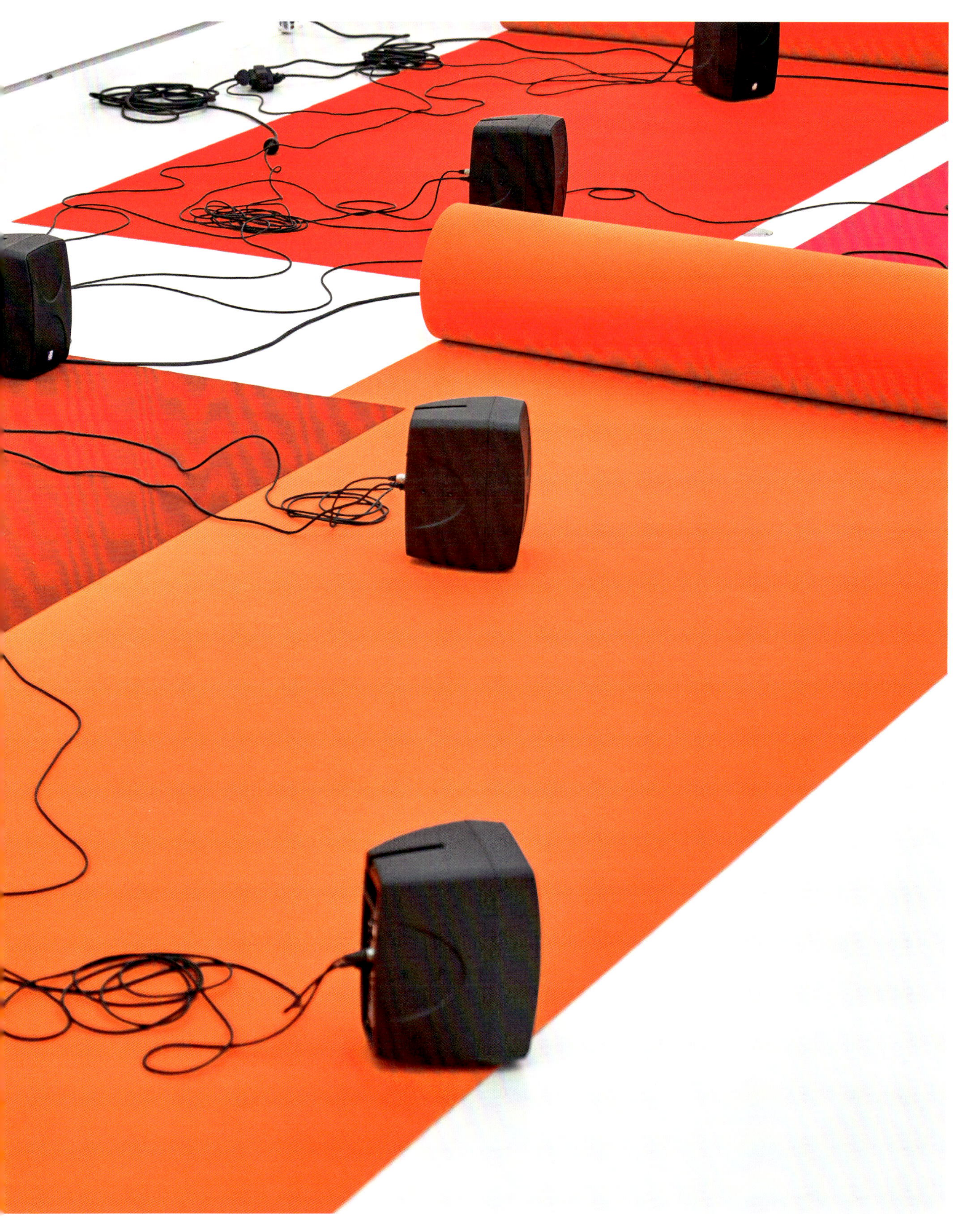

Žilvinas Kempinas

SPIN

Ortsspezifische Installation,
magnetische Bänder, Industrieventilator,
Fahrradvorderrad, HD-Video
Site-specific installation, magnetic tapes,
industrial van, bicycle wheel, HD Video

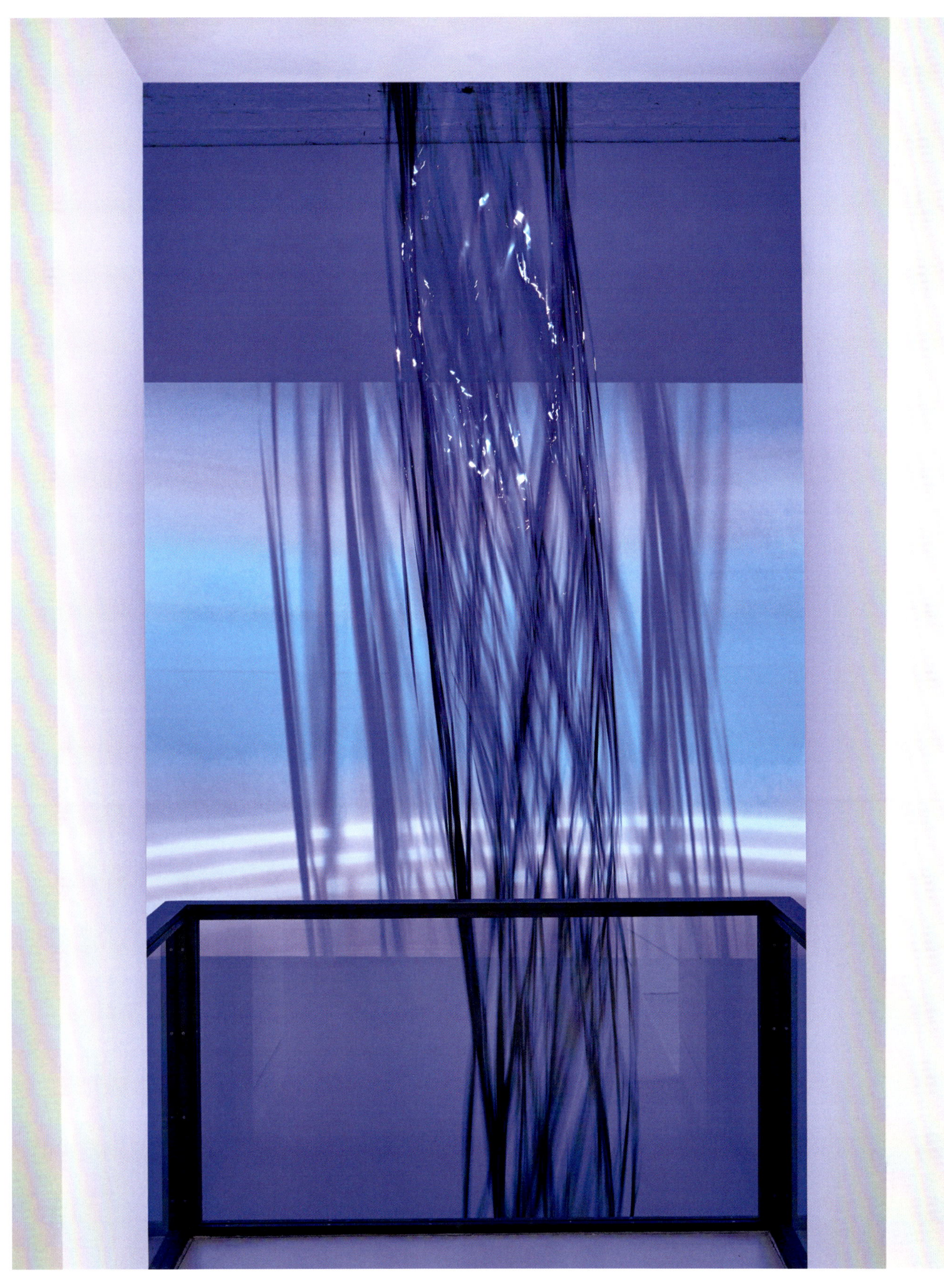

Lina Louisa Krämer: **Wie sieht dein Beitrag für *Between Us* aus?**

Žilvinas Kempinas: Mein Beitrag ist eine 10 Meter hohe ortsspezifische kinetische Installation, die den Titel *SPIN* trägt. Sie besteht aus VHS-Tapes, einer Fahrradfelge, die an einem Industrieventilator befestigt wurde, und über drei Wände erstreckt sich eine Videoprojektion.

Lina: **Von drei Seiten aus werden farbige, flimmernde Bilder auf die Magnetbänder projiziert, die an einer sich drehenden Fahrradfelge von der Decke hängen. Die Bänder verweisen auf ihre Materialität und Funktion, nicht jedoch als Bildträger, sondern vielmehr als Spiegel, der das Licht der Projektion reflektiert. Wie würdest du das Verhältnis zwischen der Projektion und den Bändern beschreiben?**

Žilvinas: Die Körperlichkeit der Bänder kann auf die Vorstellung des Körpers als Behälter übertragen werden. Die Projektionen von Licht und Farbe im Hintergrund können wiederum auf die Funktionsweise unseres Geistes bezogen werden – Gedanken, Visionen, Halluzinationen, Träume, Ideen usw. Ich bin daran interessiert, diese Überschneidung in allen möglichen poetischen Veränderungen zu sehen, die sich daraus ergeben. Es werden auch Schatten auf die Wände geworfen, Geräusche gehen vom Ventilator und der dadurch erzeugten Luftströmung aus. All diese simplen Elemente sollen zusammenarbeiten, um ein System zu erschaffen, das auf den ersten Blick chaotisch wirkt, aber seiner eigenen Logik folgt. Ich freue mich, diese Elemente nun in Aktion zu sehen. Ich mag die experimentelle Natur dieses Projekts. Das macht es lebendig und aufregend für mich.

Lina: **Strategien zur Besetzung von Räumen spielen in deinem künstlerischen Ansatz allgemein eine große Rolle. Deine Installation *SPIN* im Alten Turm der Kunsthalle Mainz ist eine Neuproduktion, die die Raumhöhe von zwölf Metern fast gänzlich ausnutzt. Die physische Begegnung der Besucher*innen mit deiner Arbeit ist jedoch auf einen kleinen Balkon beschränkt. Robert Morris hat einmal argumentiert, dass Kunst – insbesondere Skulptur – nicht durch das Sehen allein erlebt werden kann, sondern auf einer körperlichen Betrachtung beruht, einer Beteiligung, die sich aus spezifischen räumlichen Narrativen ergibt.**

„Luftströmung, flackernde Reflektionen, das Geräusch des Ventilators und der Bänder, Lichtstrahlen der Projektoren und flirrende Farben an den Wänden hinter der zentralen Skulptur, die sich wie ein Tornado von Magnetbändern konstant vor unseren Augen dreht."

Žilvinas Kempinas

Es gibt keinen direkten Zugang zu *SPIN*, die Besucher*innen können sie nicht umwandeln und von unterschiedlichen Standpunkten aus sehen. Verschiebt sich die Ebene, auf der die Begegnung der Rezipient*innen mit deiner Arbeit stattfindet?

Žilvinas: Mich inspiriert die Phänomenologie der Werke von Robert Morris schon seit langer Zeit – eigentlich seit ich Anfang der 1990er Jahre an der Kunstakademie in Vilnius anfing zu studieren. Ich sah seine Kunst damals nur auf Fotografien, schätzte sie aber trotzdem sehr. Nach einiger Zeit zog ich nach New York und hatte das Glück, dass Robert Morris mein Professor am Hunter College wurde. Ich habe immer daran geglaubt, dass Kunstwerke persönlich, im realen Raum und in der Zeit erlebt werden müssen, um sie zu verstehen – selbst die besten Fotografien sind irreführend. Auch Videodokumentation bietet nicht genügend Informationen über eine Arbeit. Das Körpergefühl in Bezug auf das Kunstwerk, die physische Nähe dieser Beziehung bewirkt einen signifikanten Unterschied in der Wahrnehmung. Ich schätze dies ganz besonders in unserem digitalen Zeitalter.

In dem konkreten Fall des Alten Turms der Kunsthalle Mainz – einer wirklich sehr speziellen Umgebung – mache ich mir keine Sorgen um Einschränkungen, die der Balkon vorgibt. Denn die Arbeit ist visuell äußerst fordernd, und von ihr geht eine starke körperliche Präsenz aus: Luftströmung, flackernde Reflektionen, das Geräusch des Ventilators und der Bänder, Lichtstrahlen der Projektoren und flirrende Farben an den Wänden hinter der zentralen Skulptur, die sich wie ein Tornado von Magnetbändern konstant vor unseren Augen dreht. Es gibt keinen Grund, sich um die Installation herumzubewegen. Die Kulisse des Alten Turms ist leicht theatralisch und etwas unheimlich – von einer festen Position im Raum aus kann man ein Kunstwerk beobachten, das sich in Lichtstrahlen zur Schau stellt.

Lina: **In drei Disziplinen, drei Ansätzen, drei ästhetischen Formaten untersucht das Projekt *Between Us* die Übertragung und Transformation von Informationen. Die ständige Veränderung ist auch in deinen kinetischen Skulpturen vorhanden. Kann diese Bewegung auch auf der Metaebene als Symbol für die Übertragung und Transformation von Informationen gesehen werden?**

Žilvinas: Ja, bitte. Was auch immer man hier sieht, man muss es mitnehmen.

Lina: **Du hast einmal gesagt, dass ein Band wie eine Linie ist, der man folgen kann, eine Aneinanderreihung endloser Punkte, die alles beschreiben können. Was passiert, wenn sich die Linien in Bewegung setzen?**

Žilvinas: Sie tanzen. Sie werden lebendig und surfen in den Luftströmungen. So wie Surfer auf den Wellen der Ozeane reiten.

Lina: **Bewegung und Motiv des Kreises sind zwei mögliche Verbindungen zur Choreografie *Effect* von Taneli Törmä. Wo siehst du weitere Zusammenhänge, und was hat dich am meisten an der Idee fasziniert, mit einer auf Zirkulation basierenden Choreografie zu arbeiten?**

Žilvinas: Moment, Zufall, Störsequenzen, Effizienz der Mittel, Turbulenzen, Geschwindigkeit, Einfachheit, Wiederholung, rituelle Monotonie ... – all das schwingt in unserem alltäglichen Leben, wie wir es kennen, mit. Kombinationen dieser einfachen Elemente in richtigen Verhältnissen zueinander können einen ästhetischen Wert erzeugen. Dennoch kann ich nicht sagen, dass ich im traditionellen Sinne mit Choreografie gearbeitet habe. Wenn ich zuvor mit Choreografie gearbeitet hätte, hätte ich vielleicht ein völlig anderes Ergebnis erzielt – eines, bei dem die Choreografie selbst fester Bestandteil des Projekts geworden wäre.

Lina: **In den 1990er Jahren hast du bereits mit Theatern zusammengearbeitet und das Bühnenbild für verschiedene Aufführungen entwickelt. Was unterscheidet deine früheren Kollaborationen mit Choreograf*innen und Tänzer*innen von der heutigen? Gibt es Parallelen?**

Žilvinas: Bevor ich diese Frage beantworte, möchte ich klarstellen, dass meine Beschäftigung mit dem Theater kurz, aber intensiv war und sich auf die Zusammenarbeit mit einem Theaterregisseur beschränkte – Oskaras Koršunovas –, dessen Erstaufführung 1990 das Nationaltheater in Litauen aus den Fugen hob und neue bahnbrechende Maßstäbe setzte. Mit Oskaras habe ich an seiner zweiten, dritten und vierten Theateraufführung zusammengearbeitet, und wir haben auch eine Oper (*Der fliegende Holländer* von Wagner) gemeinsam produziert. Ich habe mich nie als Bühnenbildner gesehen, der eine Kulisse für eine Aufführung schafft, vielmehr sehe ich das Bühnenbild als gleichwertigen Partner zwischen den anderen in diese komplexe Kunstform involvierten Sparten – Spiel/Text, Musik/Sound, Schauspiel, Regie ... Als bildender Künstler wollte ich ebenso wie die anderen auf ihrem Gebiet einen Beitrag dazu leisten, dass die gesamte Aufführung des Dramas zu einem einzigen eigenständigen System aus kreativen Elementen werden kann, in dem alles wie ein Schweizer Uhrwerk reibungslos aufeinander abgestimmt abläuft. Ich habe oft an den Proben teilgenommen, nicht weil ich das musste, sondern weil ich es liebte, zu sehen, wie sich alles entwickelt, und ich es mochte, meine Ideen zu diskutieren und, wenn nötig, mein Feedback zu geben.

Für *Between Us* gab es keine solche Aufgabenstellung. Eigentlich war es sogar eher gegensätzlich – wir arbeiteten jeder für sich und präsentierten unsere Werke in gänzlich autonomen architektonischen Räumen. Alle Künstler*innen sind in *Between Us* über Fragestellungen miteinander verbunden, die sich wiederholen, aber wir alle agieren unabhängig voneinander als Künstler*innen. Mit anderen Worten: Weder brauche ich Tänzer*innen in meinem Raum, die meine Arbeit lebendig werden lassen, noch brauchen die Tänzer*innen meine Arbeit, um die sie herumtanzen können, um zu einem besseren Ergebnis zu gelangen. Die Idee war jedoch, dass erste Impulse von der Choreografie ausgehen – die so zum Startpunkt für alle wurde. Das Erste, was ich vom Tanz sah, war eine 25-minütige Videoaufzeichnung. Mein Ziel war es dann, meine Version der Performance in eine kinetische Installation umzuwandeln, die als autonomes Kunstwerk funktionieren sollte. Es ist also von Anfang an ein völlig anderer Ansatz, wenn man *Between Us* mit einer Theaterproduktion und einem Bühnenbild vergleicht.

Lina: ***Between Us*** **ist ein Projekt, das aus gegenseitigen Einflüssen und Transferprozessen besteht, aber basierend auf einem fest definierten Quellmaterial. Worin liegt der Reiz dieses Projekts für dich? Worin die kritischen Aspekte?**

Žilvinas: Eigentlich war ich anfangs sehr skeptisch gegenüber der Grundidee von *Between Us*, da Interpretation meist im Zentrum der darstellenden Künste, wie Theater, Musik oder Tanz, steht, aber die bildende Kunst frei davon ist. Was ich damit meine, ist, dass man sich beim Malen eines Gemäldes oder bei einer Installation nicht auf bestimmte existierende Noten oder ein vorhandenes Drehbuch verlässt. Es schien mir deshalb eine schlechte Idee, einen Tanz / eine Performance als Ausgangsmaterial für mögliche Kunstwerke zu nehmen. Aber diese „schlechte Idee“ hat mich gerade fasziniert, und ich entschied mich, die Herausforderung anzunehmen.

Ich ziehe es vor, falsch zu liegen, aber mich damit vielleicht selbst zu überraschen, als immer richtig und vorhersehbar zu agieren. Man muss gelegentlich seine eigenen Regeln brechen. Das ist die einzige Möglichkeit, um voranzukommen, an einen neuen Ort zu gelangen, an dem man noch nie zuvor gewesen ist. Ich war wirklich neugierig darauf, die Choreografie zu sehen, um herauszufinden, ob es irgendetwas gibt, das mich ansprechen und mir eine Erwiderung entlocken würde. Ich sah den Mitschnitt auf einem Computerbildschirm und erkannte einige grundlegende Elemente, die ich in meiner eigenen Praxis wertschätzen und anwenden konnte. Und dann war da noch dieser ungewöhnliche architektonische Ort – ein alter Turm. Das passte alles für mich zusammen. Die Tänzer*innen führen ihren „Kreistanz“ auf, und ich gestalte meine Installation wie eine Art wirbelnden Derwisch, der sich im Turm dreht. Und das tue ich auf meine eigene Art und Weise.

‘Airflow, flickering reflections, the sound of the fan and tapes, light beams from projectors, and colors flickering on the walls in the background of a central piece, which is a tornado of magnetic tapes conveniently spinning in front of you, meaning there is no reason to move around it.’

Žilvinas Kempinas

Lina Louisa Krämer: **What is your contribution to *Between Us*?**

Žilvinas Kempinas: It’s a 10-meter-high, site-specific kinetic installation called *SPIN*, made of VHS tapes, a bicycle wheel attached to an industrial fan and three video projections for three walls.

Lina: **By projecting flickering colorful images from three sides onto the magnetic tapes that hang on the rotating bicycle wheel from the ceiling, the tapes refer back to their materiality, not as a medium for images, but rather a mirror that reflects the light from the projection. How would you describe the relation between the projection and the tapes?**

Žilvinas: The physicality of tapes could be referenced to the idea of the body as a vessel, and projections of light and color in the background could be linked to the ways our minds operate—thoughts, visions, hallucinations, dreams, ideas, etc., I am interested in seeing this overlap with all the inherent possible poetic alterations it triggers. There will also be shadows cast on the walls, the sound of the fan, and currents of air. All these simple elements should work together, creating a system, which looks chaotic at first glance but has its own logic. This was something I was looking forward to seeing in action myself. I like the experimental nature of this project, that’s what makes it alive and exciting to me.

Lina: **In general strategies to occupy spaces play a big role in your artistic approach. Your installation *SPIN* in the Old Tower at Kunsthalle Mainz is a new commission that exploits the height (12 m) of the space. However the visitors' ability to physically engage with your work is limited to a small balcony. Robert Morris once argued that art—in particular sculptures—cannot be experienced through seeing, but draw on a physical consideration, an involvement, which can be experienced in a specific spatial narrative. By limiting access to walking around your work and seeing it from different angles, have you shifted the level at which the engagement takes place?**

Žilvinas: I was inspired by the phenomenology of Robert Morris works a long time back while still studying at the Vilnius Art Academy in the early 1990s. At that time, I only knew his art from photographs, but appreciated it nevertheless. Some time passed, I moved to New York and was fortunate enough to have Mr Morris as my professor at Hunter College. I have always believed that artwork has to be experienced in person, in real space and time, that even the best photographs are misleading; video documentation doesn't provide enough information about the work. The feeling of your own body in relation to the artwork, the physical proximity of this relation makes a significant difference to your perception. I value it especially in this digital age.

In the particular case of the Old Tower at Kunsthalle Mainz, a special setting indeed, I am not concerned about the restrictions of the balcony, because the piece is visually aggressive and I expect quite a lot of visceral physicality from it: airflow, flickering reflections, the sound of the fan and tapes, light beams from projectors, and colors flickering on the walls in the background of a central piece, which is a tornado of magnetic tapes conveniently spinning in front of you, meaning there is no reason to move around it. The setting is a little bit theatrical and somewhat sinister—from a fixed position you can observe an artifact performing in a light beam.

Lina: **In three disciplines, three approaches, three aesthetic formats, the *Between Us* project explores the transfer and transformation of information. Continuous change is also innate in your kinetic sculptures. Can this movement also be seen at a meta-level as symbolic of the transfer and transformation of information?**

Žilvinas: Yes, of course. Whatever you might see here is for you to take.

Lina: **You once said that the tapes are a line to follow, a succession of endless points that can describe anything and everything. What happens when these lines are set in motion?**

Žilvinas: They dance. They become animated and surf the currents of the air, just like surfers ride ocean waves.

Lina: **Movement and the theme of the circle are two possible links to the *Effect* choreography by Taneli Törmä. Where do you discern further connections and what fascinated you most about the idea of working with a choreography that is based on circulation?**

Žilvinas: The present moment, chance, accidents, the efficiency of means, turbulence, speed, simplicity, repetition, ritualistic monotony… all this resonates with mundane life as we know it. Combinations of these simple elements in the right ratios can produce aesthetic value. But I can't say that I 'worked with choreography' in the traditional sense. If I would have worked with choreography, I might have ended up with a totally different result—one where choreography itself became an integral part of the project.

Lina: **In the 1990s, you worked with theaters and developed the stage sets for different performances. In what way were your previous collaborations with choreographers and dancers different from those today? Are there parallels?**

Žilvinas: Before answering this question, I would like to clarify that my involvement with theater was brief but intense, and limited to a single drama theater director—Oskaras Koršunovas. His first piece in 1990 blew the roof off The National Drama Theater in Lithuania, it was groundbreaking by any standards. I worked with Oskaras on his second, third, and fourth drama performances, and we also produced one opera (Wagner's *Flying Dutchman*). I never saw myself as someone who merely provides the backdrop for a performance, but considered set design as equal in status to the other

elements involved in this complex form of art—play/text, music/sound, acting, directing …
As a visual artist, I wanted to contribute just as much as others do in their fields in order to enable the whole drama performance to become a single interdependent system of creative elements, where everything is in sync and proceeds as smoothly as a Swiss watch. I used to hang out in rehearsals a lot, not because I had to, but because I loved seeing everything evolving, loved to discuss ideas, give my feedback if needed.

For *Between Us* there was no such task. Actually, the opposite was true—we worked separately and presented our works in entirely autonomous architectural spaces. All the artists are connected in *Between Us* by the fact they echo some ideas, but we all act independently as artists. In other words, I don't really need dancers in my space in order to animate my work, nor do they need my piece to dance around for better results. However, the idea was that the initial impetus came from seeing the choreography—a kind of a starting point for us all. The dance had developed into a 25-minute piece when I first saw it on my computer. My goal—as I saw it—was to present my version of the performance, albeit converted into a kinetic installation that could stand on its own as an autonomous artwork. So from the very start it's an entirely different approach if you compare *Between Us* with theater production and stage design.

Lina: ***Between Us*** **is a project based on mutual influences and transfer processes, but which nevertheless relied on well-defined source material. What is the attraction of this project for you? What are the critical aspects?**

Žilvinas: Actually, I was skeptical about the whole idea of *Between Us* at first, because interpretation usually is at the core of performing arts, like theater, music or dance, but the visual arts are free of that; I mean, you don't rely on a given score or script to make a painting or installation. So to take a dance/performance as a source for a possible artwork seemed to me like a bad idea. That said, this kind of 'bad idea' was exactly what intrigued me the most and I decided to take on the challenge.

I prefer to be wrong and possibly surprising to myself, rather than be right and predictable.
You have to toss your own rules overboard occasionally; that's the only way to move forward if you want to get somewhere you have never been before. I was genuinely curious to see the performance in order to find out whether there was anything that would trigger a response in me in some way or another. I watched the dance on a computer screen and saw some basic elements used, which I can appreciate and use in my own practice. And then there was this rather unusual architectural location—the Old Tower, so it all fell into place for me. The dancers will perform their circular dance, and I am going to have my installation like some kind of whirling dervish spinning in the tower, and I will do it my way.

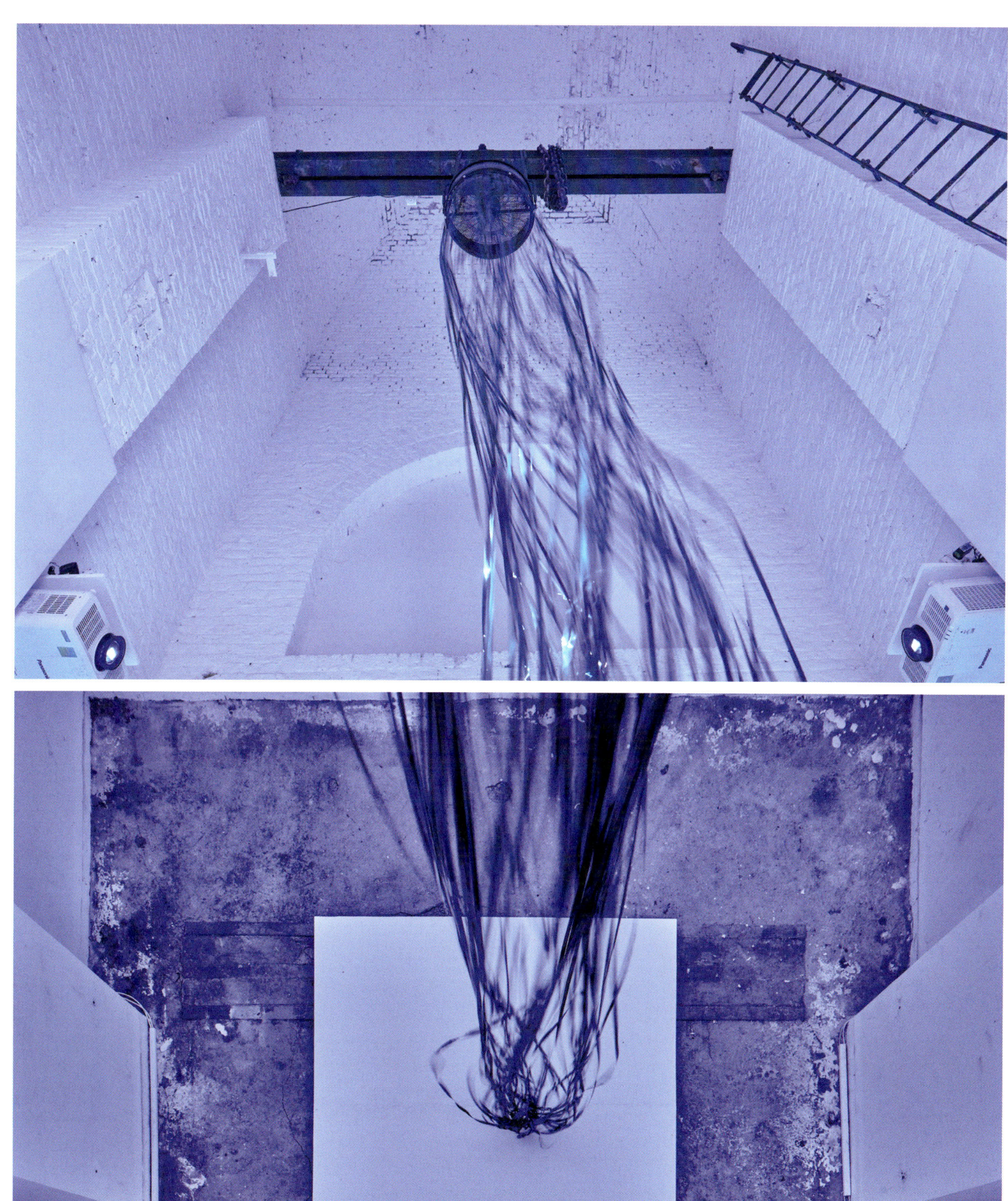

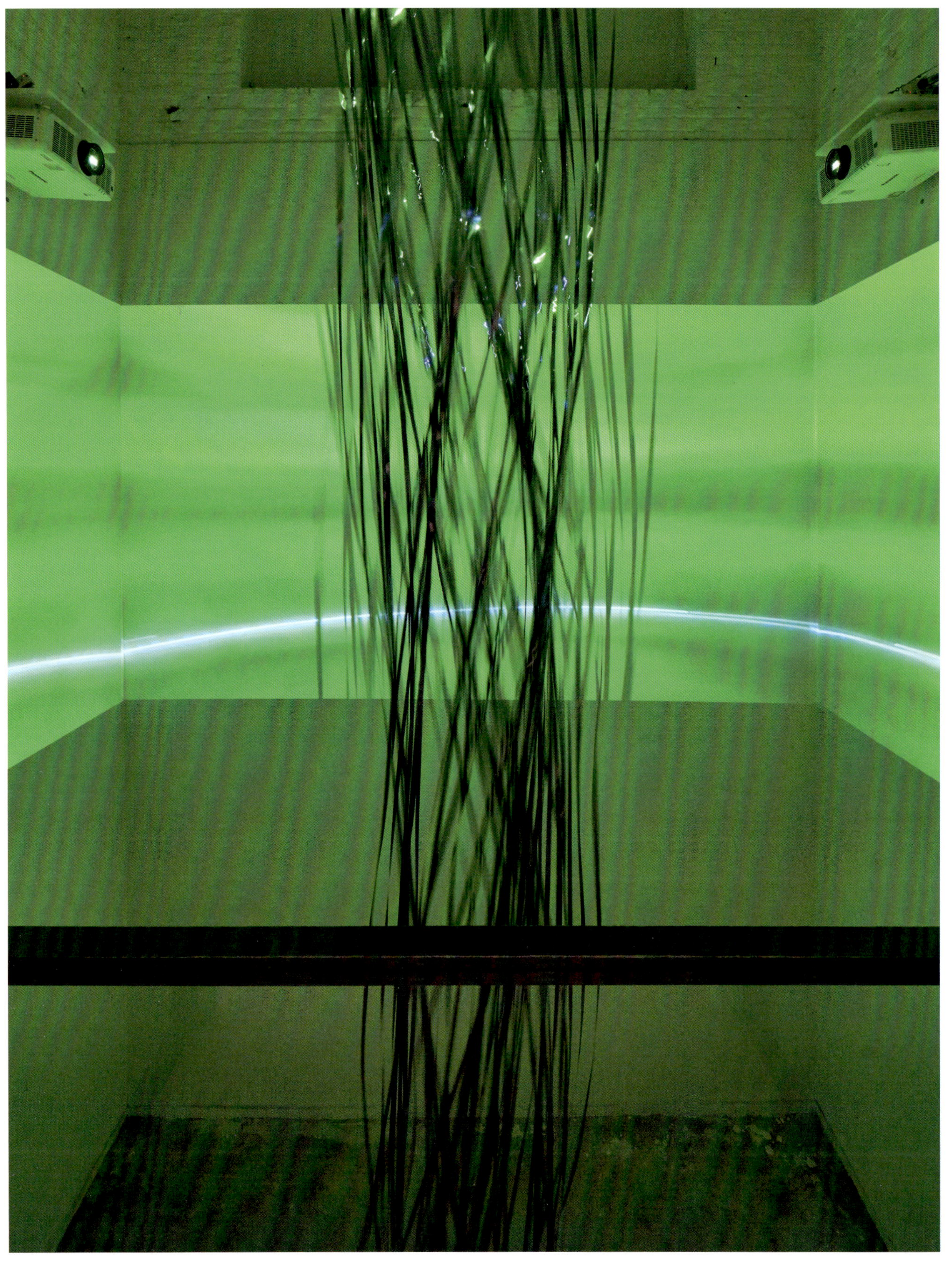

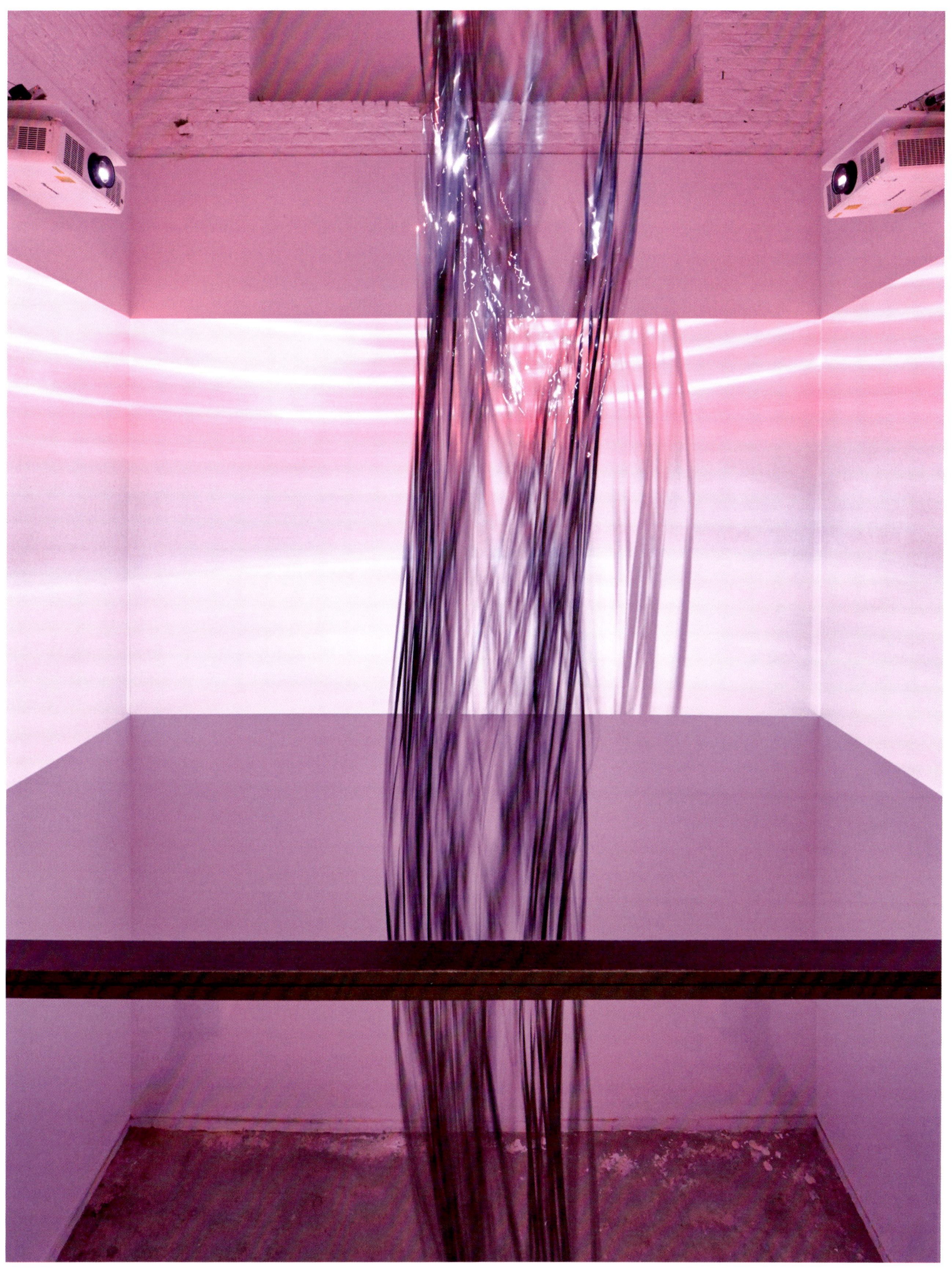

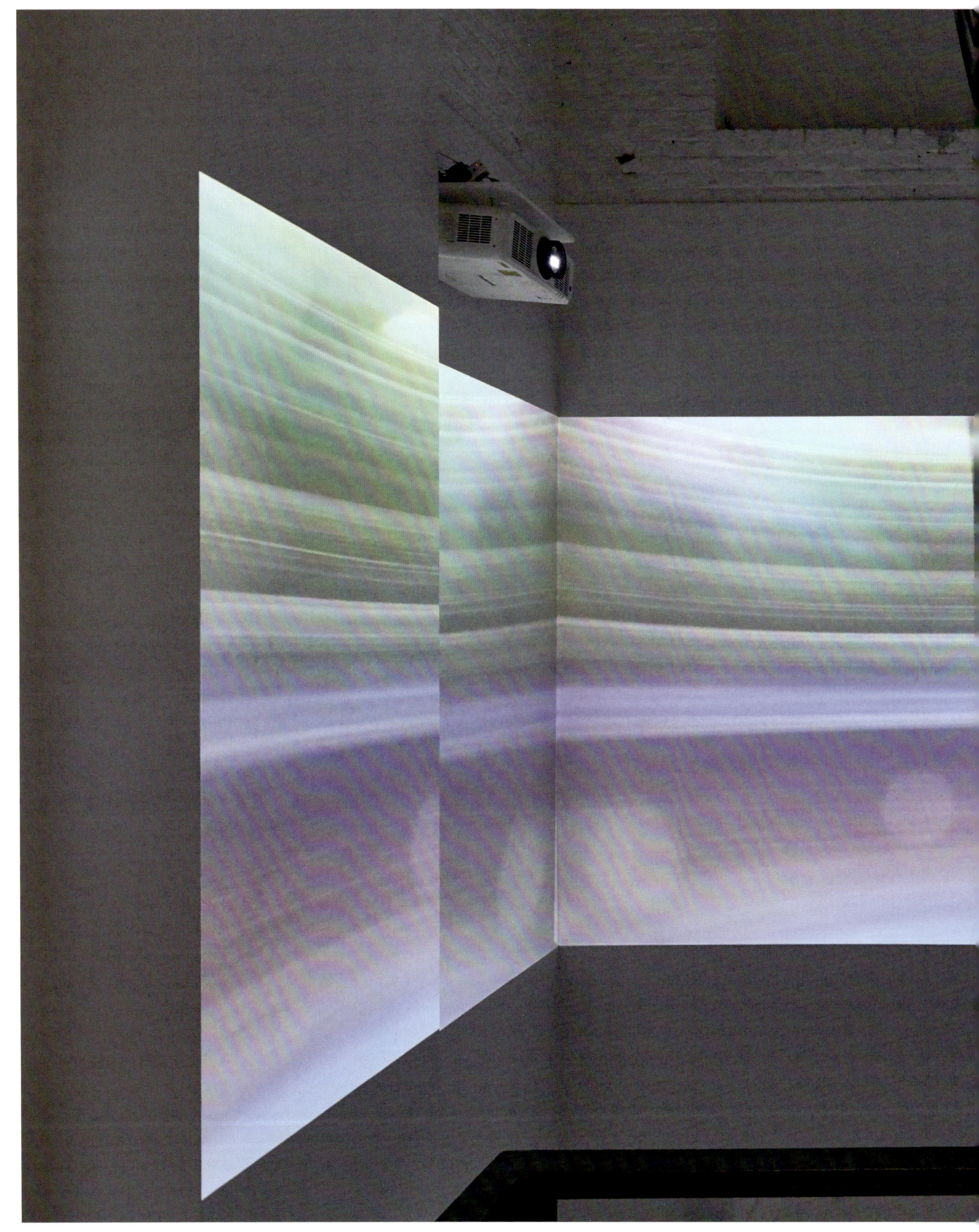

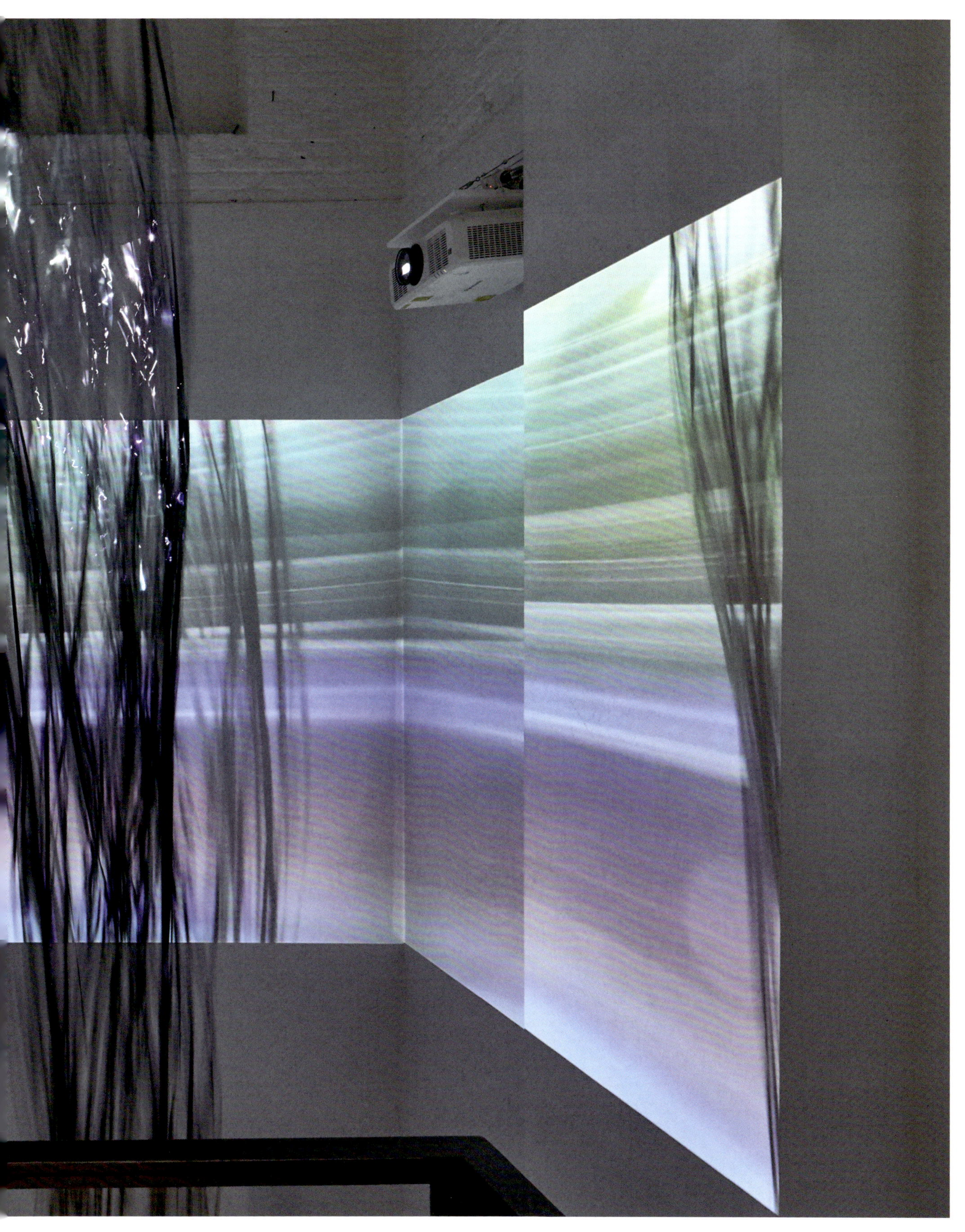

Søren Lyngsø Knudsen

Figure Eight

24-Kanal-Soundinstallation, Transducer,
Sperrholz, Elektronik
*24-channel-sound-installation, transducer,
plywood, electric*

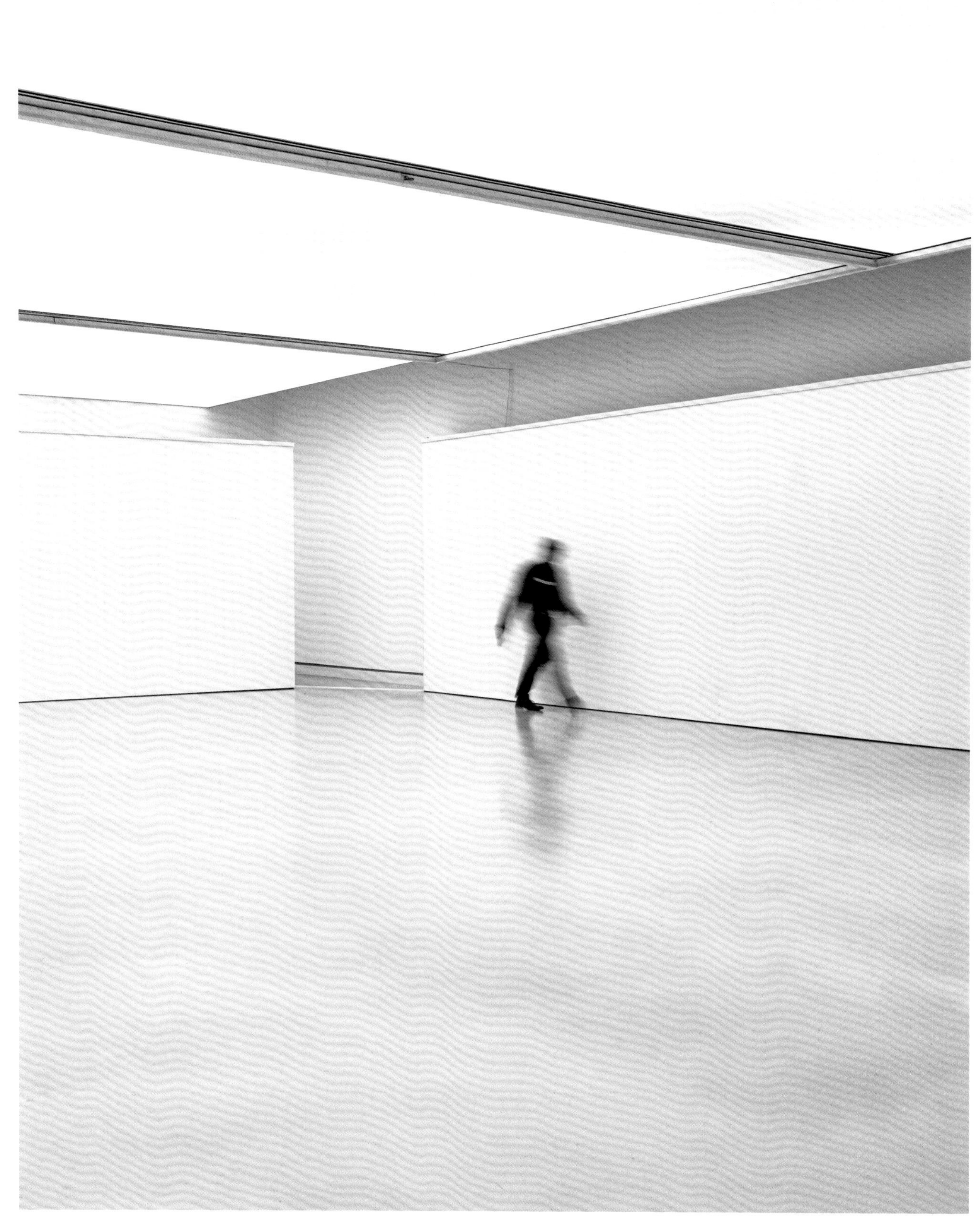

Lina Louisa Krämer: **Für die Ausstellung *Between Us* hast du zwei Projekte verwirklicht: Du hast den Sound für die Choreografie *Effect* komponiert und eine weitere Soundarbeit, die jenseits der Aufführungen in dem Raum läuft und einen eigenständigen Beitrag für die Ausstellung bildet. Wie sah die Zusammenarbeit mit dem Choreografen Taneli Törmä aus? Was sind die Unterschiede zwischen beiden Herangehensweisen, mit denen du dich für das Projekt auseinandergesetzt hast?**

Søren Lyngsø Knudsen: Für die Performance *Effect* habe ich mit der Arbeit an der Komposition angefangen, als die Choreografie noch am Anfang ihres Entstehungsprozesses stand und bevor die Bewegungen der Tänzer*innen aufgezeichnet wurden. Daher ist auch die Musik einer der Startpunkte des gesamten Projekts. Die später entstandene Datensammlung, in Form von z. B. 3-D-Trackings von Motion Bank, dient als eine Basis für meine Soundinstallation. Für die Choreografie habe ich die Musik von zwei selbst entwickelten Computerprogrammen komponieren lassen – eines war für die Komposition zuständig, und eines erzeugte die synthetischen Klänge. Ich habe Algorithmen geschrieben, die auf den musikalischen Ideen basieren, die im Austausch zwischen mir und dem Choreografen Taneli Törmä entstanden sind. Mittels Musik wollten wir ein kontemplatives Gefühl in den Köpfen des Publikums erzeugen. Sie sollte in den Fokus der Aufmerksamkeit hinein- und dann wieder aus dem Bewusstsein herausgleiten. Mithilfe einer Mehrkanal-Klanginstallation war ich in der Lage, mit dem Sound räumliche Transformationen zu erzeugen. Ich konnte etwas erschaffen, das sich bewegt und den Raum gestaltet, das sich auf musikalischer Ebene konstant verändert, aber auch irgendwie am selben Ort verbleibt.

Mein Ansinnen war es, eine Klanginstallation zu kreieren, die so transparent wie möglich ist und doch nicht wie eine Demonstration technischer Möglichkeiten daherkommt, weil 24 Lautsprecher im Raum zum Einsatz kommen. Deshalb hatte ich die Idee mit Lautsprechern, die in die Wände integriert sind, um den Raum von jeglicher visueller Interferenz dieses technischen Equipments, wie z. B. der Lautsprecher, zu befreien, die ansonsten den Raum in der Kunsthalle Mainz einnehmen würden.

Der Sound für meine Installation wurde ebenfalls von den Computerprogrammen erzeugt. Der Unterschied besteht jedoch darin, dass anstelle des generativen Algorithmus die durch Motion Bank aufgezeichneten Daten alles Material hervorbringen. Meine Aufgabe bestand darin, die Daten in Form einer musikalischen Komposition in eine Tonfolge umzuwandeln, die räumliche Informationen der aufgezeichneten Daten auf akustische Weise veranschaulicht und das kontemplative Grundgefühl der dort regelmäßig stattfindenden Performances mit aufnimmt, um ein kohärentes Zusammenspiel zwischen den beiden Werken zu schaffen.

„Wenn man mit Kunst oder Musik arbeitet, arbeitet man meiner Meinung nach immer auch mit einer Art Algorithmus. Das Werk ist dann das Ergebnis dieses Algorithmus."

Søren Lyngsø Knudsen

Lina: **In deiner Soundarbeit *Figure Eight*, die für die Ausstellung entstanden ist, hast du ausschließlich mit den aufgezeichneten Daten von Motion Bank gearbeitet. Kannst du noch einmal erläutern, wie du die digitalen Codes in Tonfolgen umgewandelt hast und wie das wiederum die Bewegungen der Tänzer*innen aufgreift?**

Søren: Dieser Prozess erforderte viel Computerprogrammierung, und die Herausforderung für mich bestand darin, die rohen Trackingdaten in eine ästhetische und musikalische Form zu bringen. Ich erhielt eine große Menge Rohdaten. Meine erste Aufgabe bestand darin, ein Programm zu schreiben, um den riesigen Datenstrom auf eine sinnvolle Weise lesen zu können. Zeitgleich suchte ich auch nach einem Weg, um die Daten zu visualisieren, sodass ich eine Vorstellung von der Beziehung zwischen der Bewegung und meinem generierten Ergebnis in Form von Klang bekommen konnte. Der nächste Schritt bestand darin, die Daten zu analysieren und die relevanten Parametersätze zu extrahieren, die meiner Meinung nach aus musikalischer Sicht interessant waren. Die Komposition basiert auf den berechneten Daten aus der Position jedes*r Tänzer*in auf dem Tanzboden, der Entfernung zwischen ihnen, der Bewegung und den Abständen der jeweiligen Gliedmaßen und Gelenke zueinander sowie der Entfernung der Tänzer*innen zum Mittelpunkt der Tanzfläche. Alle Daten wurden dann zu musikalischen Parametern verschlüsselt, die letztlich den Klang erzeugen. Wenn also Bewegungen in den Daten vorhanden waren, spiegelten die Audiodaten diese wider.

Lina: **Was hat dich am meisten daran gereizt, mit den Trackingdaten von Motion Bank zu arbeiten?**

Søren: Die rohen Daten enthalten keine ästhetischen Eigenschaften im Gegensatz zu aufgenommenen Ton- oder Videomitschnitten. Ich fand es interessant, dieses ansonsten „tote" Material zu nehmen und es klanglich wiederzubeleben. Zudem faszinierte es mich, einen Datensatz zu verwenden, der Bewegungsdaten enthält, und ihn in einen völlig anderen Datensatz, der aus Ton besteht, umzuwandeln. In vielen meiner früheren Arbeiten habe ich auch daran gearbeitet, einen Datensatz auszuwählen und ihn in etwas völlig anderes zu konvertieren oder auf etwas Neues anzuwenden. Dies ist zum Beispiel der Fall, wenn ich aus Audioerzeugnissen Visualisierungen oder abstrakte Digitaldrucke erstelle.

Lina: **Die Wiedererkennung der fünf Tänzer*innen erfolgt durch individuelle Melodien, die ihnen zugewiesen wurden. Diese Melodien wiederum basieren alle auf Algorithmen. Kann man also sagen, dass du den Prozess des „Machens" völlig aus der Hand gegeben hast?**

Søren: Wenn man mit Kunst oder Musik arbeitet, arbeitet man meiner Meinung nach immer auch mit einer Art Algorithmus – auch wenn es sich dabei nicht direkt um ein Computerprogramm handelt. Das Werk ist dann das Ergebnis dieses Algorithmus. Aus diesem Grund sehe ich die Computerprogrammierung als nichts anderes als ein Hilfsmittel an, um einen bestimmten Inhalt zu erzeugen. Die Werkzeuge, die ich für die Installation erstellte, wandelten die Daten auf eine bestimmte ästhetische Weise in Sound um und basierten auf meinen Ideen für die Komposition. Ich würde also sagen, dass der Schöpfungsprozess immer in meinen Händen lag. Der künstlerische Prozess bestand eher darin, die Qualitäten in den Daten zu erkennen und sie auf eine bestimmte Weise zu formen, die in meiner Soundarbeit mündete.

Lina: **Während man durch den Raum deiner Soundarbeit läuft, bewegt man sich als Besucher*in gleichzeitig durch die Choreografie von *Effect*, indem man ein Gefühl dafür entwickelt, was wo zu einem bestimmten Zeitpunkt an einem bestimmten Ort passiert ist. Wie würdest du die Verbindung von den Klängen und dem Ort beschreiben?**

Søren: Abgesehen von dem durch die Daten erzeugten Klangmaterial, das Bewegungen wie Schritte usw. in bestimmten Teilen der Komposition akustisch erkennbar macht, besteht auch ein direkter Zusammenhang zwischen der Position der Tänzer*innen in den Daten und der Klangbewegung innerhalb des Raums. Den fünf Tänzer*innen sind also jeweils eine Reihe von Sounds zugeordnet, die dreidimensional widerspiegeln, wie sie sich im Raum bewegen, und ihre Position anhand der aufgezeichneten Daten auf den 24-Kanal-Lautsprecher-Wänden nachvollziehbar machen. Die Kreisbewegung in der Choreografie reizte und inspirierte mich zu vielen meiner Entscheidungen. Für mein Kunstwerk habe ich die physischen Bewegungsdaten verwendet, um detaillierte Sounds zu erzeugen. Dies beruhte hauptsächlich auf der Herausforderung, aber auch Faszination, die gesammelten Datensätze, die erst mal nur eine lange Liste an Zahlen sind, die wirklich alles sein könnte – beispielsweise eine Steuererklärung –, zu konvertieren. Danach habe ich sie auf direkteste Weise in Musik verwandelt und dabei die Anmutung von Musik beibehalten. Ich wollte die Bewegung außerdem nutzen, um den Sound im Raum zu verorten, um den Eindruck zu vermitteln, dass die Tänzer*innen in den Klangfolgen tatsächlich anwesend sind. Es war ein Experiment, zu schauen, wie viel von der ursprünglichen Information bei der Übertragung der Rohdaten in tatsächliche Musik noch übrig bleiben würde.

Lina: **Unter anderem fragt *Between Us* danach, wie Informationen von einem zum anderen weitergereicht werden können. Was macht für dich den Reiz des Projekts aus?**

Søren: Besonders am Projekt gefällt mir wahrscheinlich die Idee, sehr konkrete Informationen basierend auf der Analyse eines Kunstwerks – in diesem Fall einer Tanzperformance – als Grundlage für neue Kunstwerke zu verwenden. Ich fand die Datenerhebung dabei besonders interessant, weil sie große Ähnlichkeiten dazu aufweist, wie Informationen digital in unserem Alltag gesammelt werden. Jeder Schritt wird im Grunde sowohl online als auch von der Öffentlichkeit überwacht. Die Computeranalyse der Daten wird immer weiter standardisiert, um Profile anzulegen, um zu „lernen", wer wir sind, um unseren nächsten

Schritt bereits im Voraus zu „kennen" und daraus berechnen zu können, was wir vorhaben. Zum Beispiel sind Datensätze, die von öffentlichen Videoüberwachungen erfasst werden können, Bewegungsmuster. Die daraus resultierenden Algorithmen werden dafür benutzt, Personenprofile basierend auf dem persönlichen Laufstil aufzustellen. Die Polizei setzt diese ein, um maskierte Kriminelle auf der Flucht aufzuspüren. Andere Analysen können Informationen über Gesundheit, Stimmung usw. liefern oder, noch direkter, zum körperlichen Erscheinungsbild. Interessant wäre, zu sehen, wie sich diese weit verbreiteten Profilanalysen in einer alternativen Darstellungsform wie der Performance zeigen ließen. Was sagen Analysen wirklich über uns aus, wenn wir uns nicht so verhalten, wie es von uns erwartet wird?

'As I see it, whenever you're working with art and music you're working with some sort of algorithm. The work is then the outcome of that algorithm.'

Søren Lyngsø Knudsen

Lina Louisa Krämer: **You worked on two different levels for this exhibition. You composed the sound for the *Effect* choreography and a sound piece for the performance space that is an independent contribution to the exhibition. What shape did the collaboration with choreographer Taneli Törmä take and what is the difference between the two tasks you had to fulfill?**

Søren Lyngsø Knudsen: For the *Effect* performance I started to work on the composition while the choreography was still in the making and before any tracking had taken place. In this sense, the music was one of the starting points for the whole project. The later data collection in the form of 3-D-tracking by Motion Bank formed the basis of the exhibition and therefore also of my installation. For the performance I composed the music by writing computer programs for the composition itself as well as for the synthesized sounds. For this purpose, I created algorithms based on the musical ideas that evolved between me and the choreographer Taneli Törmä. We wanted a contemplative feeling in the music that would go in and out of focus in the mind of the audience. I wanted to use multichannel sound to be able to work with spatial transformations in the sound, to make something that could be moving and interesting spatially, and which would musically speaking be in constant change, but also in a way would stay in the same place.

I tried to make the sound work as transparent as possible and not seem like a technical demonstration although there would be 24 speakers in the room, and I had the idea of relying on transducer walls to free the space of any visual interference that technical equipment such as speakers would otherwise introduce into a place like Kunsthalle Mainz.

The sound of the installation was also generated by computer programs, but the difference was that instead of a generative algorithm, all of the material came from the tracking data, and thus my task was to convert the data into sound in the form of a musical composition that sonically illustrated the spatial information provided by the tracked data and also reflected the contemplative feeling of the performance taking place in there to offer a coherent expression straddling the two works.

Lina: **In your *Figure Eight* sound piece for the exhibition you work with the data captured from the motion tracking. Can you explain how you transform the digital codes into sounds and how they refer back to the dancers movements?**

Søren: This process required a great deal of computer programming and the challenge was to change the raw tracking data into something aesthetic and musical. I received a set of completely raw data files with the tracking data and my first task was to build a program that enabled me even to read the massive stream of data in a way that would make sense. I also needed a means of visualizing the data in order to gain some sort of an idea about the relationship between the movement and my generated outcome in the form of sound. The next step was to analyze the data and extract the relevant parameter sets that I found would be interesting to work with in a musical perspective. The composition is based on the data calculated from the position of each dancer, the distance between them, the movement of each tracked joint of each dancer and their distance from the center. All the data were then mapped into musical parameters that would then generate the sound—so whenever there was movement in the data, the audio would reflect that.

Lina: **What interested you the most working with the captured date from Motion Bank?**

Søren: The raw data files did not contain any aesthetic characteristics and only a recorded sound or video. I found it interesting to take this otherwise 'dead' material and reanimate it sonically. What I also found interesting was to take a data set that contains movement data and convert it into a completely different one for sound. In many of my earlier works I have also worked by taking one set of data and converting or applying it to another set. This is, for example, the case in the way I have created audio generative visuals and abstract digital prints from audio.

Lina: **The recognition of the five dancers works by individual melodies that have been assigned to each of them. The melodies themselves are based on an algorithm, meaning you rendered the process of creation completely independent of yourself?**

Søren: As I see it, whenever you're working with art and music you're working with some sort of algorithm, even though it might not be in the sense of a computer program. The work is then the outcome of that algorithm. For this reason I don't see the computer programming as anything other than a tool to achieve a certain content. The tools I created for the installation transformed the data into sound in a certain aesthetic way based on my ideas for the composition. So I would say that the process of creation was always in my hands—and the process was more about seeing the qualities in the data and shaping them in a certain way that then became the sound work.

Lina: **While walking around the space your sound piece escorts the visitors through the *Effect* choreography, while giving them a sense of what is performed here at a certain time at a certain position. How would you describe the linkage of the sounds and the space?**

Søren: Apart from the sound material generated by the data that makes movements such as footsteps etc. sonically recognizable in certain parts of the composition, there is also a direct connection between the position of the dancers in the data and the way sound travels in the installation. So the five dancers each have a set of sounds that moves in the space and reflects their position in 3-D from the recorded data panned on the 24 channel speaker walls. The circular motion in the choreography was interesting to work with and inspired many of the choices I made along the way. I used the physical movement data for my piece in order to generate detailed music and sound. This was mostly based on the challenge and fascination of converting the collected dataset—which resembled a long list of numbers that could really have been anything, a tax return for example—and turning it into music in the most direct way while upholding the impression of music. I also wanted to use the movement to pan the sound in the room to create the impression the dancers were actually present in sonic form. It was an experiment to see how much you would recognize of the original information in the translation between raw data to actual music.

Lina: **Among other things, *Between Us* asks how information can pass from one medium into the other. What fascinated you the most about the project?**

Søren: What I liked most about the project was probably the idea of taking very concrete information based on the analysis of a piece of art—in this case a dance performance—and using it as the basis for new artworks. I found the data collection especially interesting because I think it has some resemblance to the way information on us is collected digitally, in our everyday lives. Every move is subject to surveillance both online and in public. Computer analysis of the data is being standardized in order to profile us and 'learn' who we are with a view to 'knowing' our next move and calculating what we're up to. For example, one of the data types that can be collected from public video surveillance is movement and the algorithms used to profile people based on their personal gait has actually been used by the police as a way of identifying criminals on the run who are in disguise. Other analyses can generate information related to health, mood etc. plus all the more direct details such as physical appearance. What would be interesting would be to see how these profiling analyses, which are widely used, perform in the alternative setting of the performance. What do they really say about us if we don't behave as expected?

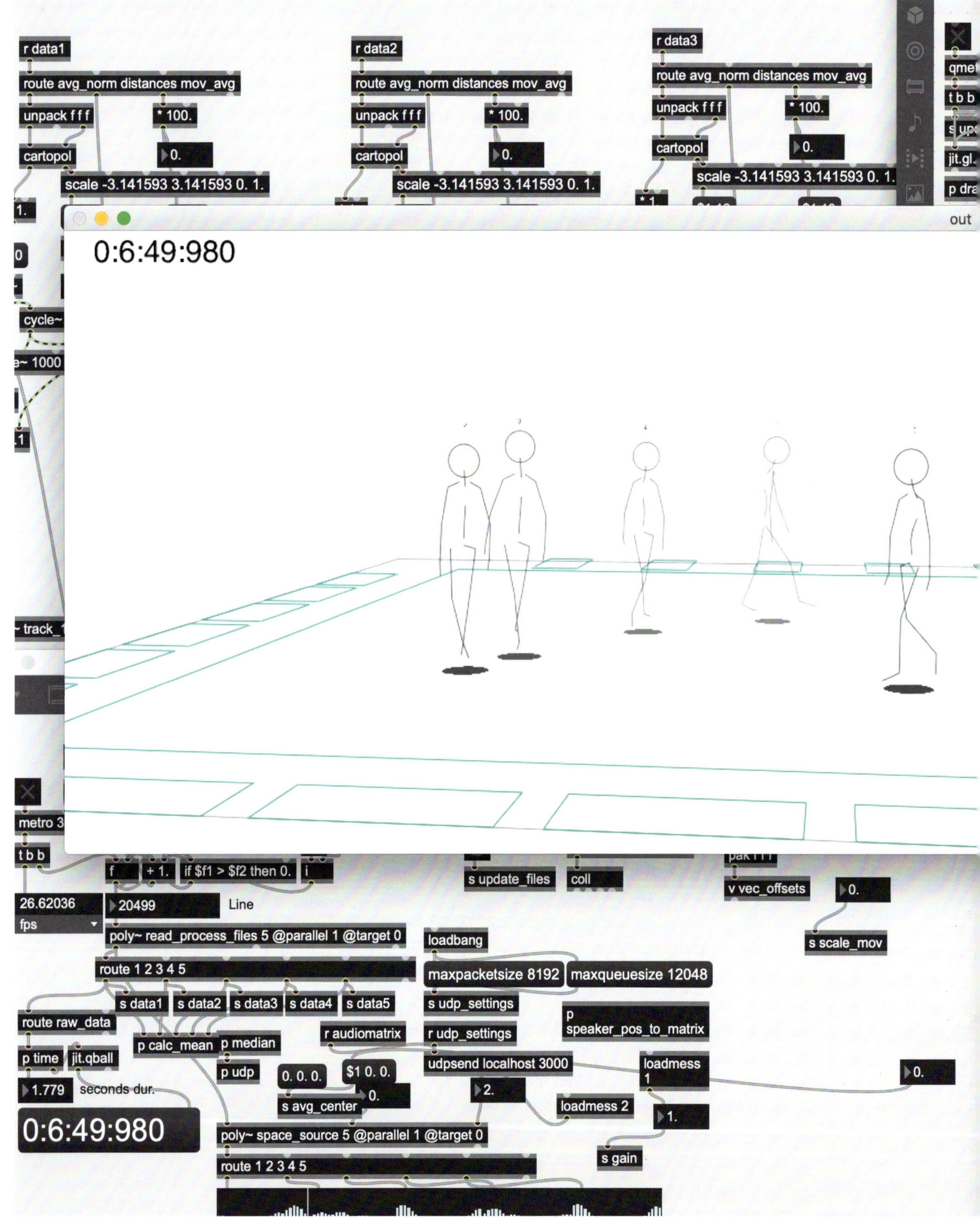
r data1
route avg_norm distances mov_avg
unpack f f f
* 100.
cartopol
0.
scale -3.141593 3.141593 0. 1.
r data2
route avg_norm distances mov_avg
unpack f f f
* 100.
cartopol
0.
scale -3.141593 3.141593 0. 1.
r data3
route avg_norm distances mov_avg
unpack f f f
* 100.
cartopol
0.
scale -3.141593 3.141593 0. 1.
out
0:6:49:980
metro
t b b
f
+ 1.
if $f1 > $f2 then 0.
i
s update_files
coll
v vec_offsets
0.
26.62036
fps
20499
Line
poly~ read_process_files 5 @parallel 1 @target 0
loadbang
s scale_mov
route 1 2 3 4 5
maxpacketsize 8192
maxqueuesize 12048
s data1
s data2
s data3
s data4
s data5
s udp_settings
route raw_data
p speaker_pos_to_matrix
r audiomatrix
r udp_settings
p time
jit.qball
p calc_mean
p median
udpsend localhost 3000
loadmess 1
p udp
0. 0. 0.
$1 0. 0.
0.
1.779
seconds dur.
s avg_center
0.
2.
loadmess 2
1.
0:6:49:980
poly~ space_source 5 @parallel 1 @target 0
s gain
route 1 2 3 4 5

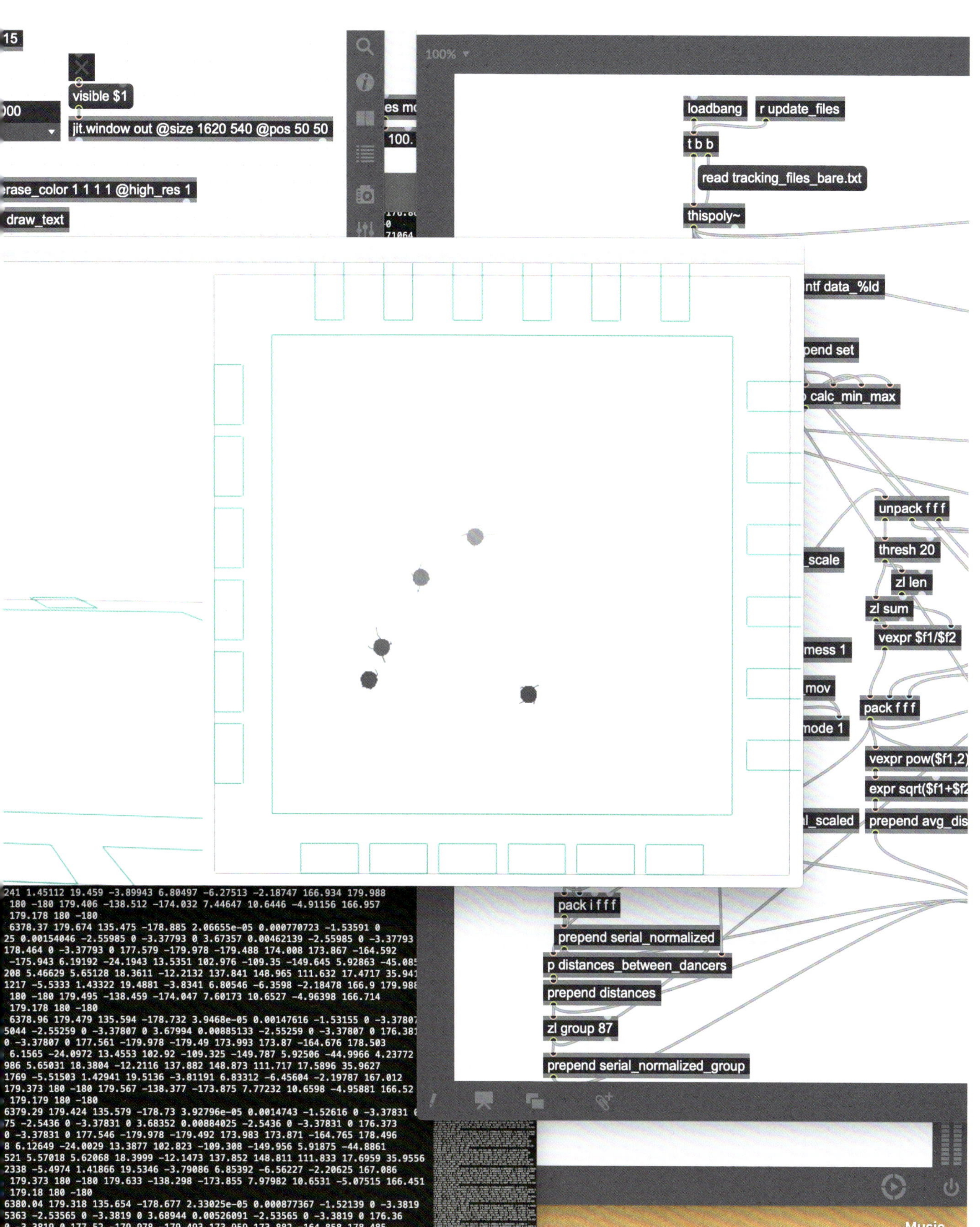
visible $1
jit.window out @size 1620 540 @pos 50 50
erase_color 1 1 1 1 @high_res 1
draw_text
100%
loadbang
r update_files
t b b
read tracking_files_bare.txt
thispoly~
ntf data_%ld
pend set
calc_min_max
unpack f f f
thresh 20
scale
zl len
zl sum
vexpr $f1/$f2
mess 1
mov
pack f f f
mode 1
vexpr pow($f1,2)
expr sqrt($f1+$f2
l_scaled
prepend avg_dis
pack i f f f
prepend serial_normalized
p distances_between_dancers
prepend distances
zl group 87
prepend serial_normalized_group
Music

Isabel Lewis

Social Dances as Cultural Storage Systems

Video-Collage, aufgenommener Text
der gleichnamigen Performance von Isabel Lewis,
ortsspezifisches Ausstellungsmobiliar,
diverse Materialien
Video-collage, recorded text of the eponymous
lecture-performance by Isabel Lewis, site-specific
exhibition furniture, various materials

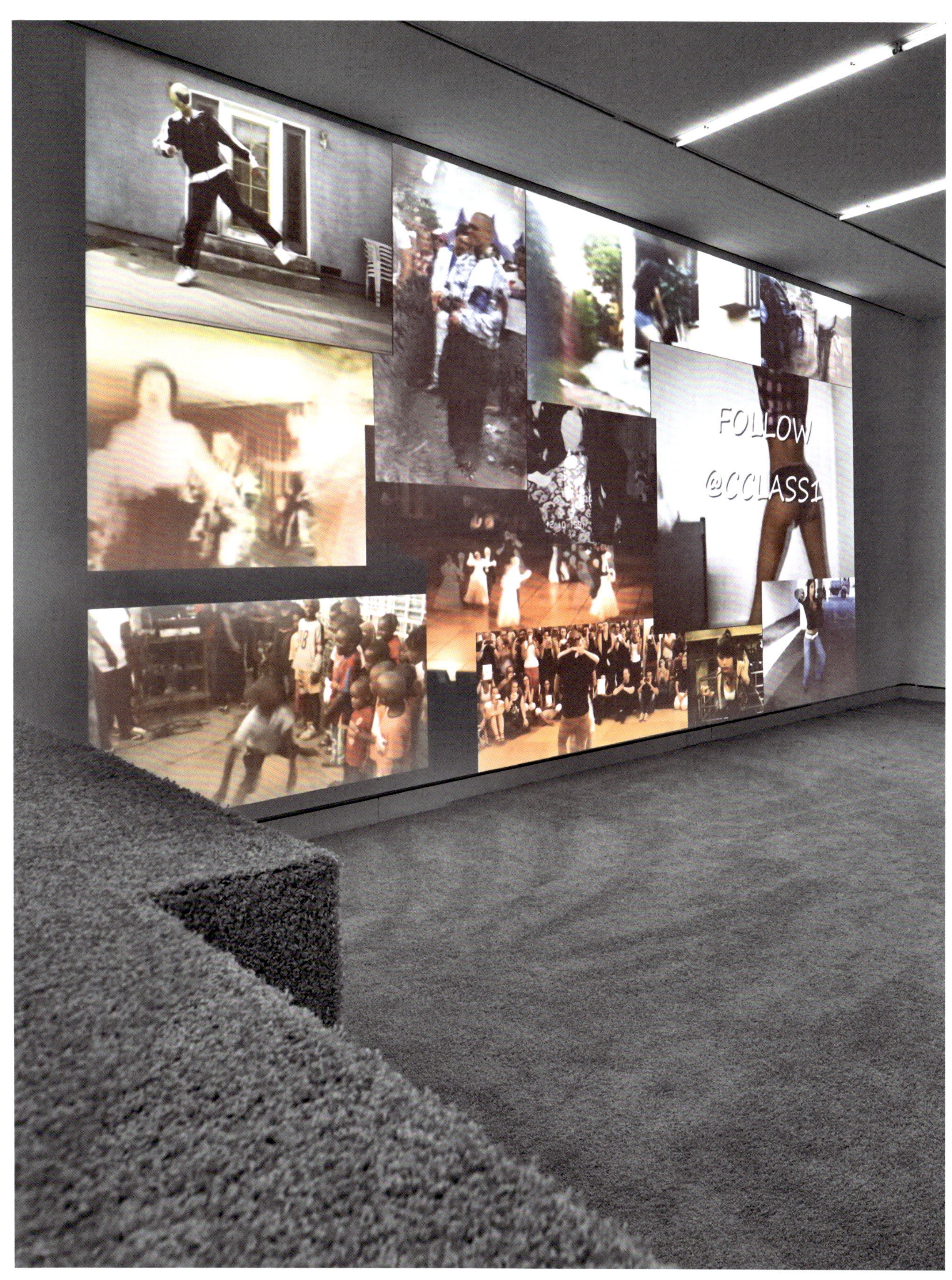
FOLLOW
@CCLASS1

Stefanie Böttcher: ***Between Us* basiert auf der neu entwickelten Choreografie *Effect*. Zusammen mit dem durch Motion Bank gewonnenen Material gaben wir sie an sechs bildende Künstler*innen weiter. Welche Aspekte des Ausgangsmaterials haben dich zu deinem Beitrag zu *Between Us* inspiriert?**

Isabel Lewis: Als ich mir die Videoaufzeichnung von *Effect* angeschaut habe, zogen die Verbindungen zwischen den Technikern, die das Motion-Capture-Verfahren angewendet haben, und den Tänzer*innen meine Aufmerksamkeit auf sich – die Beziehung zwischen einer technologisch vermittelten Form der Rezeption von Tanz und den eigentlichen tanzenden Körpern auf der anderen Seite. Es scheint mir eine besondere Suche nach der schwer fassbaren „Essenz" des Tanzes zu sein, die durch die Verortung der Bewegungen von Körpern in Raum und Zeit gelingen soll. Die Körper sind im aufgezeichneten Material zu Strichmännchen abstrahiert: Geschlecht, Identität und Herkunft werden dabei augenscheinlich abgestreift. Ich frage mich aber, inwieweit man einen Tanz wirklich von seinen kulturellen Wurzeln, den Identitäten seiner Tänzer*innen und der Rezeption durch ein bestimmtes Publikum zu einer bestimmten Zeit lösen kann. Ist der zeitgenössische Tanz, den Taneli kreiert, nicht ebenso eine Form des Volkstanzes – ein kulturspezifischer, regionaler Ausdruck, wie jeder Tanz aus irgendeinem Teil der Welt? Wenn ich seine Choreografie sehe, bekomme ich Hinweise auf seine Herkunft, auf seine Kultur und deren Besonderheiten, genauso wie ich bei allen gesellschaftlichen Tänzen, die in meiner Video-Collage auftauchen, Hinweise dazu finden kann. Deswegen faszinieren mich Tänze – weil sie kulturelle Wertesysteme speichern.

Stefanie: **Macht es für dich einen Unterschied, wenn anstelle von Taneli andere professionelle Tänzer*innen unterschiedlicher kultureller Herkunft den Tanz aufführen?**

Isabel: Das ist interessant. Es ist meines Erachtens immer wichtig, wer den Tanz entwickelt, und ich denke, der Schlüssel liegt in den Besonderheiten jedes einzelnen Individuums, das den Tanz tanzt. Es gibt Möglichkeiten, wie Choreografien diese speziellen Merkmale deutlicher hervorheben können, und es gibt andere choreografische Ansätze, bei denen die Besonderheiten der Identität des Individuums nicht betont werden, die ebendiese gerade nicht in den Vordergrund stellen. Im Allgemeinen

„Die Vorstellung von Tanz als Wissenslieferant hallt durch die Räume dieser Ausstellung. Sie scheint mir eine Einladung zu sein, den Tanz tatsächlich als ein wichtiges kulturelles Phänomen zu begreifen, als etwas, das wir erlernen können, um zu lernen und auch um wichtige Dinge mitzuteilen."

Isabel Lewis

nimmt die Geschichte des zeitgenössischen, westlichen Tanzes eine neutrale Position in Bezug auf die Identität ein. Dass überhaupt ein Glaube an Neutralität hinsichtlich Technologie oder den Menschen oder sonst irgendetwas existiert, ist ein präzises Beispiel für die kulturelle Besonderheit des modernen Westens.

Stefanie: **Taneli erwähnte, dass er sich für Wanderschuhe und das Motiv des Gehens entschieden habe, weil es ihm sehr vertraut ist, der Natur nah zu sein. Und anstelle von Tanzen würden Finnen andere Formen wählen, ihre Körper in Bewegung zu setzen.**

Isabel: Die Wahl der Kostüme ist immer ein interessanter Aspekt der Arbeit, und Sport- wie auch Outdoorbekleidung sind in der Mode definitiv gerade sehr populär. Es ist interessant zu hören, dass Taneli tatsächlich eine Beziehung zu Wanderschuhen und zum Gehen als Freizeitbeschäftigung in seinem Heimatland hat. Im zeitgenössischen Tanz hat das Gehen eine besondere Geschichte – sie führt zurück in die Judson-Church-Ära und die Idee einer „Fußgängerbewegung", die Ausdruck einer egalitären Weltanschauung war. Zu dieser Zeit entstand die Idee, in den Tanz Bewegungen einfließen zu lassen, die man für demokratisch hielt, weil man dachte, dass jede*r sie ausführen könne. Natürlich ist die Idee eines „Jedermanns", die durch eine bestimmte Haltung gegenüber Zugang und Privilegien geprägt wird, niemals so umfassend, wie man sie sich vorstellt. Für mich persönlich wird aus dem Gehen, das den primären

Bestandteil der Choreografie bildet, klar, dass sich Taneli auf eine bestimmte Ausrichtung des US-amerikanischen und europäischen zeitgenössischen Tanzes bezieht.

Stefanie: **Du selbst hast lange Zeit als Tänzerin gearbeitet, bist immer noch als Choreografin tätig – auch mit deinen Projekten in der bildenden Kunst. Was verstehst du unter dem Begriff „Choreograf*in"? Was unter „Choreografie"?**

Isabel: Ein*e Choreograf*in arbeitet mit einer Komposition in Raum und Zeit. Ich arbeite mit einem erweiterten Choreografie-Begriff, der über die Vorstellung sequenzierter Bewegungen des menschlichen Körpers hinausgeht. Während der Tanz innerhalb von und zwischen Körpern ein zentraler Teil meiner Praxis bleibt, sehe ich die Zusammenstellung und Anordnung der Beziehungen zwischen Materialien, Menschen, Dingen, Gerüchen, Klängen, Geschmäckern sowie die Atmosphäre ebenso als Bestandteile der Choreografie an. Wenn ich zum Beispiel Möbel für einen Raum entwerfe oder zusammenstelle, choreografiere ich damit die Bewegung der Besucher*innen im Raum. Ich eröffne die Möglichkeit für bestimmte Arten der Anordnung von Körpern im Raum, die für die Rezeption jeder Arbeit spezifisch sind.

Stefanie: **So wie du für *Between Us* einen Raum gestaltet hast, in dem deine Sammlung aus „social dances" in einem gleichermaßen entspannenden wie aktivierenden Umfeld gezeigt wird. Er besteht aus Möbelelementen, flauschigem Teppich, deiner Video Lecture…**

Isabel: Hier in der Kunsthalle Mainz wollte ich einen einladenden Ort schaffen. Ich möchte den*die Besucher*in zum Verweilen einladen, Zeit in der Arbeit zu verbringen, weil das Voiceover – ein von mir gelesener Text einer meiner Lecture Performances – eine gewisse Länge hat und nicht wirklich zu der Idee einer klassischen geloopten Videoinstallation passt, in die die Besucher*innen hineingehen, sie ein paar Sekunden lang anschauen und sie dann wieder verlassen. Um sich auf die Arbeit einzulassen, muss man wirklich zuhören. Der Text beinhaltet theoretische und akademische Inhalte, die sich wie Erzählungen locker aneinanderreihen, und ist etwa 15 Minuten lang.

Wenn ich über „Raum" nachdenke, denke ich ihn definitiv als einladenden Ort. In diesem Raum habe ich eine Installation geschaffen, die aktivierend wirken soll: Man kann sitzen, aktiv zuhören oder sich bewegen, wenn man möchte. Wenn ich mir diese verschiedenen Tänze in der Videocollage ansehe, bin ich sehr versucht, mich selbst dazu zu bewegen. Wenn ich sehe, wie andere tanzen, lädt das den Körper ein, zu antworten. Es liegt etwas so Festliches in diesen Tänzen, was es meiner Meinung nach so reizvoll macht, sie nachzuahmen. Es gibt genügend Platz in der Installation, der diese Art der Reaktion zulässt, aber sie suggeriert auch ein gewisses Gefühl der Umfassung, um etwas Privatsphäre zu bieten.

Stefanie: **Was meint der Begriff „social dance" genau?**

Isabel: Ich glaube, dass eigentlich jede Kultur „social dances" hat. Wenn ich von „social dances" spreche, meine ich Tänze, die aus einer Kultur hervorgehen, aber nicht auf einen bestimmten Erfinder zurückzuführen sind. Es ist einfach etwas sehr Grundlegendes und sehr Menschliches, das in jeder Kultur auf unterschiedliche Art passiert. Menschen sind gesellig, und Bewegung ist eine Form der Kommunikation, die über die verbale Sprache hinausgeht. Oft haben diese Tänze feierliche Anlässe, aber natürlich werden sie in verschiedenen Kulturen auch während Ritualen und Trauerfeiern aufgeführt. Dieser Tanz ist nicht für ein Publikum geschaffen, sondern gehört zu einer Gemeinschaft und dient dazu, diese Gemeinschaft zu stärken und soziale Bindungen auszuprägen.

Stefanie: **Motion Bank hat den Entstehungsprozess von *Effect* begleitet, dokumentiert, die Aufführung der fertigen Choreografie mehrmals aufgezeichnet. Kann Tanz für dich tatsächlich vollständig „eingefangen" werden, oder wie machst du Tanz erlebbar?**

Isabel: Ich denke, dass der Datenstrom unendlich ist und dass es deshalb auch möglich ist, unendlich viele Daten zum Tanz zu generieren, aber dass es etwas anderes ist, ihn wirklich „einzufangen". Für mich ist das echte Ereignis sehr komplex. Es besteht nicht nur aus Handlungen bestimmter Körper, die in einer kausalen Beziehung zueinander stehen und aufeinander reagieren, sondern aus überlappenden Geflechten von Wechselbeziehungen, die sich zwischen Kulturen, Geschichten, Zeitmodalitäten, Präsenzbereichen, Handlungsausmaß und Energien entwickeln, die untrennbar ineinander verwoben sind. Ich denke, dass es möglich ist, den Tanz auf verschiedene Weise weiterzugeben: durch den Körper, durch schriftliche Partituren, durch das Ansehen von Videos und durch die Auswertung von erfassten Bewegungsdaten, durch schriftliche Notationssysteme und durch das Erzählen von Geschichten aus der Erinnerung heraus, deren Grad an Treue zum Ursprungsmaterial variiert. Dem Drang, ein echtes Erlebnis wahrheitsgetreu „einfangen" zu wollen, stehe ich vermutlich misstrauisch gegenüber. Das scheint mir ein besorgniserregendes Symptom einer Konsumgesellschaft zu sein, die mit der dunklen Geschichte kolonialer Unterdrückung verbunden ist …

Stefanie: **In unserem Projekt geht es um Einflüsse, Konstellationen, Beziehungen. Der Tanz bildet dabei ein spannendes Ausgangsgenre, um der Bewegung in und zwischen Körpern nachzugehen und im Weiteren zu verfolgen, wie diese außerhalb des Körpers aufgenommen werden und Veränderungen durchlaufen. Was hat dich an *Between Us* am meisten gereizt?**

Isabel: „Social dances" als Speichersysteme für Kultur zu betrachten ist ein reizvoller Ansatz, weil er es erlaubt, ebendiese nicht nur als Frivolität, als Spielerei zu begreifen, sondern als Träger wichtiger Hinweise auf bestimmte Wertesysteme einer bestimmten Zeit an einem bestimmten Ort. Ich bin sehr daran interessiert, wie wir Wissen auf anderen Wegen, über das Verbale, das Rationale hinaus, erwerben können. Deshalb verstehe ich Tanz als wichtigen Beitrag zu Wissenserwerb und Wissenserschaffung – insbesondere für diesen Teil der Welt, in dem wir viel Wert auf das Rationale, das Verbale und das Logische legen.

Die Vorstellung von Tanz als Wissenslieferant hallt durch die Räume dieser Ausstellung. Sie scheint mir eine Einladung zu sein, den Tanz tatsächlich als ein wichtiges kulturelles Phänomen zu begreifen, als etwas, das wir erlernen können, um zu lernen und auch um wichtige Dinge mitzuteilen. Tanz im Theater wurde häufig dafür eingesetzt, Erfahrungen zu repräsentieren oder um Kultur zu repräsentieren. Diese Ausstellung gibt Raum, über Tanz jenseits derartiger Instrumentalisierungen nachzudenken. Sie nimmt Tanz ernst – als etwas, das tatsächlich Bedeutung und Verständnis hervorbringen kann.

'Dance as knowledge resonates throughout this exhibition. It seems to me like an invitation to actually consider dance as an important cultural phenomenon and something that we can look at to learn and also with which to say important things.'

Isabel Lewis

Stefanie Böttcher: ***Between Us* is based on the newly developed choreography *Effect*. Together with the relevant motion capture data it has been made available to six visual artists. Which aspects of the source material inspired you in your contribution to *Between Us*?**

Isabel Lewis: What caught my attention when watching the video of *Effect* was the relation between the motion capture technicians and the dancers, the relation between a technologically mediated form of reception of a dance and the dancing bodies themselves. It struck me as a peculiar quest to capture the elusive 'essence' of a dance by mapping the bodies' trajectories in space and in time. When you see the motion capture material the bodies are rendered as abstract stick figures, gender, identity, and culture purportedly stripped away. I wonder to what degree you can really strip a dance of its cultural roots, the identities of its dancers, and its reception by a specific audience at a particular time. Is the contemporary dance that Taneli creates not also a form of folk dance—a culturally specific, regional expression just like any dance from any part of the world? When I see his dance I am given clues to his cultural specificity just as I observe clues in all of the social dances that I feature in my video collage. I think dances are fascinating in the way that they store cultural value systems.

Stefanie: **Does it make a difference for you that instead of Taneli performing his dance it is professional dancers with other cultural backgrounds doing so?**

Isabel: That's interesting. I do think that it always matters who does the dancing and I think the specificity around each particular individual who dances the dance is key. There are certain ways in which certain choreographies make those features more apparent and there are other choreographic approaches that don't highlight, don't feature or don't address the specificity of the individuals' identity. In general in the history of contemporary dance the West takes a kind of a position of neutrality in relation to identity. The fact that there is a belief in the notion of neutrality in relation to technology or humans or anything really is precisely a particular example of the cultural specificity of the modern West.

Stefanie: **Taneli mentioned that he chose hiking boots and the theme of walking because it was something very familiar to him being close to nature. And that instead of dancing, Finns would choose other forms of movement to engage the body actively.**

Isabel: Costume choice is always an interesting feature of any work and definitely this kind of aesthetics of sport or outdoor wear is really popular right now in fashion. It's interesting to hear that he actually has a specific relationship to hiking boots and the act of walking in nature as a leisure-time pursuit in his home country. Walking in performance in contemporary dance has a very specific history—dating back to the Judson Church era and the idea of 'pedestrian' movement which was an expression of an egalitarian ideology. There was this idea about making dances with movements that were thought to be democratic because it was thought that anyone could perform these movements. Of course the idea of an 'anyone' formed from a specific position of access and privilege is never as inclusive as you might think it is. For me by using walking as the primary vocabulary in the work it is clear that Taneli associates himself with a particular lineage in American and European contemporary dance.

Stefanie: **You have worked as a professional dancer for a long time and you are still working as a choreographer—that includes with your projects in the fine arts world. What distinguishes a choreographer? What is your concept of choreography?**

Isabel: A choreographer works with composition in space and time. I work with an expanded sense of the word 'choreography' beyond just the notion of sequenced movements of the human body. While dance within and between bodies remains a central part of my practice I also see the composition and arrangement of the relations between materials, people, things, smells, sounds, tastes, atmosphere as choreography as well. When I create or arrange furniture in a space, for example, I am choreographing the movement of the visitors in space, I am opening up the potential for particular kinds of body arrangements that are specific to the reception of each work.

Stefanie: **Like for *Between Us*, where you decided to create a space that shows a part of your social dance collection in a both relaxing and energizing environment. The room consists of furniture elements of fluffy carpet, a video lecture of yours…**

Isabel: Here at Kunsthalle Mainz I wanted to think about a way to create a space that was inviting. I would like to invite the visitor to linger and spend time with the work because the voice-over which is a text from a lecture performance of mine is of a duration that doesn't really fit the idea of a video-looped installation where typically a visitor can kind of walk in and observe things for a few seconds and leave. To enter the work you have to really listen. The text has theoretical and academic aspects but is delivered in a casual way, more like storytelling, and it's around 15 minutes long.

I definitely think about space as a place of hosting. In this space I create the installation as a way of inviting activation in different kinds of ways, be it sitting and actually listening actively or moving if you wish so. When I look at these different dances in the video collage I'm very tempted to move myself. For me, seeing others dance invites the body to respond and there's something so celebratory about these dances that I think this makes it appealing to try to approach them. There is enough space in the installation to allow for that kind of response and it also provides a certain sense of enclosure to give some privacy.

Stefanie: **What does the expression 'social dance' actually mean?**

Isabel: I actually think every culture has social dances. When I say 'social dance', I mean a dance that emerges out of the culture, but isn't actually authored by one particular individual. Instead, it's just something very basic and very human that actually every culture does in different ways. Humans are sociable and movement is a form of communication that goes beyond verbal language. You often find these dances where people gather to celebrate, but of course in different cultures they are also used for ritual and for mourning. Social dance is not created to be performed for an audience, but rather belongs to a community and it is used in a function that's related to strengthening that community and form social bonds.

Stefanie: **Motion Bank accompanied the entire creation process of *Effect*, documented it, and recorded the finished choreography several times. Do you think dance can really be completely 'captured' or how do you enable others to experience dance?**

Isabel: I think, that data is infinite and it is possible to generate infinite amounts of data in regard to a dance; however that is not the same as really being able to 'capture' it. For me, the live event is very complex, not just the particular actions of particular bodies in a direct causal relationship, but entire overlapping webs of interrelations between cultures, histories, modalities of time, ranges of presence, degrees of agency, and energies that can never be untangled from one another. I think it is possible to pass dance on in a variety of means, through the body, through written scores, by watching videos and assessing motion capture data, through written notation systems, and by telling stories from memory with varying degrees of fidelity to the original iteration. I guess I'm suspicious of the urge to faithfully 'capture' a live experience anyway; that it seems to me like the anxious symptom of a consumer society tied to a dark history of colonial oppression …

Stefanie: **Our project is based on questions of influences, constellations, relationships. The dance forms an exciting starting point to follow the movement in and between bodies and to further follow how they are absorbed outside the body and undergo changes. What was the most interesting part of this project for you?**

Isabel: Thinking about social dance as a storage system for culture is a compelling idea in the sense that it allows us to consciously reflect on social dance not as a mere frivolity, as just fun. It also offers important clues to or elements of a particular value system from a particular time and place. I'm very interested in the ways in which we can acquire knowledge in ways beyond the verbal and beyond the rational, and I look at dance as an important mode of knowledge acquisition and knowledge creation—especially for this part of the world, where we have a very heavy emphasis on the rational, the verbal, and the logical.

Dance as knowledge resonates throughout this exhibition. It seems to me like an invitation to actually consider dance as an important cultural phenomenon and something that we can look at to learn and also with which to say important things. Dance in theater has often been used to represent experiences, or represent culture. In this exhibition there is space to reflect upon dance beyond those functions. There's a certain sense of taking dance seriously as something that can actually produce meaning and understanding.

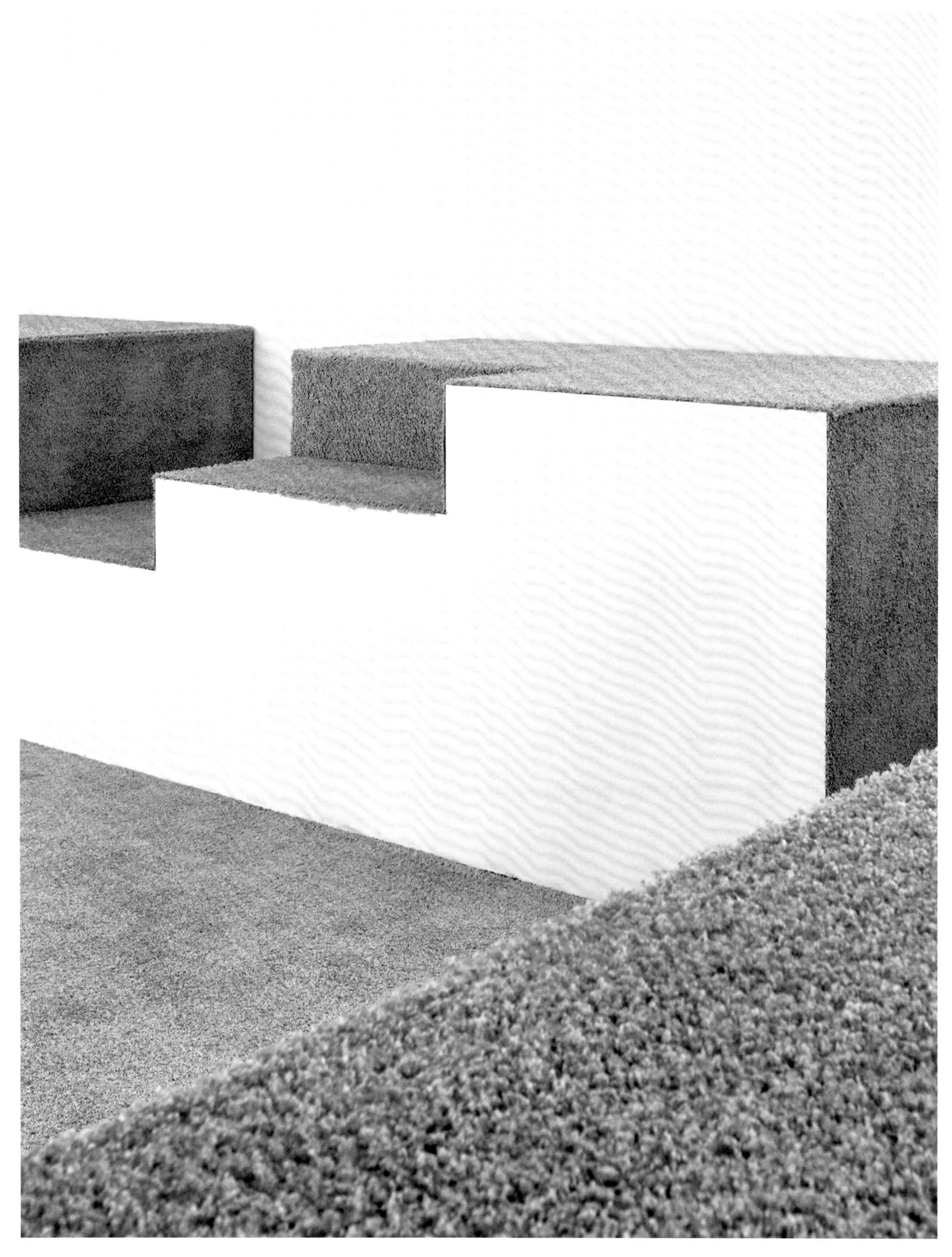

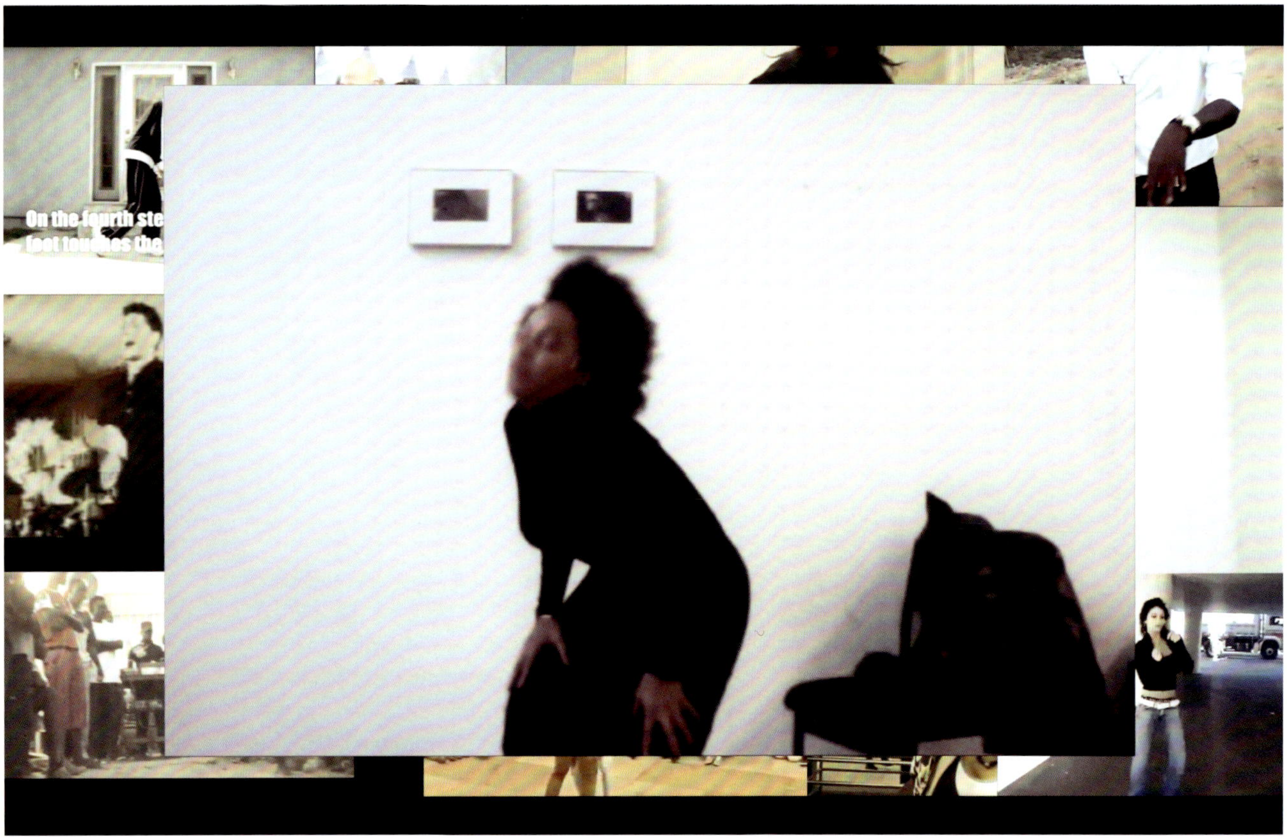

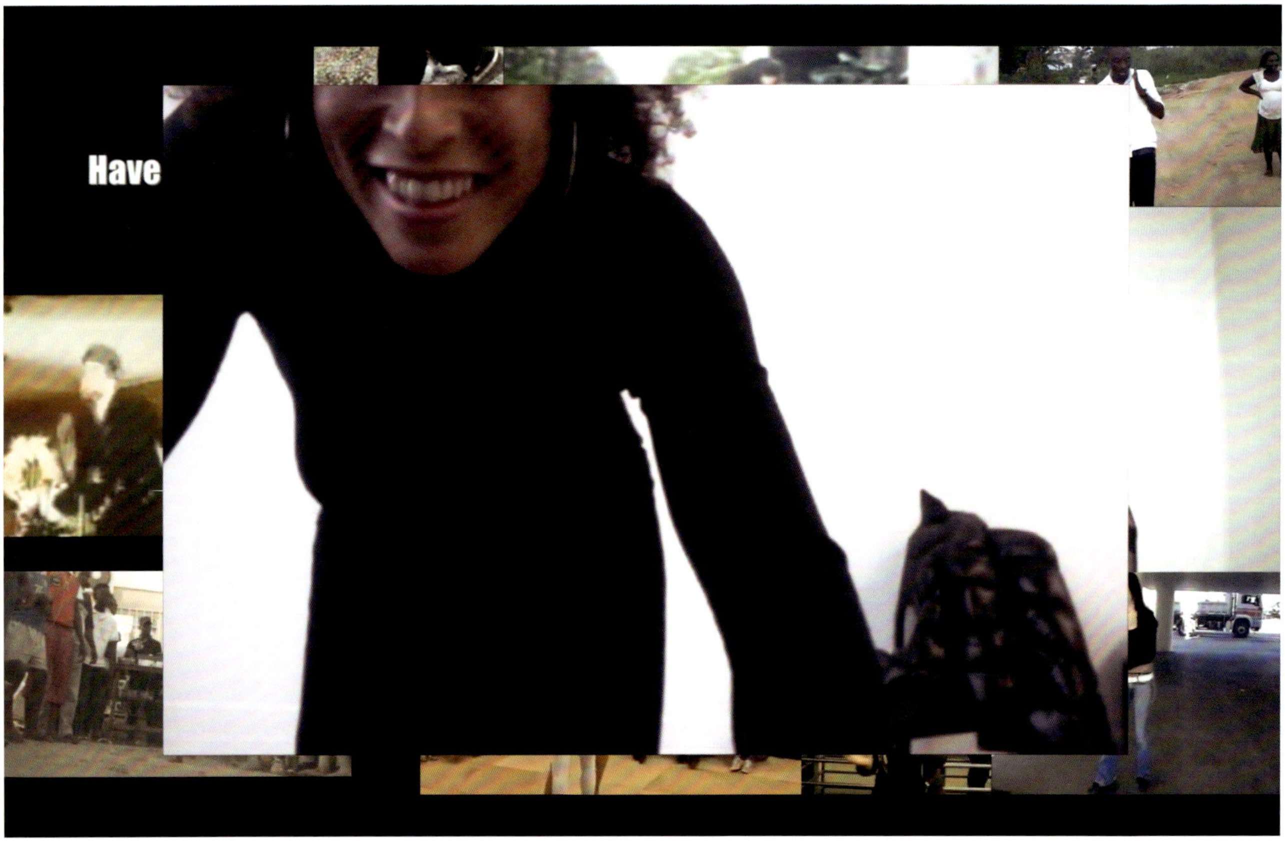

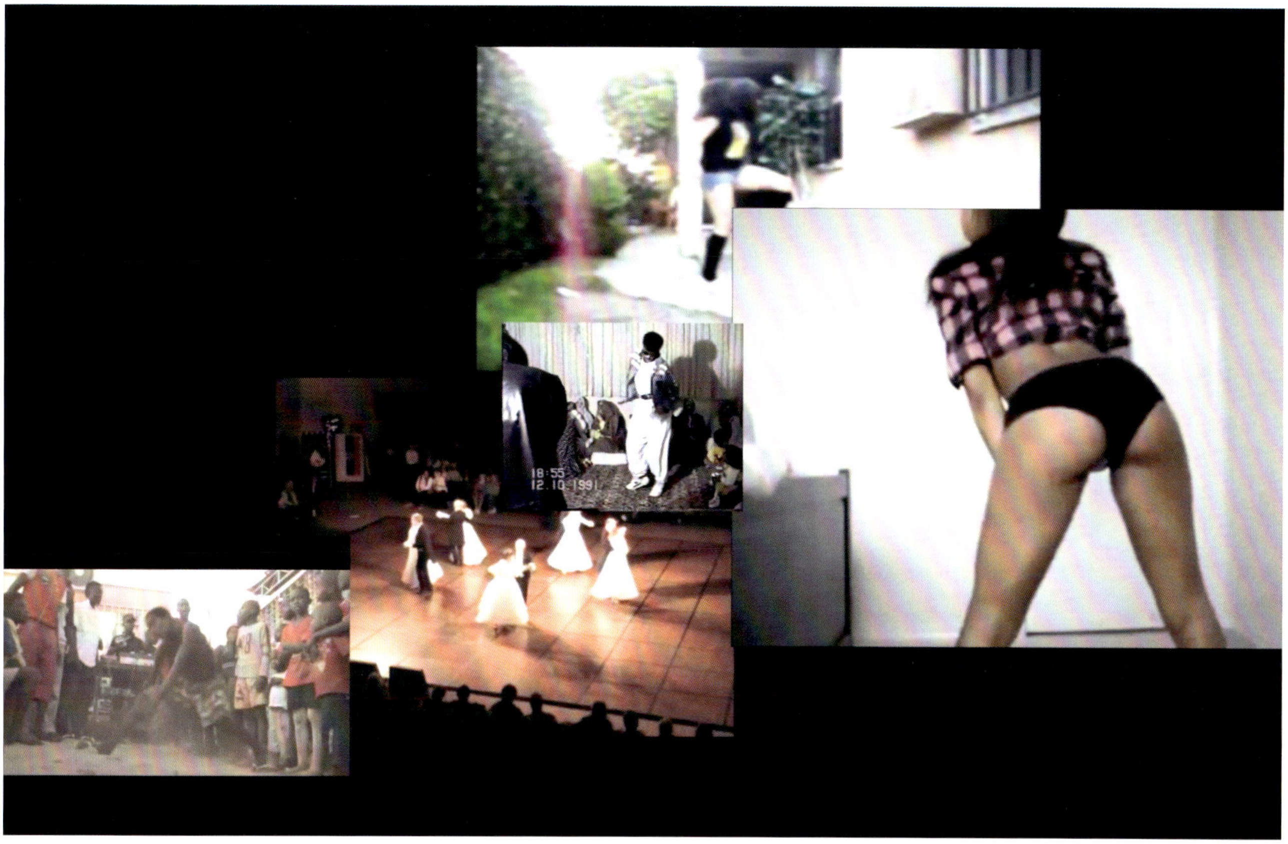

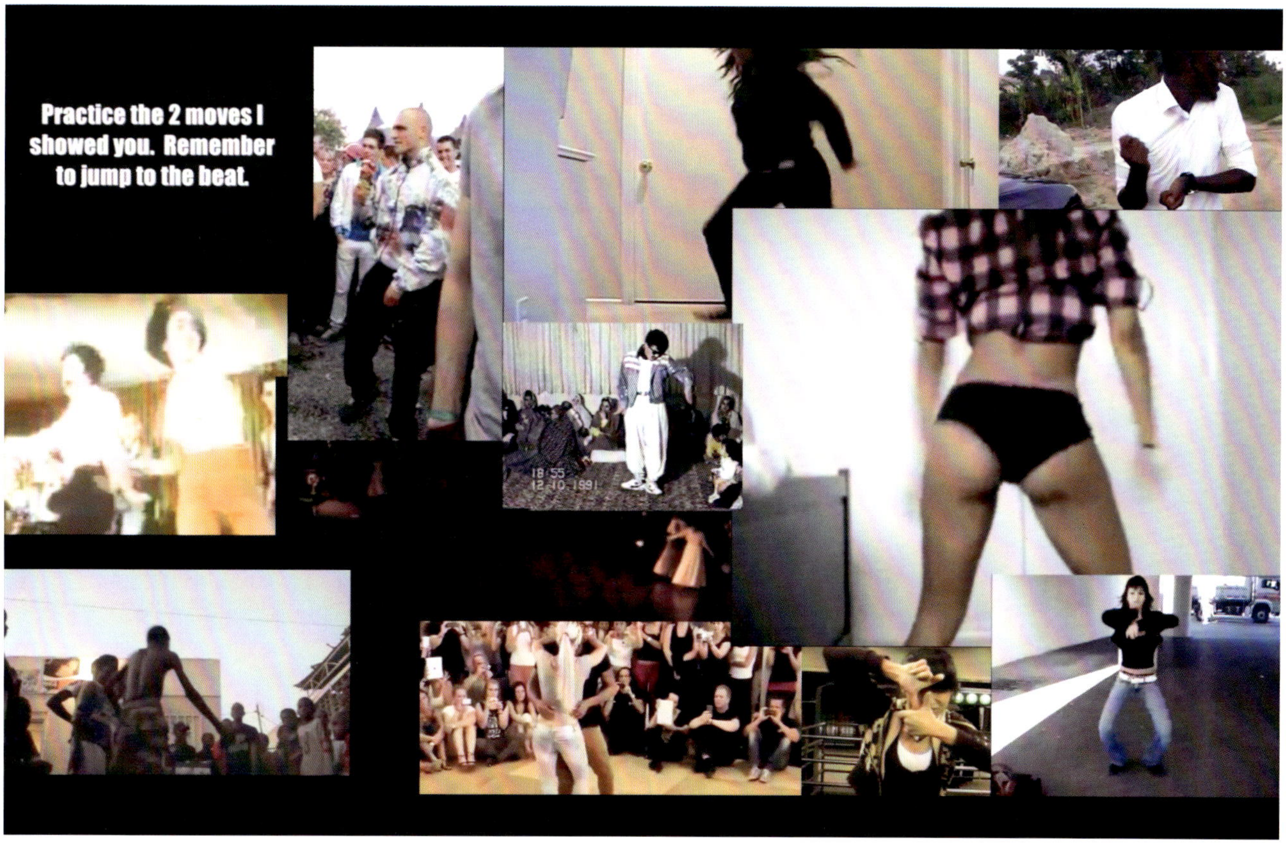

Practice the 2 moves I showed you. Remember to jump to the beat.

18:55
12.10.1991

18:55
12.10.1991

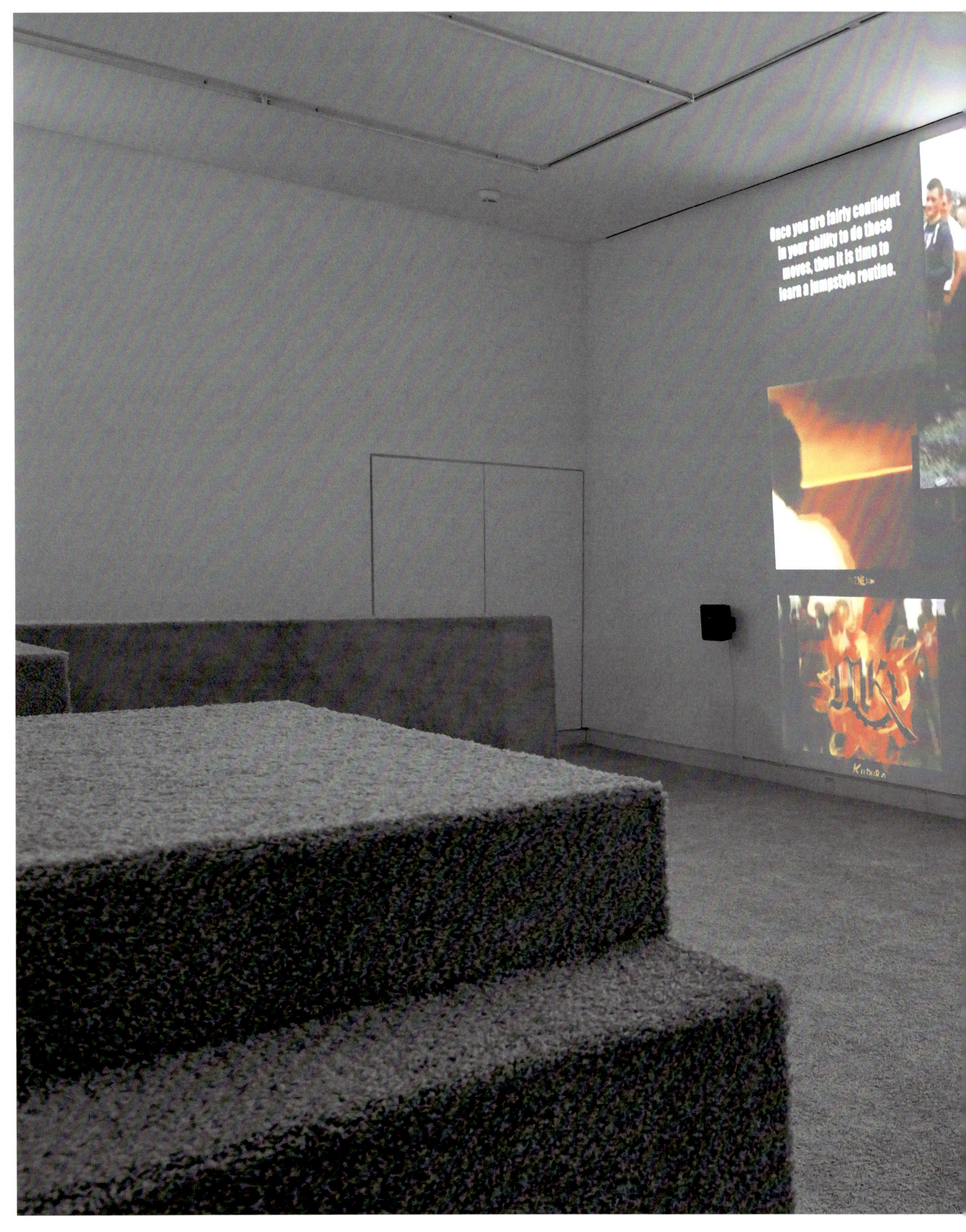
Once you are fairly confident
in your ability to do these
moves, then it is time to
learn a jumpstyle routine.

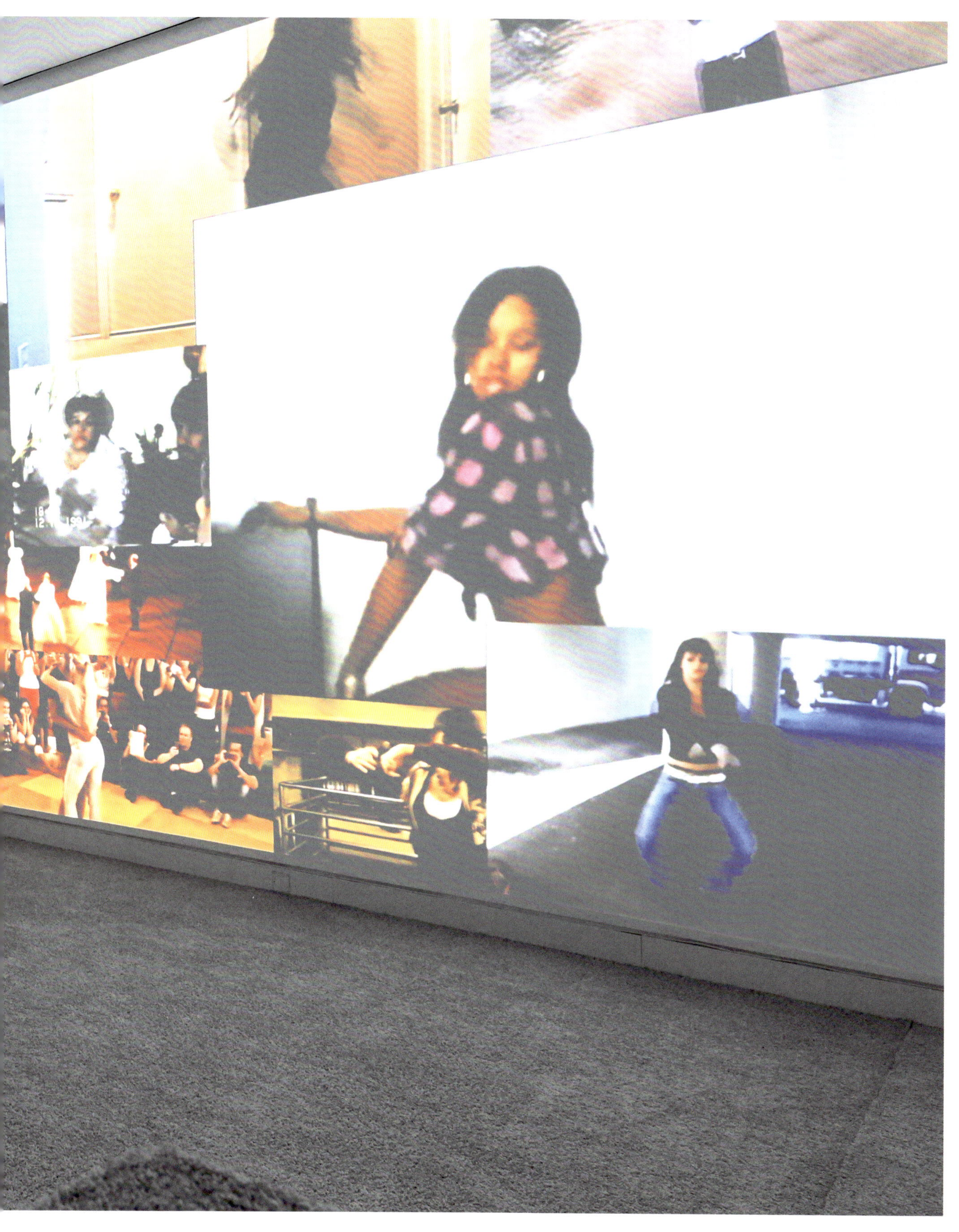

Sissel Tolaas

In_Between Us

—

SmellCoding / Air Movement

14 porzellanene
Apparaturen auf Sockeln mit
Geruchsmolekülen
14 porcelain appliances on pedestals
with odor molecules

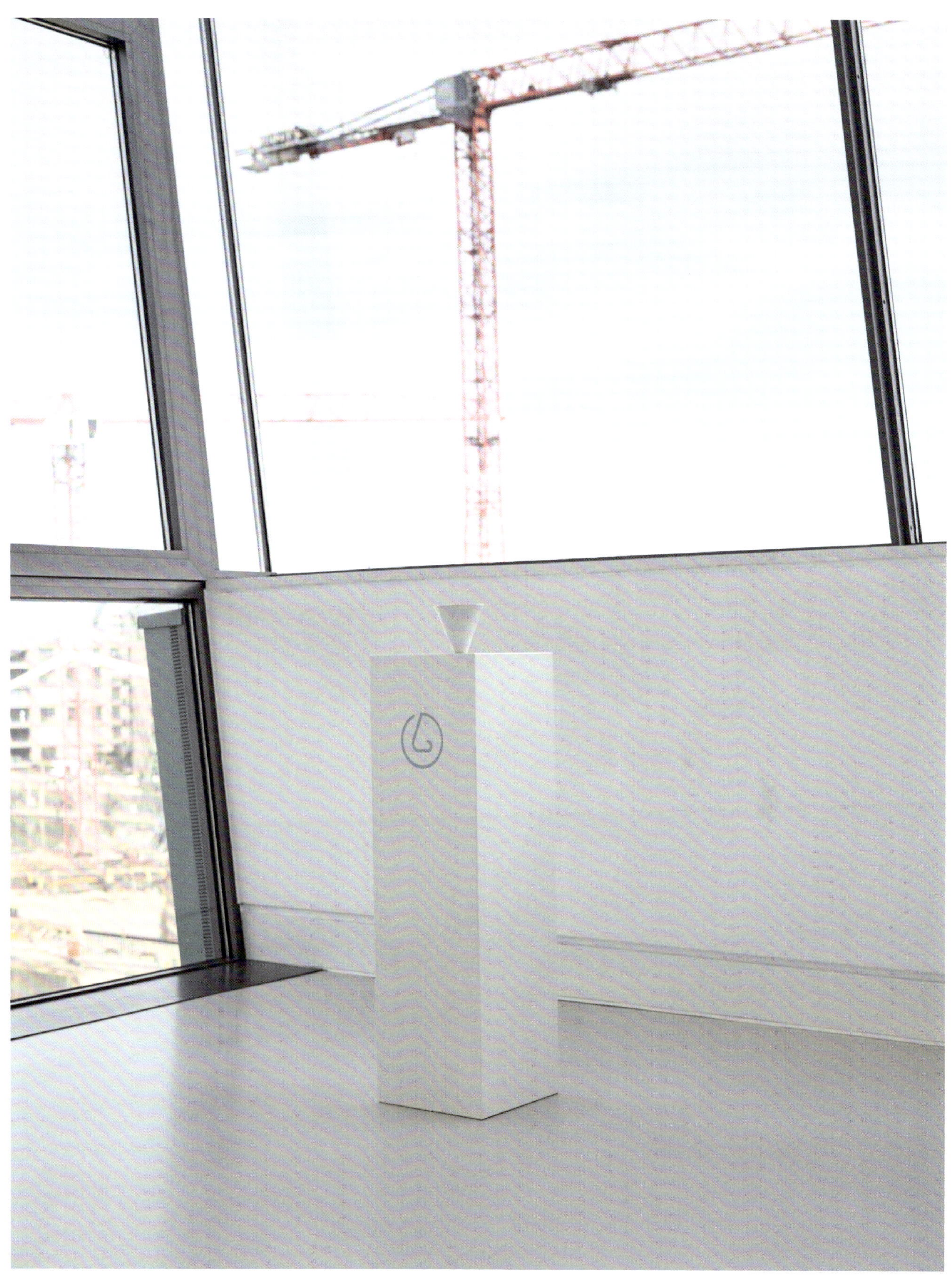

Lina Louisa Krämer: **Du leistest Pionierarbeit bei der Wiederentdeckung des Geruchssinns und arbeitest aktiv daran, dass wir diesen Sinn ernster nehmen, ihn bewusster einsetzen und ausbilden. Wie bist du dazu gekommen, mit Gerüchen zu arbeiten?**

Sissel Tolaas: Ich habe mich immer schon mit dem beschäftigt, was unsichtbar ist. Sehr früh in meinem Leben fragte ich mich: „Was ist in der Luft los? Was bedeutet Unsichtbarkeit? Was ist Wetter?" Ich war aber zu jung, um das zu verstehen. Ich komme aus Skandinavien und wuchs umgeben von viel Luft auf, in der Natur und am Meer. Meine Sinne waren schon immer sehr wach, und ich benutzte sie bereits früh, um zu verstehen, zu navigieren, zu kommunizieren, zu tolerieren und das Leben wertzuschätzen. Später habe ich das zu meiner Profession gemacht. Beim Geruch geht es um Luft und um das Atmen – um das Leben und darum, am Leben zu sein. Meine Arbeit ist in der Welt verankert und beschäftigt sich gleichzeitig mit ihr. Ich bezeichne mich als professionelle „Wanderin zwischen den Welten". Es gibt eine komplette Welt des Geruchs und eine komplette Welt des Erlernens des Riechens, sodass ich mich nicht auf eine Disziplin oder ein Thema beschränken möchte.

Lina: **Was unterscheidet deine wissenschaftliche Beschäftigung mit Gerüchen von deiner künstlerischen?**

Sissel: Meine Methoden sind wissenschaftlich, meine Lösungen, Darstellungen und Produkte sind kreativ. Ich habe einen wissenschaftlichen Hintergrund in Chemie, Kunst, Sprachen, mein Hauptfokus liegt aber auf dem Geruch. Etwa 50 % meiner Projekte und Experimente werden im kreativen Kontext präsentiert. In der kreativen Welt ist es einem erlaubt, subjektiv zu sein. Diese Freiheit ist sehr wichtig für die Fragen, die ich stelle. Ich bekomme dort eine direkte Reaktion von ganz unterschiedlichen Personen. In der Welt der Wissenschaft kann ich die gleichen Fragen stellen, muss aber objektiv bleiben und meine Thesen in trockenen Thesenpapieren schildern. Außerdem bekomme ich erst Monate oder Jahre später Antworten von einer kleinen Gruppe von Wissenschaftler*innen.

Lina: **Allgemein kann man sagen, dass Kunst auf etwas reagiert, wie auch Gerüche auf etwas reagieren. Welche Aspekte von *Between Us* – die aufgezeichneten Daten oder der Tanz selbst – haben dich zu deiner Beteiligung inspiriert?**

„Das Fantastische am Geruch ist, dass in ihm das einzigartige Potenzial steckt, uns aus unserer Komfortzone direkt ins tiefe Wasser zu schmeißen. Zurück ans Ufer zu gelangen kann eine große Aufgabe sein, aber sie ist es wert."

Sissel Tolaas

Sissel: Am Ende geht es beim Tanz auch um chemische Vorgänge. Es geht um Bewegungen, um chemische Vorgänge zwischen Menschen, und es geht um chemische Vorgänge zwischen den Tänzer*innen und ihrer Umgebung. In all diesen Fällen ist eine Komponente essenziell: die Bewegung; Bewegung der Luft und Bewegung der Körper. In meiner Arbeit für die Kunsthalle Mainz verstärke ich die Luft, die den Körper umgibt, und die durch die spezifische Choreografie verursachte Bewegung. Ich versuche, diese Bewegungen aus der Perspektive der Chemie zu verstehen, und hebe die Moleküle hervor, die vom Körper an die Luft abgegeben werden, und deren Reaktion mit der Luft, die den Körper umgibt. Man kann sich das wie eine Interaktion zwischen unsichtbarer Realität und sichtbarer Realität vorstellen.

Lina: **Kannst du deinen Beitrag für *Between Us* näher erläutern? Wie funktioniert deine Arbeit genau?**

Sissel: Ich habe 14 Porzellanobjekte in zwei verschiedenen Größen anfertigen lassen. Es gibt also zwei identische Sets. Sieben sind in der dritten Turmebene ausgestellt. Die anderen sieben verteilen sich in der Kunsthalle Mainz. Jedes Objekt beinhaltet ein anderes Molekül, es gibt sieben unterschiedliche Geruchsmoleküle in den sieben

Objektpaaren. Wenn man alle sieben Moleküle zusammenbringt, ergibt sich eine Komposition. Der Grund, warum die Objekte diese Form haben, liegt darin, dass die Besucher*innen sie halten und mit ihnen interagieren können, sie sollen ihren Geruchssinn aktivieren und können durch einen Raum oder das Gebäude getragen werden. Alle Objekte dürfen angehoben, gehalten und möglicherweise in unterschiedlichen Kombinationen zusammengebracht und berochen werden. Die ausgestellten Moleküle beeinflussen die Bewegung der Besucher*innen. Sie bringen einen dazu, zu agieren und zu reagieren. Das Wesentliche dabei ist, dass sie dazu anregen, aufmerksamer, fokussierter zu sein, gleichzeitig führen sie aber auch dazu, dass man selbst mehr Aufmerksamkeit erfährt. Das sind also die verschiedenen „Funktionsweisen" dieser Moleküle. Einzeln oder in Kombination lösen sie bei den Besucher*innen ein Verhalten aus. Vielleicht beeinflusst das letztendlich auch die Art und Weise, wie man die eigenen Bewegungen im Raum interpretiert und wie man auf andere Personen, die durch das Gebäude gehen, reagiert. Beim Tanzen verwendet man seinen gesamten Körper; sämtliche Körperbewegungen und die Atmung sind wesentlich. Wir atmen bis zu 24.000 Mal am Tag. Wir bewegen jeden Tag 12,7 Kubikmeter Luft durch das Ein- und Ausatmen, und jedes Nano-Bit dieser Luft enthält Geruchsmoleküle. Die Luft enthält Moleküle, Billionen von Molekülen. Es herrscht nie Langeweile.

Lina: **Ist es nicht sehr interessant, dass in Verbindung mit dem Tanz die Luft ephemer, flüchtig ist? Aber beide haben doch eine gewisse Körperlichkeit, oder?**

Sissel: Natürlich ist die Luft, die uns umgibt, nicht einfach nichts. Sie enthält Milliarden über Milliarden von Molekülen, die von Geruchsquellen ausgehen. Das schließt alles ein – vom Körper über den Boden bis hin zur Straße, vom Licht bis zum Papier. All diese Informationen gehen in das Gehirn und in unser Gedächtnis und lösen dort innerhalb kürzester Zeit sensorische Prozesse aus. Wenn man keine spannende Referenz dazu findet, beginnt man zu schauen, welche Erinnerung man mit einem Geruch verbinden möchte. Lange bevor das Sehen einsetzt, weiß die Nase schon Bescheid. Wir leben in einer Welt, in der es nur darum geht, wie die Dinge visuell wahrgenommen werden. Beim Sehen wird der rationale Teil des Gehirns angesprochen, dann folgt ein Übertrag, und schließlich lösen die Informationen vielleicht unsere Erinnerungen und / oder Emotionen aus, vielleicht aber auch nicht.

Lina: **Lösen die Moleküle, die du für *Between Us* ausgesucht hast, bei jedem Menschen die gleiche oder unterschiedliche Reaktionen aus?**

Sissel: Ja und nein. Wir haben Beweise, dass diese Moleküle Wachsamkeit, Erinnerungen, Aufmerksamkeit, Ablenkung usw. auslösen können. Wir haben nicht nur Geruchsrezeptoren in der Nase – die Rezeptoren verteilen sich über die Haut, und man findet sie sogar im Inneren des Körpers. Also gelangen diese Moleküle, die Luft, der aus den Objekten strömende Geruch auch durch die Haut in den Körper und können sogar die Leber oder das Herz anregen. Und natürlich wird Geruch individuell wahrgenommen. Wenn man damit anfängt, einen anderen Sinn richtig zu stimulieren, verhalten sich die Sinne anders. Plötzlich verstehen wir alles, was uns umgibt, und die Welt unterschiedlich. Wir werden mit erstaunlichen Anlagen geboren, die wir Sinne nennen, aber wann werden wir herausgefordert, sie richtig einzusetzen? In meiner Welt spielt Aufklärung deshalb eine wichtige Rolle.

Lina: **Aber es gibt keine Bilder oder Situationen, die man sofort mit den ausgewählten Molekülen verbindet? Bestimmte Gerüche wecken bei mir Erinnerungen aus meiner Vergangenheit.**

Sissel: Bei einem konkreten Geruch sucht jeder nach Assoziationen, nach einem Bild oder einem Wort. Der Geruch wird als etwas Eigenes und Emotionales wahrgenommen, und jeder nimmt Gerüche individuell wahr, deshalb ist es schwierig, generelle Aussagen zu treffen. Noch einmal zurück zur Aufklärung: Hätten wir „die Sinne" als wichtige Lehreinheit unserer Bildung, wären wir wohl durchaus in der Lage, langsam, aber sicher mehr übergeordnete Begrifflichkeiten zu verwenden. Aber je abstrakter der Geruch wird, desto weniger existieren individuelle Assoziationen oder Erinnerungen. Dort setzt meine Arbeit an … Wenn man etwas zum ersten Mal riecht, ist das eine Referenz, die man für den Rest seines Lebens behält. Das Verhalten gegenüber diesem Geruch bleibt dann für immer gleich. Alle weiteren Male sind nur Wiederholungen. Nehmen wir als Beispiel das erste Mal, wenn man einen Apfel riecht. Je nachdem ob dieser Moment positiv oder negativ war, bleibt das Verhältnis zu einem Apfel ebenfalls entweder positiv oder negativ.

Es sei denn, man bringt sich dazu, die eigene Komfortzone zu verlassen und sich der Herausforderung zu stellen, neue Praktiken zu lernen, vergleichbar mit jeder Art von Detox oder Rehabilitation. Das Fantastische am Geruch ist, dass in ihm das einzigartige Potenzial steckt, uns aus unserer Komfortzone direkt ins kalte Wasser zu schmeißen. Zurück ans Ufer zu gelangen kann eine große Aufgabe sein, aber sie ist es wert. Plötzlich versteht man dann die immensen Eigenschaften, die der Geruch schon immer hatte. Bevor es eine Welt gab, gab es den Geruch.

'What is so fantastic about smell is that it has this unique potential to take you out of your safety zone and throw you into deep water. Getting to the next shore might be a big task, but it is worth it.'

Sissel Tolaas

Lina Louisa Krämer: **You are pioneering the rediscovery of the sense of smell and you are working actively to make this sense more serious, use it more consciously and train it. How did you come to work with smells?**

Sissel Tolaas: I have always been concerned with invisibility. Very early on in my life, I wondered, 'What's going on in the air? What does invisible mean? What is weather?' I was too young to understand. Coming from Scandinavia, I grew up with a lot of air, in nature and next to the ocean. My senses were always very alert and I used them properly, from very early on, to understand, navigate, communicate, tolerate, and appreciate life. Later I made this my profession. Smell is about air and about breathing—about life and being alive. My work is very much in the world about the world. I call myself a professional 'in-betweener.' There is a whole world of smell and a whole world to educate on how to smell, so I can't limit myself to one discipline or topic.

Lina: **What makes your scientific study of smells different from your artistic work?**

Sissel: My method is scientific, my solutions, display and products are creative. I have a background in chemistry, art and languages and my main focus is on smell. Around 50 % of my projects and experiments are displayed in different creative contexts. In the creative world you are allowed to be subjective and this freedom is very important for the questions I am asking. I get an immediate response from a diversity of people. In the science world you can ask the same questions but you have to remain objective and express yourself with dry academic papers and you get a response months or years later from a small group of academics.

Lina: **So in general art reacts to something, as well as smells. Which aspect of *Between Us*—the captured data or the dance itself—inspired you to your contribution?**

Sissel: In the end dance is very much about chemistry. It's about movement, about air and breathing and it's about chemistry between people and it's about chemistry between the dancers and the surroundings. And most of all there is the core compound: the movement; movement of air and movement of body. What I do in my work at Kunsthalle Mainz is to amplify the air that surrounds the body and the movements caused by this certain choreography. I try to understand these movements from the perspective of chemistry and highlight smell molecules that are emitted from the body and their reaction to the air that surrounds that body. It's like an interaction between an invisible and a visible reality.

Lina: **Can you explain your contribution to *Between Us*? How does it work?**

Sissel: I created fourteen porcelain objects in two different sizes, so there are two similar sets. Seven for the third tower level will be stationary, and seven to be placed around Kunsthalle Mainz. Each object contains one molecule, seven different smell molecules in seven objects pairs. If you put all seven molecules together, you have a composition. The reason why I place the molecules in such a shape is that I wanted the audience to activate their noses while moving around in either the room or the building. All objects can be lifted, held, smelled, and potentially moved around in different combinations. The molecules that are on display will influence your movement; will make you react and act differently in the surroundings. What is essential here is that they prompt you to be i.e. more alert, be more focused, get more attention. The molecules have different 'functions.' Individually and in combination they start to trigger your behavior. And maybe that in the end influences the way you interpret your own movements in the room, your reaction to other people walking through the building and the building itself. In terms of dance you use the entire body, so all the body movement and breathing is essential. We breathe up to 24,000 times a day. Each of us moves 12.7 cubic meters of air by breathing every day and every nano-bit of that air contains smell molecules. That air contains molecules, trillions of molecules. There is never a dull moment.

Lina: **It's very interesting that in connection to dance air is also ephemeral, but both certainly have a materiality …**

Sissel: Of course the air you're surrounded by is not just nothing. It contains billions and billions of molecules that are emitted from smell sources that include everything from the body to the floor to the street to the light to the paper. All this information enters the brain and triggers your emotions and memory faster than any other form of sensory processing. If you don't find exciting references in your memory already, you start to look for what kind of memory you want to code it with. Long before visions ever start to set in, the nose already knows. We live in a world driven by vision; when you see something, you trigger the rational part of the brain, then render it and finally the information might end up triggering your memory or/and emotions, but maybe not at all.

Lina: **And do the molecules you chose for *Between Us* trigger the same reaction in every person or different one?**

Sissel: Yes, and no. There is a lot of evidence that certain smell molecules trigger i.e. alertness, memory, attention, distraction. The fact is that we not only have smell receptors in the nose, we have receptors all over the skin and even inside our bodies. So the air that emits from these smell objects, might go through your skin and activate or trigger even your kidney or your heart. And of course then, smell perception and reactions are very individual. In general, when we start to trigger the senses properly they behave differently; suddenly we understand our surroundings and the world differently and even more holistically. We are born with the amazing interfaces called the senses but when are we challenged to use them properly? In my world education plays a prime role.

Lina: **Do you have any images or situations you connect with these specific molecules? For example, sometimes if I smell something, it reminds me of something, a certain memory of my past.**

Sissel: With every concrete smell everybody is searching for an association, an image or a word. Smell is perceived as something private, intrinsic, emotional, and everyone perceives smell very differently, so operating with a general system is problematic. Again back to education: if we would have 'the senses' as an important block within a curriculum, we could slowly be able to approach it using more generic terms. But the moment the smell becomes abstract, the less there is of the individual association and memory. That is where my work begins … The first time you smell something, it's a reference you have for the rest of your life, so you behave towards the smell exactly the same way forever. Later it's just a repetition, for example of the first time you smelled an apple. If that moment was positive or negative, your relationship to that smell remains positive or negative forever. Unless you want to challenge yourself, to get out of your comfort zone, to learn new practices, similar to any kind of detox or rehabilitation. What is so fantastic about smell is that it has this unique potential to take you out of your safety zone and throw you into deep water. Getting to the next shore might be a big task, but it is worth it. Suddenly you will understand the immense capacity that smell has always had. Before there was the word there was the smell.

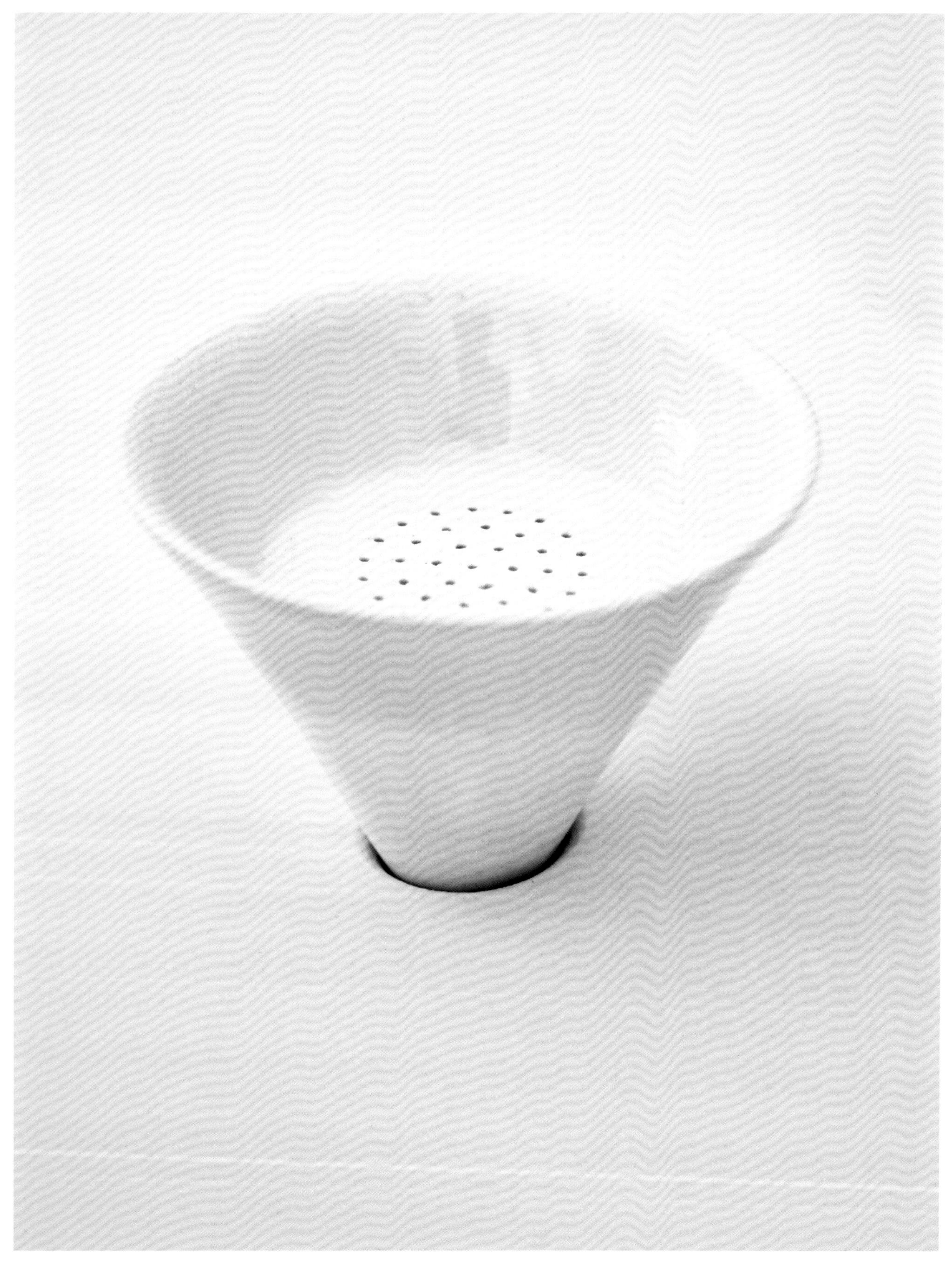

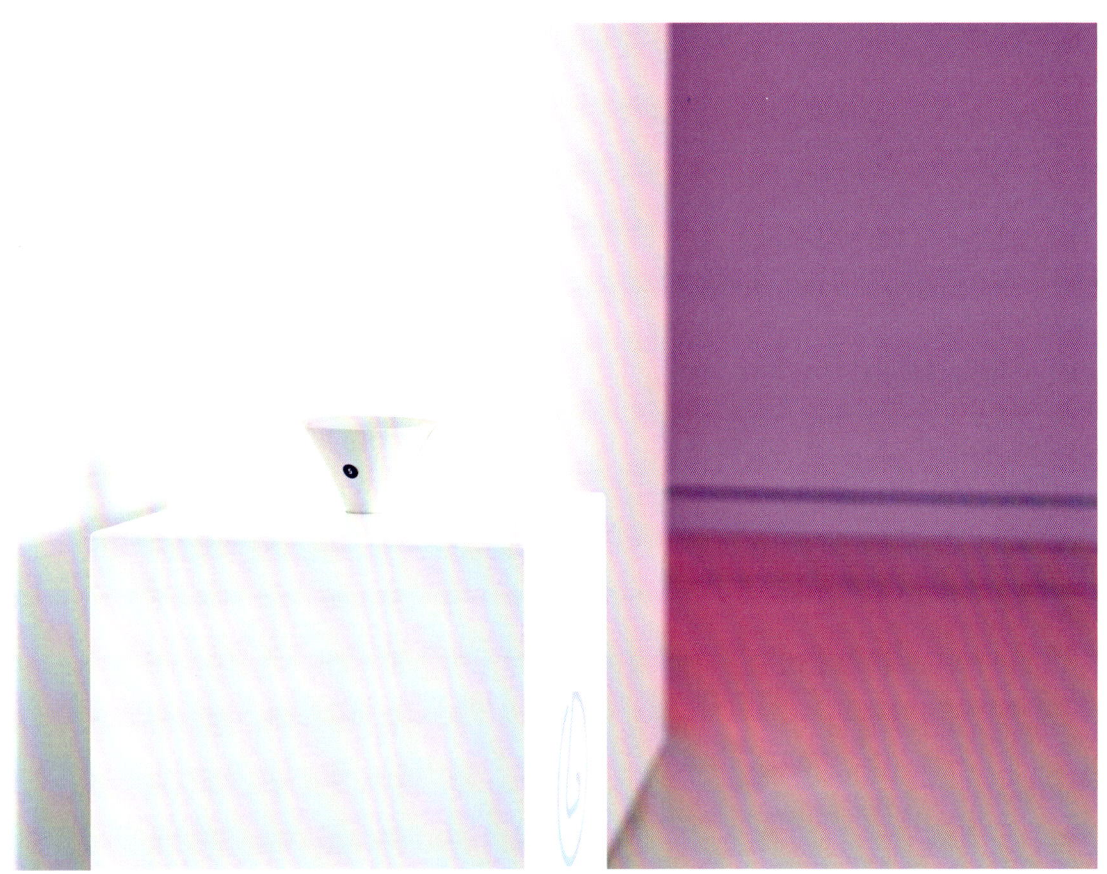

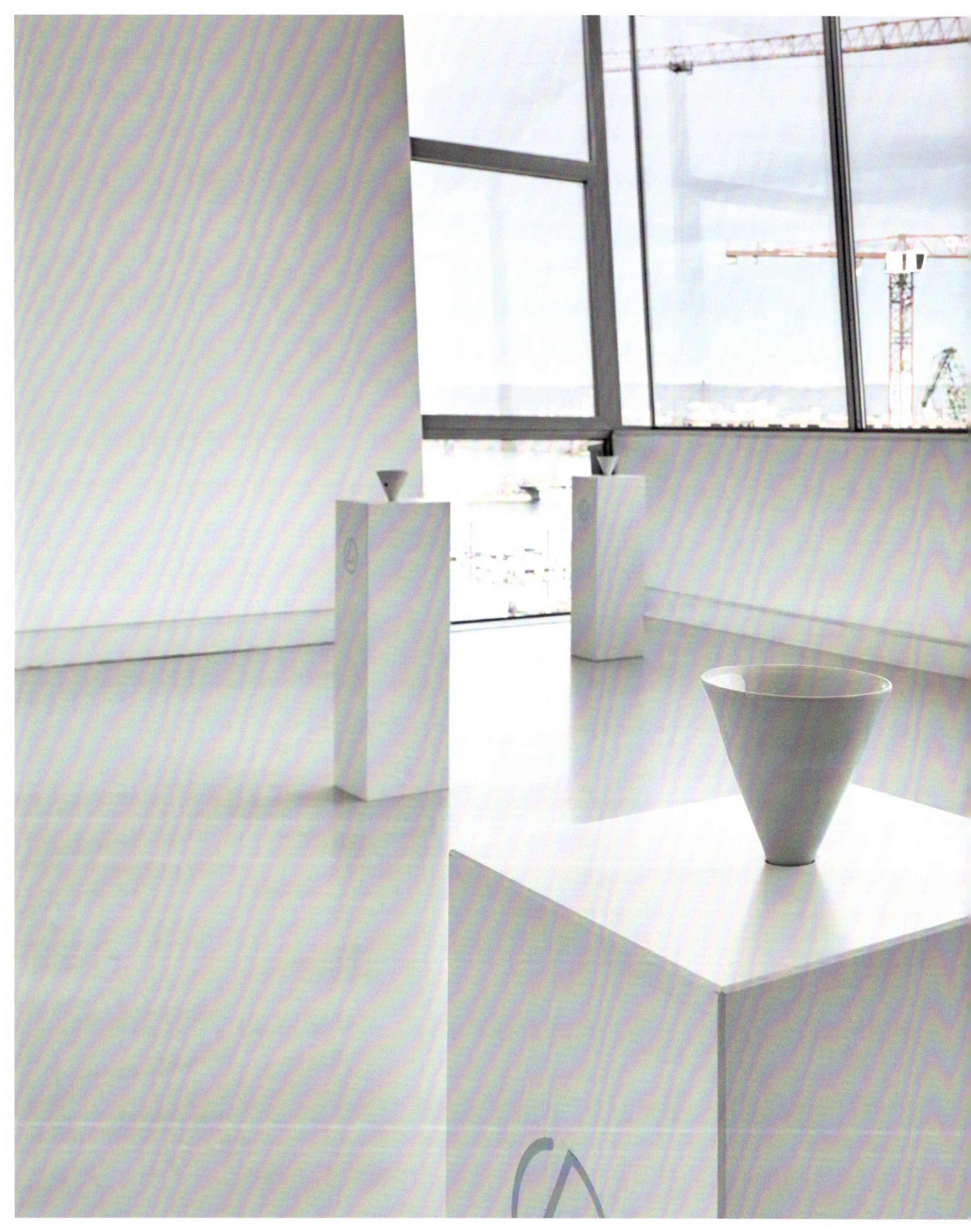

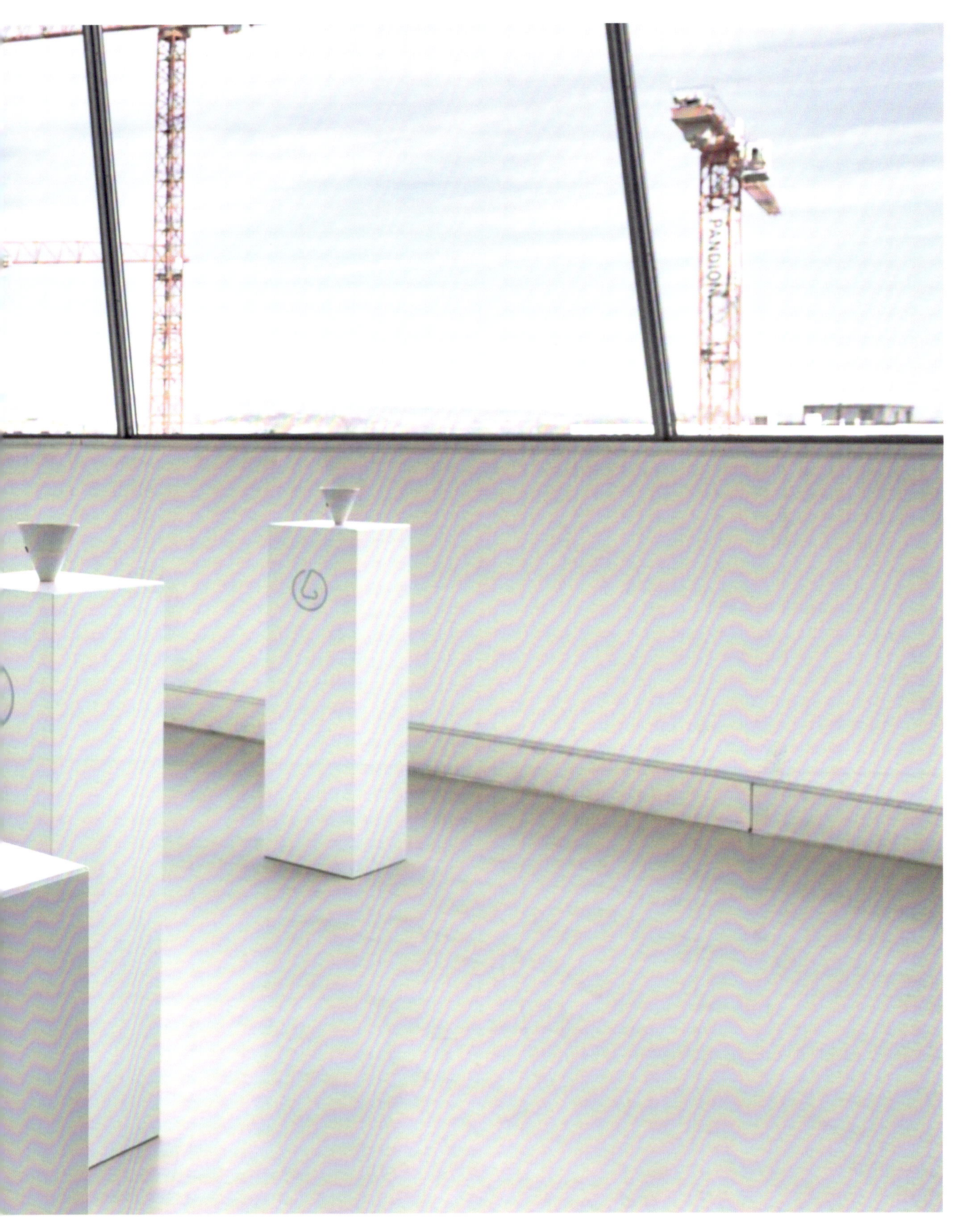
PANDION

ANHANG
APPENDIX

Werkverzeichnis
List of Works

Tim Etchells

SEITE Tim Etchells *TRY*, 2019, Sperr-
PAGE holz, CNC-Zuschnitt, 240 cm ×
57 274 cm × 5 cm; Foto: Norbert
64 Miguletz, courtesy of the artist
Tim Etchells, TRY, *2019,*
Plywood, CNC cutting, 240 cm ×
274 cm × 5 cm; photo: Norbert
Miguletz, courtesy of the artist

SEITE Tim Etchells, *PUSH*, 2019,
PAGE Sperrholz, CNC-Zuschnitt,
45 410 cm × 315 cm × 5 cm;
57 Foto: Norbert Miguletz,
65 courtesy of the artist
Tim Etchells, PUSH, *2019,*
Plywood, CNC cutting,
410 cm × 315 cm × 5 cm;
photo: Norbert Miguletz,
courtesy of the artist

SEITE Tim Etchells, *LOOK*, 2019,
PAGE Sperrholz, CNC-Zuschnitt,
45 480 cm × 304 cm × 5 cm; Foto:
57 Norbert Miguletz, courtesy of
63 the artist
64 *Tim Etchells,* LOOK, *2019,*
Plywood, CNC cutting,
480 cm × 304 cm × 5 cm; photo:
Norbert Miguletz, courtesy of
the artist

SEITE Tim Etchells, *STAND*, 2019,
PAGE Sperrholz, CNC-Zuschnitt,
44 381 cm × 331 cm × 5 cm;
57 Foto: Norbert Miguletz,
63 courtesy of the artist
64 *Tim Etchells,* STAND, *2019,*
67 *Plywood, CNC cutting,*
381 cm × 331 cm × 5 cm;
photo: Norbert Miguletz,
courtesy of the artist

SEITE Tim Etchells, *NO REASON*,
PAGE 2019, Neon-Schriftzug,
44/45 50 cm × 938 cm; Foto: Norbert
57 Miguletz, courtesy of the artist
65 *Tim Etchells,* NO REASON,
2019, Neon sign, 50 cm × 938 cm;
photo: Norbert Miguletz,
courtesy of the artist

SEITE Tim Etchells, *ONE PLACE*
PAGE *TO ANOTHER*, 2019, Neon-
57 Schriftzug, 23 cm × 734 cm;
64 Foto: Norbert Miguletz,
66/67 courtesy of the artist
Tim Etchells, ONE PLACE TO
ANOTHER, *2019, Neon sign,*
23 cm × 734 cm; photo: Norbert
Miguletz, courtesy of the artist

Tamara Grcic

SEITE Tamara Grcic, *movements*,
PAGE 2019, 16-Kanal-Sound-
50/51 installation, 6 Min., looped,
69 16 Lautsprecher, Kabel, Player,
74/75 11 Teppichrollen; Tonschnitt:
76/77 Raphaël Languillat und
Tamara Grcic; Aufnahmen und
Tontechnik: Lennart Scheuren;
Foto: Norbert Miguletz,
courtesy of the artist
Tamara Grcic, movements,
2019, 16-channel-sound-instal-
lation, 6 min., looped, 16 speak-
ers, cables, player, 11 rolled
carpets; sound editors: Raphaël
Languillat and Tamara Grcic;
recordings and sound engineer-
ing: Lennart Scheuren; photo:
Norbert Miguletz, courtesy of
the artist

Žilvinas Kempinas

SEITE Žilvinas Kempinas, *SPIN*, 2019,
PAGE ortsspezifische Installation,
54/55 4,65 m × 4,65 m × 10 m, magne-
79 tische Bänder, Industrieventi-
85 lator, Fahrradvorderrad, HD-
86 Video, looped; Foto: Norbert
87 Miguletz, courtesy of the artist,
88/89 © VG Bild-Kunst, Bonn 2019
Žilvinas Kempinas, SPIN,
2019, site-specific installation,
4,65 m × 4,65 m × 10 m,
magnetic tapes, industrial van,
bicycle wheel, HD Video,
looped; photo: Norbert Miguletz,
courtesy of the artist,
© VG Bild-Kunst, Bonn 2019

Søren Lyngsø Knudsen

SEITE Søren Lyngsø Knudsen, *Figure*
PAGE *Eight*, 24-Kanal Sound-Instal-
52/53 lation, Transducer, Sperrholz,
91 Elektronik, 50 Min., looped;
96/97 Foto: Norbert Miguletz,
courtesy of the artist
Søren Lyngsø Knudsen, Figure
Eight, *24-channel-sound-in-*
stallation, transducer, plywood,
electric, 50 min., looped;
photo: Norbert Miguletz,
courtesy of the artist

Isabel Lewis

SEITE Isabel Lewis, *Social Dances*
PAGE *as Cultural Storage Systems*,
48/49 2019, Video-Collage, 23 Min.,
99 aufgenommener Text der
105 gleichnamigen Performance
106 von Isabel Lewis, ortsspezi-
107 fisches Ausstellungsmobiliar,
108/09 diverse Materialien, Dimen-
sionen variabel; Foto: Norbert
Miguletz, courtesy of the artist
Isabel Lewis, Social Dances
as Cultural Storage Systems,
2019, video-collage, 23 min.,
recorded text of the eponymous
lecture-performance by Isabel
Lewis, site-specific exhibition
furniture, various materials,
dimensions variable; photo:
Norbert Miguletz, courtesy of
the artist

Sissel Tolaas

SEITE Sissel Tolaas, *In_Between*
PAGE *Us – SmellCoding / Air Move-*
46/47 *ment*, 2019, 14 porzellanene
111 Apparaturen auf Sockeln mit
116 Geruchsmolekülen; Foto: Norbert
117 Miguletz, courtesy of the artist,
118/19 © VG Bild-Kunst, Bonn 2019
Sissel Tolaas, In_Between Us –
SmellCoding / Air Movement,
2019, 14 porcelain appliances
on pedestals with odor mole-
cules; photo: Norbert Miguletz,
courtesy of the artist,
© VG Bild-Kunst, Bonn 2019

Impressum
Colophon

Dieser Katalog erscheint anlässlich des Projekts
This catalog is published on the occasion of the project

Between Us

15.03.–16.06.2019
Kunsthalle Mainz

Konzept- und Projektidee
Concept and Project Idea
Stefanie Böttcher, Kunsthalle Mainz
Honne Dohrmann, Staatstheater Mainz
Florian Jenett, Hochschule Mainz

Dieses Projekt wurde gefördert durch
This project was funded by
Kulturstiftung des Bundes
German Federal Cultural Foundation

Mainzer Stadtwerke AG

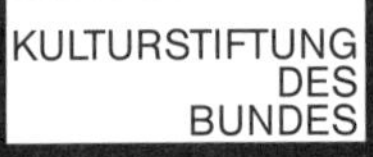

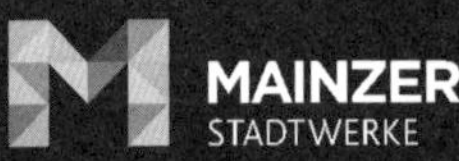

Besonderer Dank an
Special Thanks to
Königlich Norwegische Botschaft

Kunsthalle Mainz

Künstler*innen
Artists
Tim Etchells, Tamara Grcic, Žilvinas Kempinas, Søren Lyngsø Knudsen, Isabel Lewis, Sissel Tolaas

Künstlerische Leitung
Artistic Director
Stefanie Böttcher

Kuratorische Assistenz
Curatorial Assistant
Lina Louisa Krämer

Assistenz, Presse und Projektmanagement
Public Relations, Administration
Laura Günther

Kunstvermittlung
Art Mediation
Lisa Weber

FSJ Kultur
Voluntarily Social Year
Valeria Hertel

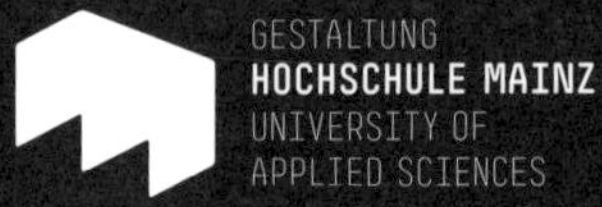

Fachbereich Gestaltung – Kommunikationsdesign
Hochschule Mainz — University of Applied Sciences
Institut Designlabor Gutenberg

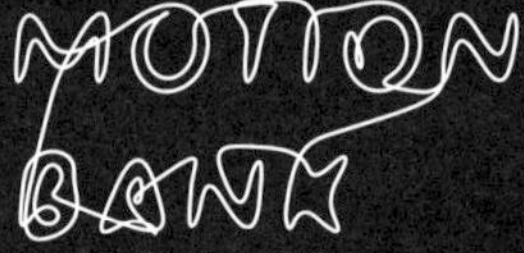

Motion Bank
Tanzforschung und Transfer
Dance Research and Transfer

Leitung
Directors
Florian Jenett, Scott deLahunta

Mitarbeiter*innen
Team
Mathias Bär, Ronja Butschbacher, Christian Hansen, Moritz Jentgens, Danae Kleida, Denis Klein, Anton Koch, David Rittershaus

Staatstheater Mainz

Choreograf
Choreographer
Taneli Törmä

Tänzer*innen
Dancers
Zachary Chant, Finn Lakeberg, Bojana Mitrović, Amber Pansters, Milena Wiese

Understudy
Thomas Van Praet

Kostüme
Costumes
Ute Noack

Tongestaltung
Sound Design
Søren Lyngsø Knudsen

Lichtdesign
Light Design
Petri Tukhanen

Proben- und Abendspielleitung
Rehearsal and Evening Direction
Andrea Svobodova

Inspizienz
Stage Manager
Marcel Tabrea

Technische Produktionsleitung
Technical Production Management
Justus Matla

Direktor tanzmainz
Director tanzmainz
Honne Dohrmann

Künstlerische Produktionsleitung
Artistic Production Management
Lisa Besser, Julia Danila

Assistentin der Tanzdirektion
Assistant to the Dance Direction
Maria Eckert

Presse & Öffentlichkeitsarbeit
Press & Communication
Kathrin Doering, Sylvia Fritzinger

Katalog
Catalog

Herausgeber
Editors
Stefanie Böttcher, Honne Dohrmann, Florian Jenett

Gestaltung
Design
Pixelgarten, Frankfurt am Main
Catrin Altenbrandt, Adrian Nießler

Texte
Texts
Stefanie Böttcher, Zachary Chant, Honne Dohrmann, Tim Etchells, Tamara Grcic, Florian Jenett, Žilvinas Kempinas, Søren Lyngsø Knudsen, Anton Koch, Lina Louisa Krämer, Finn Lakeberg, Isabel Lewis, Bojana Mitrović, Amber Pansters, David Rittershaus, Sissel Tolaas, Taneli Törmä, Milena Wiese

Übersetzung
Translation
Dr. Jeremy Gaines, Lina Louisa Krämer

Lektorat
Copy Editing
Stefanie Böttcher, Julia Danila, Kathrin Doering, Honne Dohrmann, Frauke Franckenstein, Dr. Jeremy Gaines, Valeria Hertel, Florian Jenett, Lina Louisa Krämer, David Rittershaus

Fotonachweis
Photo Credits
Ronja Butschbacher (S./*p.* 41)
Zachary Chant (S./*pp.*18, 20–23, 28)
Andreas Etter (S./*pp.* 1–8, Vorsatz/*front endpaper*)
Vanessa Liebler (S./*pp.* 124–128, Nachsatz/*endpaper*)
Norbert Miguletz (S./*pp.* 30–31, 44–55, 57, 63–67, 69, 74–77, 79, 85–89, 91, 99, 105, 108–109, 111, 116–119)

Lithografie & Produktion
Image Editing & Production Management
Pixelgarten, Frankfurt am Main

Gesamtherstellung
Printing and Binding
DZA Druckerei zu Altenburg GmbH

Vertrieb
Distribution
edel Germany GmbH
www.edel.com
international-books@edel.com

ISBN 978-3-95476-292-7
Printed in Germany

Erschienen im
Published by
DISTANZ Verlag
www.distanz.de

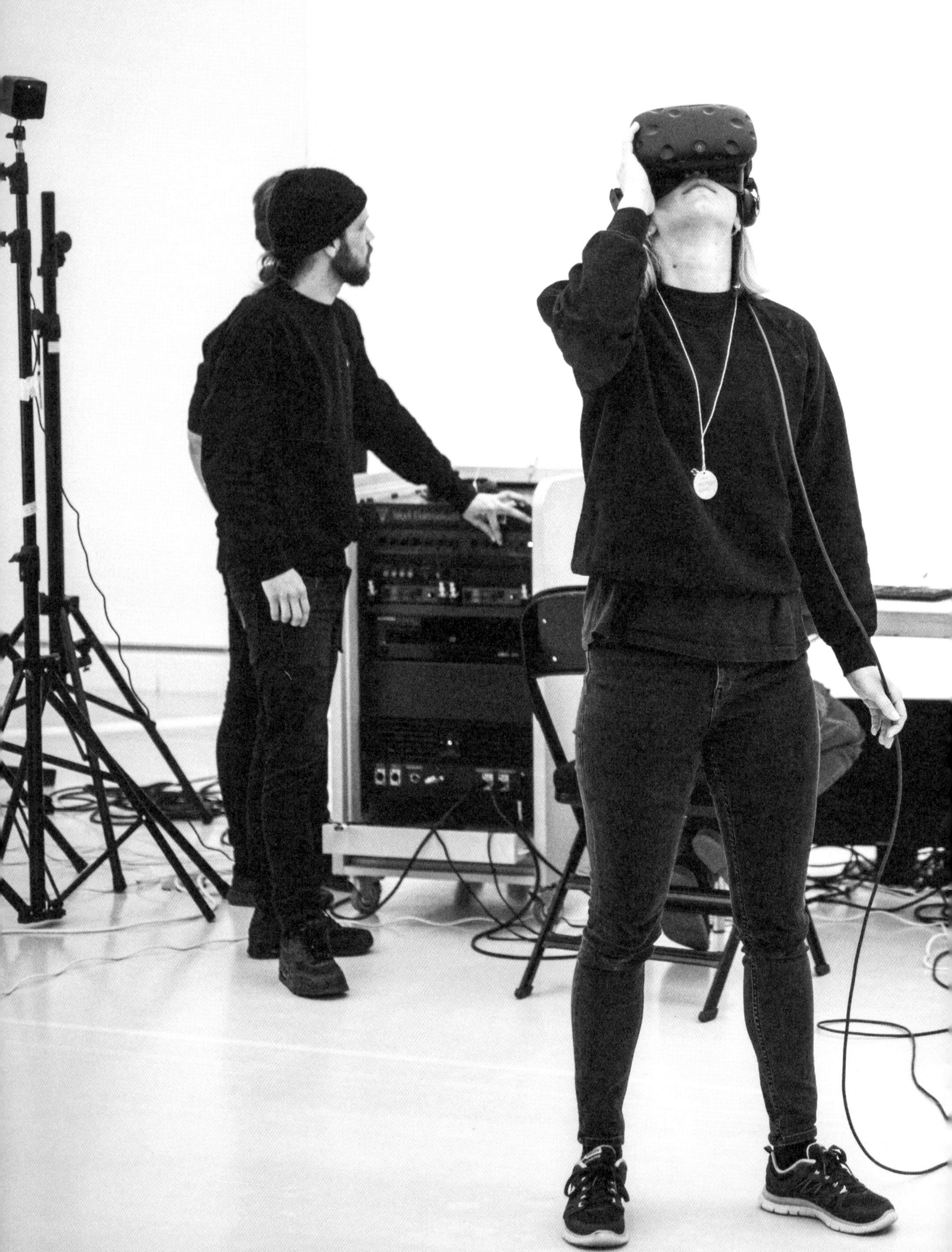

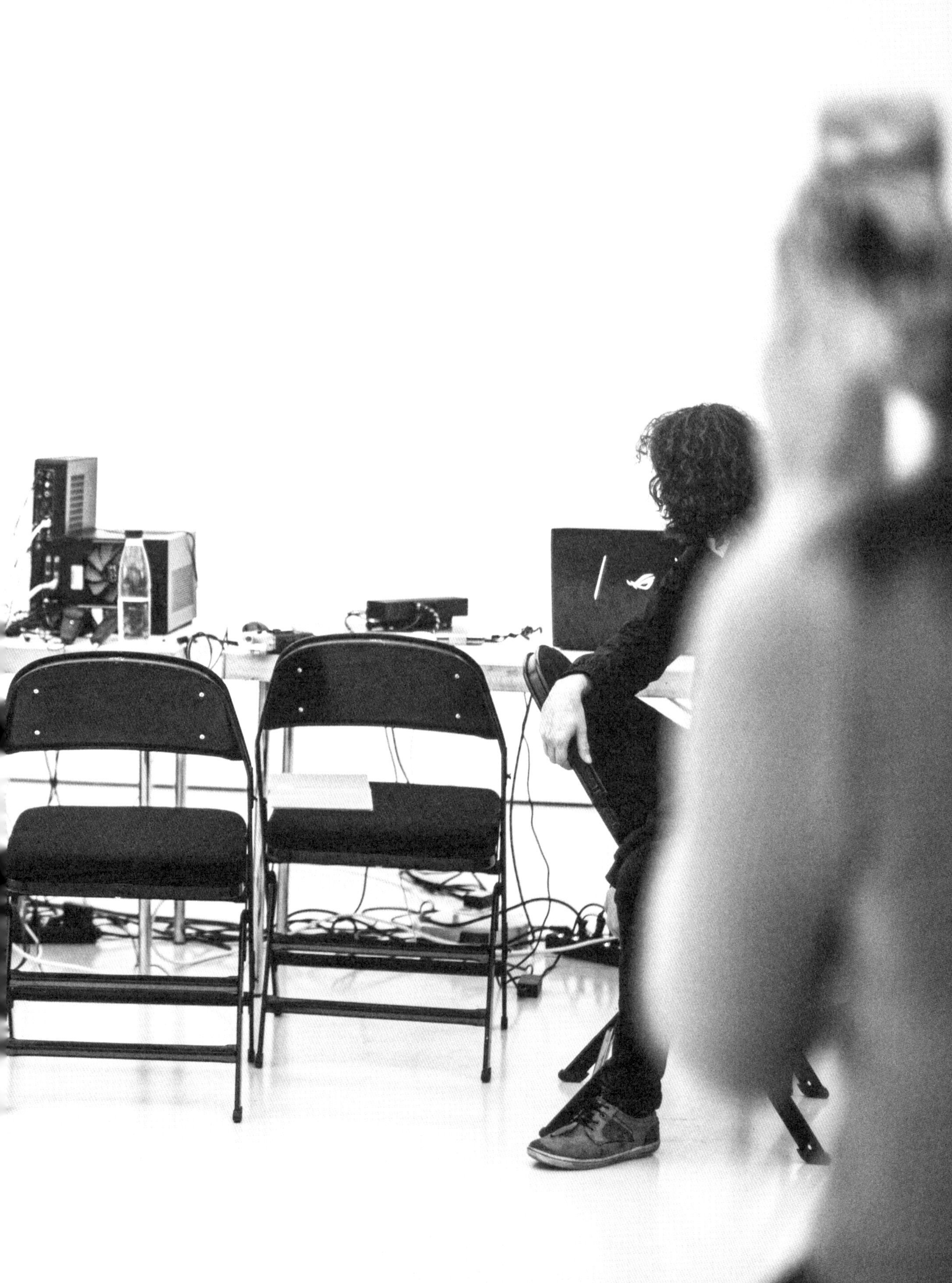

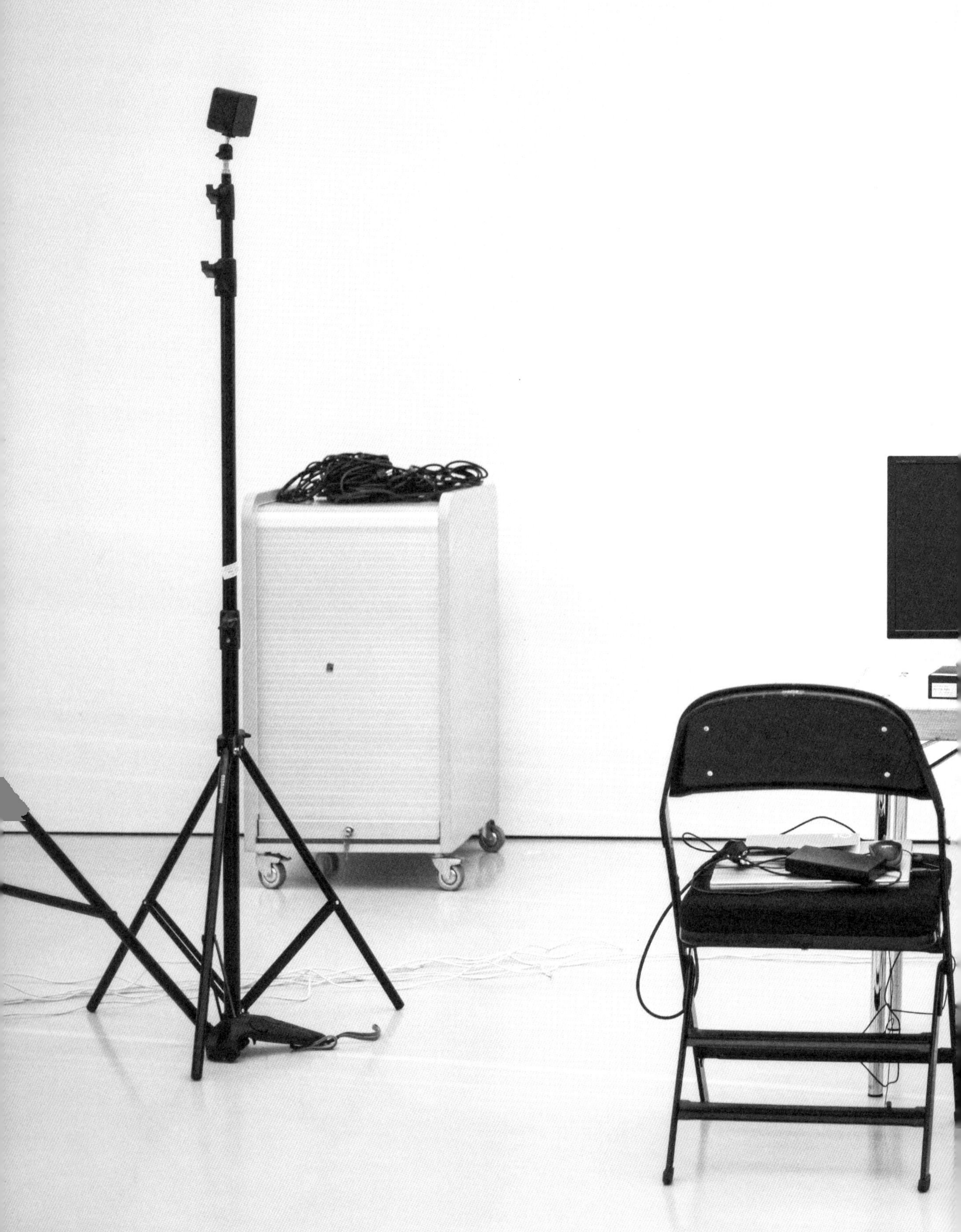

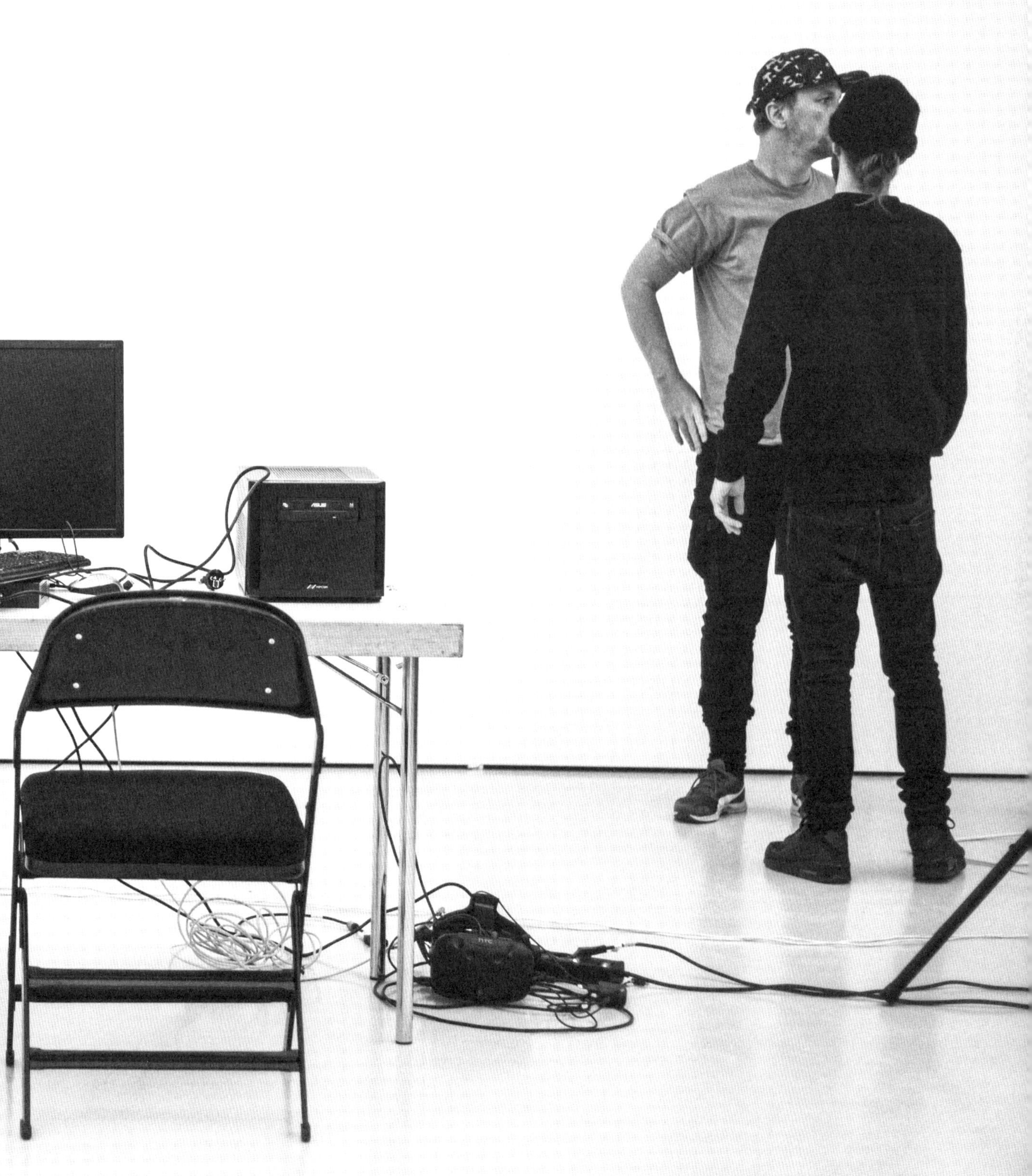

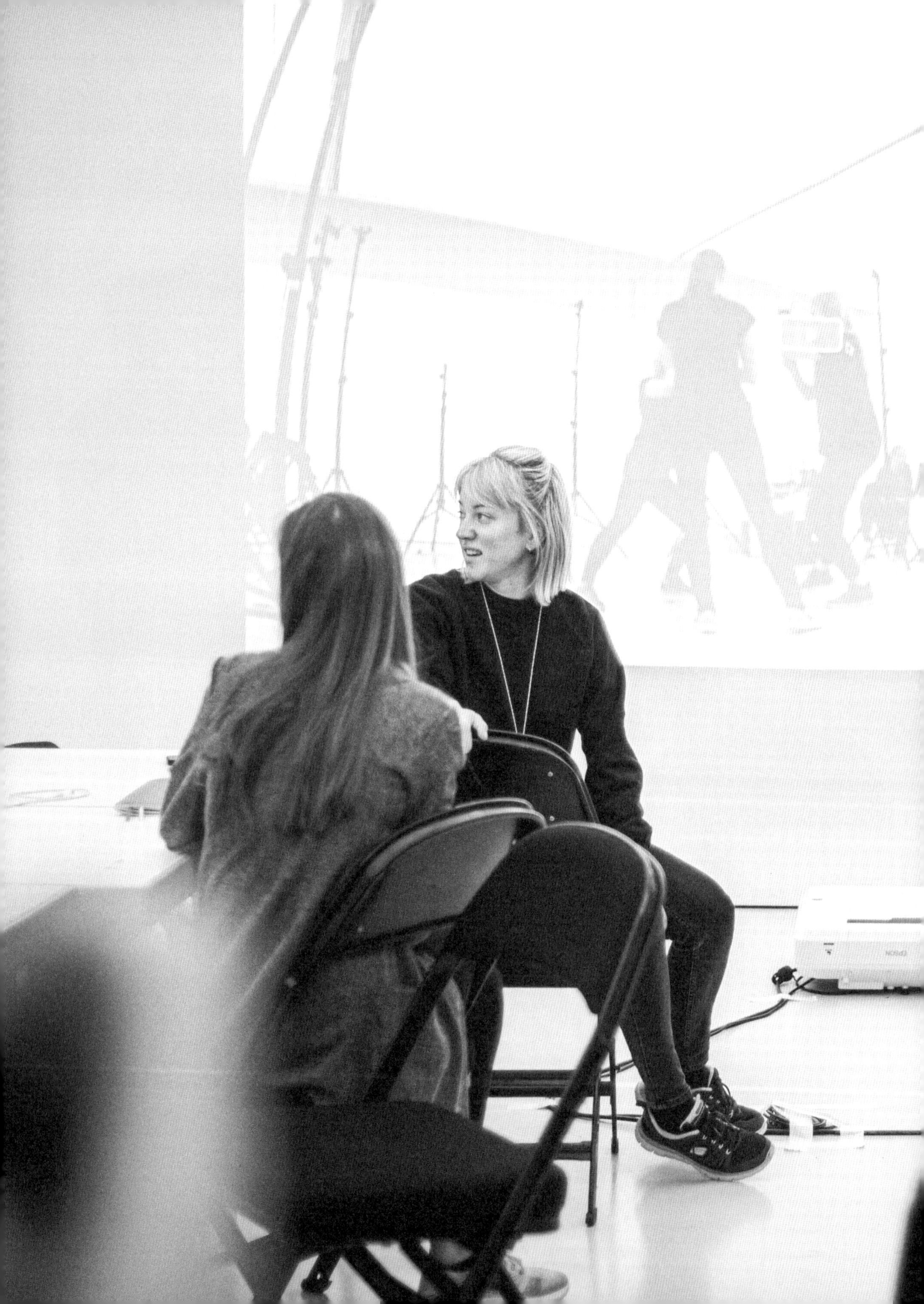

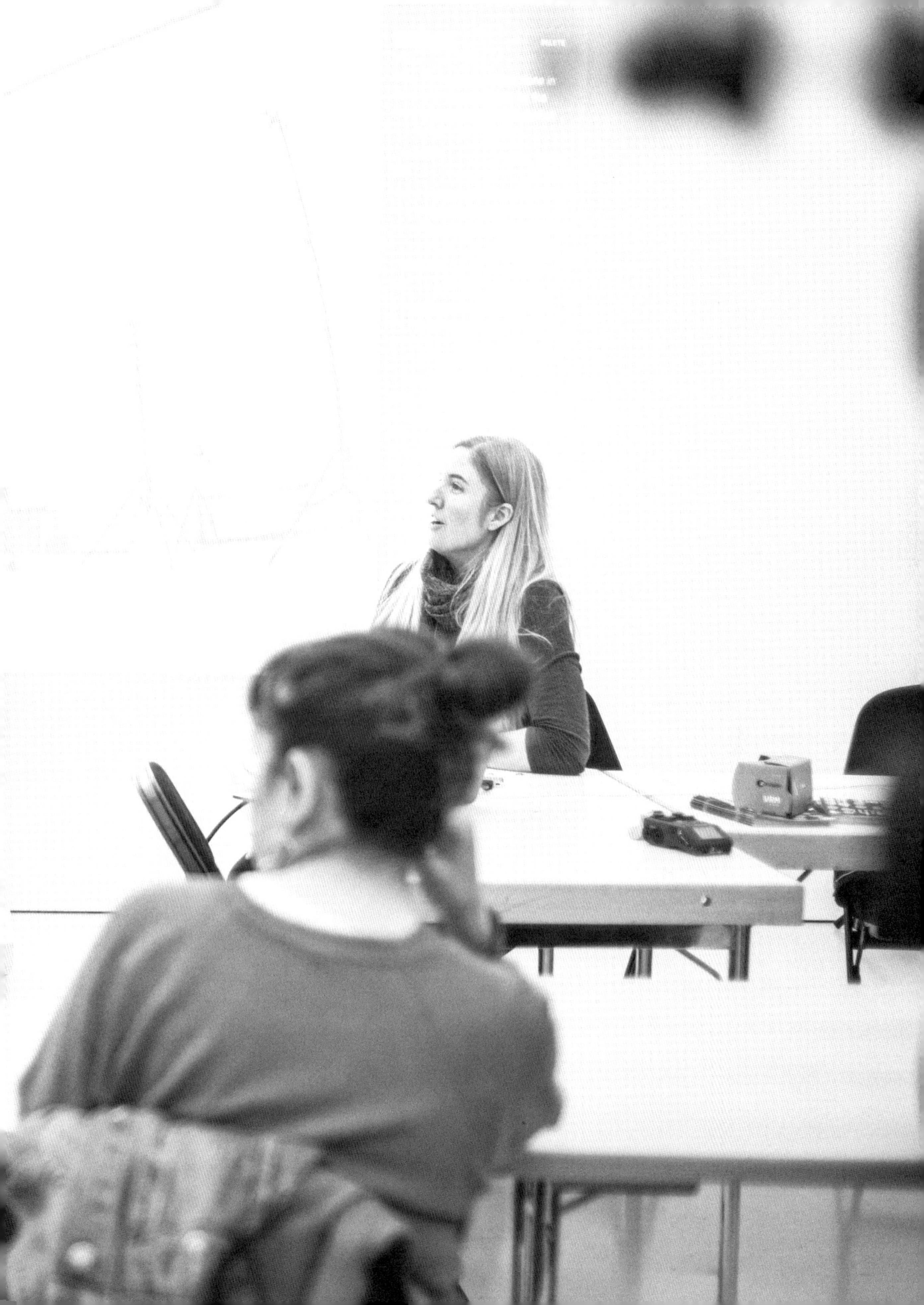

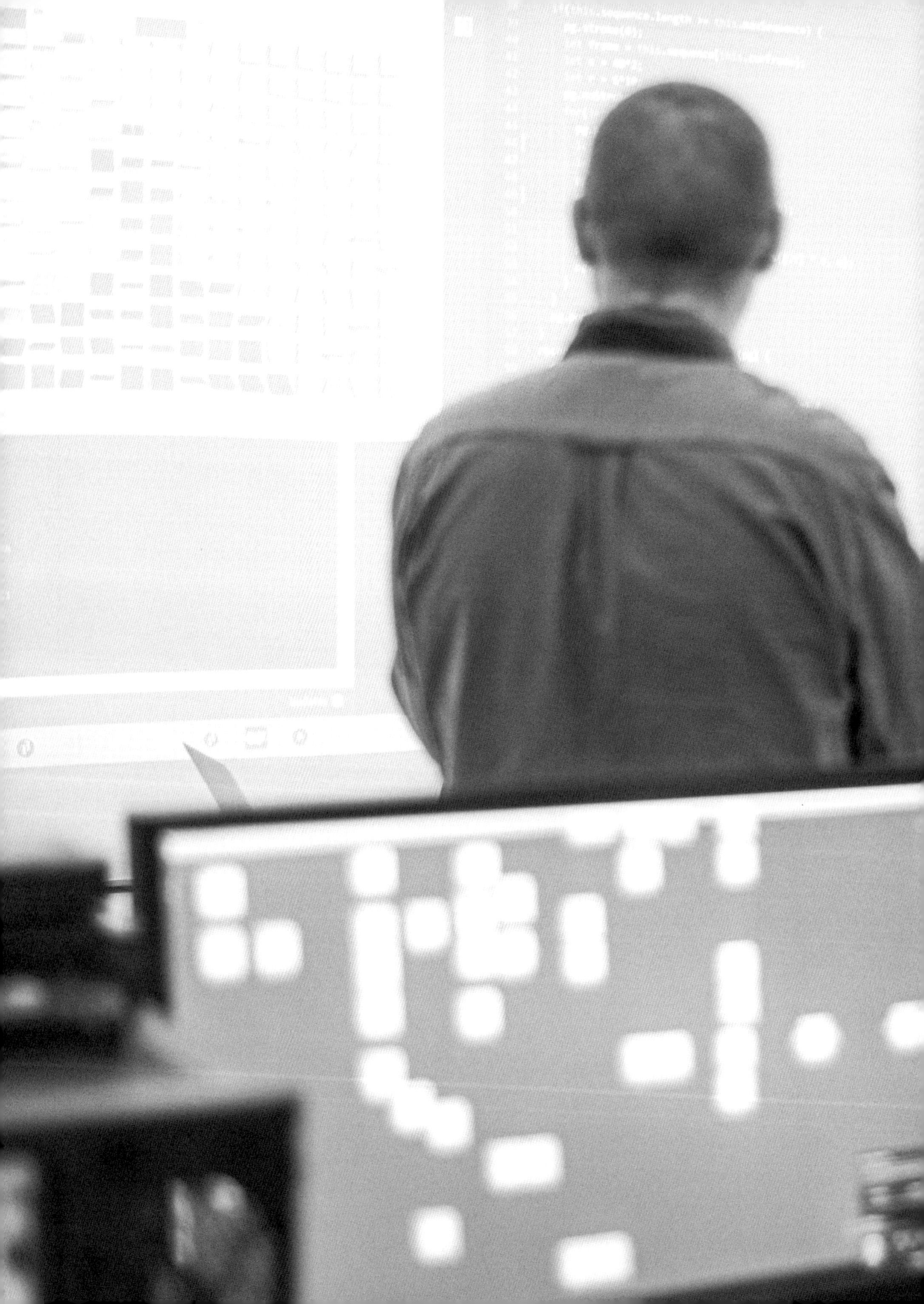